LATVIA

MARA KALNINS

Latvia

A Short History

HURST & COMPANY, LONDON

First published in the United Kingdom in 2015 by
C. Hurst & Co. (Publishers) Ltd.,
41 Great Russell Street, London, WC1B 3PL
© Mara Kalnins, 2015
All rights reserved.

Printed in the United Kingdom

Distributed in the United States, Canada and Latin America by
Oxford University Press, 198 Madison Avenue, New York, NY 10016,
United States of America

The right of Mara Kalnins to be identified as the author of
this publication is asserted by her in accordance with the
Copyright, Designs and Patents Act, 1988.

A Cataloguing-in-Publication data record for this book is
available from the British Library.

9781849044622 *paperback*

This book is printed using paper from registered sustainable
and managed sources.

www.hurstpublishers.com

History may be servitude,
History may be freedom. See, now they vanish,
The faces and the places, with the self which, as it could, loved them,
To become renewed, transfigured, in another pattern.

T. S. Eliot, 'Little Gidding', *Four Quartets*

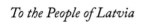

To the People of Latvia

CONTENTS

ACKNOWLEDGEMENTS

I gratefully acknowledge the many scholars and historians, both Latvian and Western, whose research informs this volume and who are cited in the Bibliography; Irēna Hamilton of the Latvian Embassy in London for her unfailing enthusiasm and help; and the many museum curators and librarians throughout Latvia who facilitated access to their archives. In particular thanks must go to Gundega Michele and Valters Nollendorfs of the Museum of Occupation in Rīga, to the directors of Rīga's History and Navigation Museum, and to Vizma Belševice (now deceased) to whom I am indebted for a greater understanding of the Soviet period in Latvia.

LIST OF MAPS AND IMAGES

Maps

Images

LIST OF MAPS AND IMAGES

NOTE ON NAMES AND SPELLINGS

The word 'Balt' can have several meanings, depending on whether it is used in a geographical, political, linguistic, cultural or ethnological context. Throughout this volume it refers primarily to the Latvians, Lithuanians and Old Prussians who belong to a single linguistic family. The Finno-Ugric Estonians speak a different language and are of different origin, so they are not included unless there is a reference to the post Ice Age migrations of peoples into the Baltic area and, in historical times, where the political fortunes of the three Baltic nations are intertwined.

The spelling of eastern European place names is notoriously fraught and controversial, given that they are so often indicators of national, political and cultural allegiance. The general policy throughout has been to give the name appropriate to the historical period under discussion (e.g. Danzig, Gdansk; Livonia, Latvia) and, where clarification might be helpful, to add the alternative name or names in parenthesis, thus: Liepāja (Libau), Klaipēda (Memel), Daugava (Düna, Dvīna). This is to preserve for readers a sense of the complex and shifting political history of the regions. In general discussion I have used the form accepted in the contemporary official national language of the country. For the Slavic territories, however, which this book only touches on, I have adopted the spellings familiar to Western readers (e.g. Kiev rather than Kyiv). Similarly, in the spellings of personal names—and in order to avoid confusion—I have used the current national forms and, with respect to émigrés, the spelling they themselves have adopted. My apologies if I have offended any sensibilities.

GLOSSARY OF PLACE NAMES IN THE BALTIC

Baltic	**German**
Alūksne	Marienburg
Cēsis	Wenden
Daugava (river)	Düna (*Russian* Dvīna)
Daugavpils	Dünaburg
Gdansk	Danzig
Ikšķile	Uexküll
Jēkabpils	Jakobstadt
Jelgava	Mitau
Klaipēda	Memel
Koknese	Kokenhusan
Kuldīga	Goldingen/Jesusburg
Kurzeme	Kurland/Courland
Latgale	Lettgallen
Latvia	Lettland (*French* Lettonie)
Liepāja	Libau
Mežotne	Mesoten
Nemunas (river)	Memel
Salaspils	Kirchholm
Tallinn	Reval
Tartu	Dorpat
Valmiera	Wolmar
Venta (river)	Windau
Ventspils	Windau
Vidzeme	Livland/Livonia
Zemgale	Semgallen

CHRONOLOGY

Early Chronology

c. 6000 BC	Finno-Ugric peoples reach Estonia Narva and Nemunas people established in the eastern Baltic
c. 2500–2000	Coming of the Kurgans (Corded Ware/Battle Axe Culture) Formation of individual Baltic Kurgan Groups
c. 1800–1600	Chalcolithic
c. 1600–1250	Early Bronze Age
c. 1250–1100	Classical Baltic Bronze Age
c. 1100–800	Late Bronze Age
c. 800–400	('Neuri' of Herodotus)
c. 400	Early Iron Age
1st century AD–	Tacitus describes the Baltic 'Aestii' who trade in amber
c. 400	Old Iron Age Baltic 'Golden Age' (to 1201)
c. 400–850	Middle Iron Age
c. 850–1200	Late Iron Age Viking Road to Byzantium (ninth to tenth centuries) *Lifland* and *Kurs* mentioned in the Scandinavian sagas

Historical Chronology

1186	Bishop Meinhard fails to establish Christian church in Rīga
1201	Teutonic Knights under Albert of Bremen, Bishop of Livonia, invade and build Rīga (founded next to an earlier settlement)
1207	Livonia (*Terra Mariana*) recognised as part of the Holy Roman Empire with Rīga as its capital
1215	Rīga granted the rights of a free city of the Holy Roman Empire
1219	Danes invade north Estonia and found Tallinn (Reval)
1225	*Chronicle of Livonia* by Henricus de Lettis
1230	Mindaugas unites Lithuania; Grand Duchy created
1237	Crusaders' Order of the Knights of the Sword becomes the Livonian Order
1282	Rīga joins the Hanseatic League
1316	Lithuanian expansion begins under Duke Gediminas
1386	Lithuania and Poland united (until 1795) through marriage of Duke Jogaila and Queen Jadwyga
1410	Dukes Vytautas and Jogaila defeat the Teutonic Order at the Battle of Tannenberg (Grünwald)
1501–3	Livonian army (under Walter von Plettenberg) halts the advance of Tsar Ivan III
1520	The Reformation establishes Lutheran faith in Livonia
1558–83	Livonian Wars between Sweden and Russia; north Livonia annexed by Sweden, south Livonia and Lithuania by Poland
1561	Teutonic Order dissolved; Gotthard Kettler becomes Duke of Courland

CHRONOLOGY

1581–1621	Rīga swears fealty to King of Poland and Lithuania
1585–6	Catholic and Protestant catechisms published in Latvian
1629	Sweden takes Livonia from Poland
1632	Publication of first Latvian newspaper, *Ahwises* Foundation of Dorpat (Tartu) University in Estonia by Sweden
1642–82	Flowering of Courland under Duke Jēkabs
1685–9	The Old and New Testaments translated into Latvian by Ernst Glück
1694	St Peter's steeple in Rīga completed (tallest in the world)
1700–21	Great Northern War between Charles XII of Sweden and Peter the Great; Russia is victorious and occupies Livonia
1712	Martha Skavronska, a Livonian peasant girl, marries Peter the Great and in 1724 is crowned Catherine, Empress of Russia
1764–9	Johann Gottfried Herder a pastor in Rīga; begins to collect Baltic folklore
1768	Rundāle Palace completed
1772	Latgale becomes part of the Russian province of Polotsk
1773	Herder's *Stimmen der Völker in ihren Liedern* published
1795	Third Partition of Poland; Lithuania becomes part of Russian Empire; Duchy of Courland becomes a Russian province
1796	Publication of *Die Letten* by Merkel
1812	Napoleon's march to Moscow through the Baltic provinces; lays siege to Rīga
1818–20	Baltic German nobility abolish serfdom in Courland and Livonia but without granting land to the peasants

1835–1923	Life of Krišjānis Barons, folklorist and nationalist whose collection of the Latvian *Dainas* strongly influenced the National Awakening movement
1849, 1856	Land reforms in Latvia and Estonia benefit the peasant population
1861	Tsar Alexander II abolishes serfdom
1860–85	Era of the 'National Awakening'
1863	Abolition of serfdom in Latgale
1869, 1873	First Latvian Song Festivals
1870	First railway in the Baltic provinces
1885	Unsuccessful uprising against Russia; intensive Russification follows under Tsar Alexander III; Baltic languages displaced
1888	Publication of *Lāčplēsis*, Latvian national epic by Andrejs Pumpurs
1905	Abortive uprising; demands for independence followed by reprisals
1909	Birth of the philosopher [Sir] Isaiah Berlin in Rīga
1914–18	First World War
1914–15	Germany occupies part of Latvia and Lithuania
1915–16	Russian Imperial Army forms Latvian Rifle Regiments
1917	Russian Revolution; Bolsheviks seize Estonia; Germans capture Rīga; Baltic national assemblies demand independence from Russia
1918	18 November: Latvian National Council proclaims independence
1918–19	November 1918–March 1919: Bolsheviks invade Baltic and capture Rīga 22 May 1919: German, White Russian and Latvian troops retake Rīga June–July: Germany forces defeated at Wenden (Cēsis) by Estonian and Latvian troops

1920–1	Baltic States sign peace treaties with Soviet Russia; Moscow recognises their independence
1920	Major land reforms in Latvia
1922	Democratic Constitution introduced; Latvia admitted to the League of Nations
1929	The Great Depression
1934	Kārlis Ulmanis dissolves Saeima (parliament)
1939	23 August: Molotov–von Ribbentrop Pact; 23 September–10 October: Soviet Union stations troops in Latvia
1939–40	Hitler orders evacuation of Baltic German community from Latvia, Lithuania and Estonia; 17 June 1940: Soviet Union invades 3–6 August: annexes Baltic states
1941	'The Terror': tens of thousands arrested, deported to Siberia or executed; 28 August: Germany re-captures Baltic states; Jewish holocaust begins
1944	August-May 1945: Soviet army re-conquers the Baltic states, destroys attempts to restore national governments; hundreds of thousands flee to be replaced by Russian-speaking immigrants
1945–54	'Forest Brothers' continue guerrilla activities against the Soviets
1947	Collectivisation begins; agricultural communities crippled
1949	March: mass deportation of Balts to Central Asia and Siberia
1953	Death of Stalin
1956–7	'Thaw' begins under Khruschev and enables some recovery of Baltic culture
1965	Brezhnev tightens economic and political control over the Baltic
1970s	'Era of Stagnation'
1982	Death of Brezhnev

1985	Appointment of Mikhail Gorbachev as Secretary-General of the Soviet Communist Party; begins to implement *glasnost* and *perestroika*
1987	Demonstrations against Soviet rule begin in all three Baltic states
1988	23 August: rallies held to denounce the Molotov-von Ribbentrop Pact; opposition parties established
1989	31 May: Latvia's Popular Front calls for full independence 28 July: Latvian Supreme Council passes declaration of sovereignty 23 August: 'The Baltic Way'/'The Singing Revolution'—two million Balts form a living human chain from Tallinn to Vilnius calling for independence

Contemporary Chronology

1990	18 March: Latvian Supreme Council elections lead to resolution calling for full independence 4 May: Declaration of Independence, Anatolijs Gorbanovs leading the country 12 May: the three Baltic leaders establish the Baltic Council and apply for membership of CSCE Autumn: Soviet hardliners attempt to sabotage the independence movement; OMON police force defects to side with Moscow
1991	11–13 January: Soviet paratroopers invade Vilnius; 20 January: OMON attacks Interior Ministry, Rīga 3 March: referendum held in Latvia with large majority voting for independence 19–21 August: unsuccessful counter-revolution in the Soviet Union; OMON kills several people in Rīga

20 August: Latvia's Supreme Council declares full independence followed by international diplomatic recognition and admission to CSCE
6 September: Soviet State Council recognises Baltic independence
18 September: Latvia joins the UN
27 November: Latvian Supreme Council passes law restoring citizenship to all those who held it before 1940 and to their descendants
25 December: Gorbachev resigns as President of the USSR and announces its dissolution

1992   20 May: Latvia joins IMF
15 September: Latvian Supreme Council demands the withdrawal of all Soviet troops

1993   5 March: Lat restored as the official currency
5–6 June: Elections to the fifth Saeima (in continuity from the first independence era)
6–7 July: Guntis Ulmanis elected first President after the restoration
25 November: new Citizenship Law passed

1994   31 August: last Soviet troops leave Latvian soil

1995   Associate membership of the EU and membership of OSCE

1998   USA proposes Charter of Partnership

1999   Vaira Vīķe-Freiberga becomes President (re-elected in 2003)

2004   29 March: Latvia becomes a member of NATO
1 May: Latvia, Lithuania and Estonia join the EU

2006   28–29 November: Latvia hosts NATO summit

2008   Global Financial Crisis
18 November: ninetieth Anniversary of Independence

2010   Economic recovery

| 2014 | Rīga becomes 'European Capital of Culture'; Latvia enters the euro-zone |
| 2015 | Latvia assumes the presidency of the Council of Europe |

The Presidents of Latvia

Jānis Čhakste	1922–27 [Democratic Centre Party]
Gustavs Zemgals	1927–30 [Democratic Centre Party]
Alberts Kviesis	1930–36 [Farmers' Union]
Kārlis Ulmanis	1936–40 [Farmers' Union]
[Latvia, SSR]	*[1940–91]*
Guntis Ulmanis	1993–99 [Farmers' Union]
Vaira Viķe-Freiberga	1999–2007 [none]
Valdis Zatlers	2007–11 [none]
Andris Bērziņš	2011–[Farmers' Union]

PREFACE

Still the debate continues: what constitutes a nation? How do we define nationality, nationalism, a national consciousness? For centuries historians and philosophers have sought to clarify and define the meanings of these terms. One thinks of Johann Gottfried Herder, the great Enlightenment figure, with his famous dictum: '*Denn jedes Volk ist Volk; es hat seine Nationalbildung, wie seine Sprache*' ('For each people is a People; it has its own national culture, like its own language'). In more recent times Erich Auerbach (*Mimesis*), Walter Benjamin (*Illuminations*), Benedict Anderson (*Imagined Communities*) and a host of historians and social scientists—J. A. Armstrong, John Breuilly, Eric Hobsbawn, Miroslav Hroch and Anthony Smith, to cite but a few—have sought to analyse the phenomenon of nationhood. The complexities of their theories and debates are necessarily outside the scope of the present study, though inevitably the findings of liberal historiography must inform it. Rather, this book takes as its premise Hugh Seton-Watson's general observation that 'a nation exists when a significant number of people in a community consider themselves to form a nation, or behave as if they formed one'[1] and adopts his widely accepted distinction between 'nation' and 'state':

> A state is a legal and political organization with the power to require obedience and loyalty from its citizens. A nation is a community of people, whose members are bound together by a sense of solidarity, a common culture, a national consciousness.[2]

The story of the Latvian people, which begins some four and a half millennia ago with the coming of the proto-Baltic Indo-

European tribes to north-western Europe, exemplifies the above distinction. The chapters that follow will consider how one branch of those Indo-European migrants coalesced into a community which evolved a distinctive and remarkably robust culture and language that in turn developed into a loose federation of discrete tribal kingdoms in the first millennium BC which stretched from the shores of the Baltic Sea to the upper reaches of the Dniepr river. Like other early feudal societies in Europe, it is likely that these small kingdoms would have merged over time, but whereas the twelve tribes of medieval Sweden were eventually united by the Folkjunker Jarls, Poland by the Piasts, and the Lithuanian peoples under Mindaugas, the Latvian chiefs remained independent but divided, and so were unable to resist the invasion of the Teutonic Knights with their advanced weaponry in 1201. That incursion initiated nearly eight centuries of helotry for the Latvians in their own domains.

Throughout the succeeding centuries when the peoples of Livonia or Lettland (as the territory was then known) were dominated by successive European powers, the indigenous inhabitants nonetheless preserved a powerful sense of identity fostered by their language, oral literature, songs and customs. These in turn informed and gave impetus to the rise of national consciousness in the nineteenth century and the political activities of the early twentieth which brought the modern nation-state of Latvia into being. This book aims to trace the genesis and growth of this eastern European nation, its endurance over centuries of conquest and oppression, the process by which it achieved its independence, and its status as a member of the European community in the twenty-first century.

Mara Kalnins, Corpus Christi College, Cambridge

1

ORIGINS

The Baltic Shield

Between the Scandinavian peninsula and the Russian steppe lies an area of geological stability known as 'The Baltic Shield'. At the close of the last Ice Age the retreating glaciers shaped the eastern Baltic into a land of river valleys rich in alluvial deposits, bounded by low ridges and hills, and by a coastline of pristine white sands and dunes through which three great rivers—the Vistula, the Nemunas and the Daugava—discharged into the sea. To the east, the legacy of the glacial moraine belt created a landscape dotted by thousands of lakes and characterised by a lighter, sandier soil which eventually met the uplands of the Dniepr river basin. To the south-east, in what is now Belarus, the gentle contours dissolved into the vast swamps of the Pripet river basin. As the climate stabilised, the area settled into a transitional zone between the weather systems of central and of northern Europe, with warm, dry summers and cold winters that supported a diversity of plant and animal species. Unlike the dominant pine and spruce forests of the Nordic region, those of the Baltic Shield are a mixture of coniferous and deciduous, with abundant oak, linden, maple, birch, ash, hazel, aspen and willow which in turn attracted a wide variety of animal life: hare, squirrel, marten, beaver, badger, wolf, elk, deer, even bison and (until comparatively recently) aurochs and wild horse. Add to this woodlands full of grouse and partridge, wetlands populated by duck and geese, rivers teeming with fish, and a plentiful supply of the nuts, fungi, wild berries, fruit and honey that were the staples of any hunter-gatherer society, and it is no wonder that the early human migrants into the area felt themselves to have found a beneficent habitat where life, for all its hardships, was rich with the bounty of the natural world.

These migrants were the Narva and Nemunas people, so-called after the two Baltic rivers (in Estonia and Lithuania, respectively) which formed the heartland of the Baltic Mesolithic group. Part of the relatively homogeneous culture of hunters and fishers which flourished throughout north-eastern Europe (extending as far as the Dniepr and Volga river basins and southwards to beyond the Vistula), they were nonetheless racially distinct from the Finno-Ugric folk, who occupied the lands that would one day become Estonia and Finland. Both groups had reached the Baltic in roughly the same period, around 6000 BC. The east Baltic Narva were skilled in the manufacture of flint and stone tools; they used baskets and pots, and are sometimes referred to as the 'Comb Ware' people, after the distinctive patterning on the pottery. They built timber houses above ground, had hunting dogs and a diverse economy supplied by sophisticated hooks, traps and nets. They used boats for both inland and coastal fishing and were almost certainly the colonisers of the islands in the Baltic Sea. Then, as happened throughout northern Europe, their culture was gradually infiltrated by that of the food-producing peoples of central and south-eastern Europe whose skills spread northwards and reached the Baltic in the fourth millennium BC. They in turn had been influenced by the dissemination of the still more sophisticated cultures of the Aegean and Near East. Such gradual diffusion was characteristic of European pre-history in general, and although the rapidity and nature of that diffusion remain a matter of scholarly debate, archaeological evidence offers a reasonably accurate system of dating and has provided timescales and patterns of migration for the early Mesolithic inhabitants and the later migration of the Indo-European speaking peoples across the face of Europe.[1]

As their grave goods and burial rituals reveal, the Narva possessed a highly developed aesthetic sense and a religious awareness. One of the most important communal burial cemeteries in northern Europe lies on the shores of Lake Burtnieks in Latvia,[2] where excavations have shown that the Narva carefully positioned their dead, covering them with furs and sprinkling the body with red ochre. In some graves the skulls were also protected by blue clay and the eye sockets filled with amber rings or discs, which may have been placed there to help the spirit 'see' on its journey from this world to the next. These graves have also yielded beautifully carved tools of flint, antler, bone and wood, in some of whose geometric patterns one can trace the origin of folk motifs that survive to this day in Latvian art. The elk, deer and boar tooth ornaments characteristic of earlier Palaeolithic man, however, have been largely replaced by carved and polished amber jewellery: large and small pendants and necklaces of oval, round and cylindrical beads; amber rings make their first appearance, as do amber totemic figures of birds and animals, perhaps hunters' talismans.

The change from Mesolithic to Neolithic came comparatively late to the hunter-gatherers of north-eastern Europe, though by about 3500 BC that transition had been made. The thousand years that followed saw the Narva communities flourishing through their new expertise in the cultivation of crops and the domestication of sheep, pigs and cattle, with a corresponding development in the sophistication and diversity of both domestic goods and outdoor implements. Grave items such as wooden distaffs, amber spindles, and intricately woven fabrics become common. This was the beginning of a period of dynamic cultural change and diversification, but many elements survived into the Neolithic and later periods—especially the central importance of amber, the sun-stone—and were also to modify the belief systems of the later Indo-European immigrants who gradually merged with the east Baltic culture. The newcomers brought the domesticated horse, more advanced weaponry, and social and religious customs very different from those of the Narva. They were the Kurgans (also known as the 'Corded Ware/Battle Axe' culture), semi-nomadic pastoralists, whose farming and stock-breeding expertise had swept north and west into Europe through a series of migrations over several millennia, reaching the lands of the eastern Baltic around 2500–2200 BC.[3]

When the Kurgans brought their Indo-European language and customs to the eastern Baltic lands, they merged with the indigenous Narva people to create a hybrid race: the proto-Balts. Their Indo-European tongue prevailed and would eventually evolve into the trio of closely related Baltic languages and associated dialects of Latvian, Lithuanian and (now extinct) Old Prussian. But although all languages change over time, the rate of that change in the Baltic trio was exceptionally conservative. Whether this was the result of its comparative geographical remoteness in the thinly populated north-east or whether it was because it was deemed too primitive or insignificant to attract the attention of later conquerors will never be known.

However, for whatever reason, the three Baltic languages which developed from the proto-Baltic remained very close to their Indo-European parent and to each other, preserving a complex, inflected grammar and an ancient vocabulary. This makes them intensely interesting to linguists and affords valuable insights into the migration patterns and cultures of archaic humanity. Indeed Baltic and Sanskrit are widely recognised as the two poles which mark the boundaries of the Indo-European homeland, with its closely related languages and dialects that evolved into the languages spoken across Europe today. The proto-Balts, then, were created from the merger of two very different races, cultures and languages. That merger in turn was to generate a sense of linguistic and cultural identity so powerful that it would enable the Baltic peoples to withstand the pressure of other invasions for millennia to come.

As elsewhere, the Kurgans brought with them not only their language but the horse, a pastoral economy, a patrilineal society with a strong hierarchical structure, and the images and symbols of their gods. Chief among them was the sky god, often depicted as a mounted warrior, who embodied the power of light and of the sun and was associated with the seasons. As archaeological findings reveal, his symbol was the sun disc, incised with rays. Such amber discs were considered powerful amulets, worn by chieftains and warriors; some would have been attached to the harness of horses. For the first time axe-shaped amber amulets appeared and tooth-shaped amber talismans copying the incisor teeth of wolves and boar, animals sacred to the sky god. The Narva belief systems, part of what Marija Gimbutas has called 'Old Europe', which were matrilineal and matricentric, were confronted by the warlike, masculine deities of the incomers. Over time, however, the two different religions and their symbolic structures combined. But whereas the patrilineal Indo-European system had dominated elsewhere on the continent—with the myths, deities and symbols of 'Old Europe' surviving in a subordinate position or as a hidden undercurrent—in the eastern Baltic the female deities and powers of the Narva flourished as a vigorous element in the new, hybrid culture. In particular, the 'Old Europe' designation of the sun and the great natural powers of fertility, life and death as specifically feminine remained, in equal partnership with the Kurgan gods. The enriched mythology of this dual heritage would survive the coming of Christianity and is apparent even today, preserved in the languages and oral traditions of Latvia and Lithuania, as well as in the ancient signs and symbols which appear in contemporary Baltic art and design.

It is generally accepted that by the end of the third millennium a certain formalisation of cultures and languages had taken place across Europe. As the Neolithic period gradually gave way to the Bronze Age (c.1800 BC), the various Kurgan groups evolved into more differentiated societies. Their territories demonstrate more clearly defined spheres of cultural and linguistic change and influence, as shown by archaeological excavations of their burial mounds. This period of diversification was also characteristic of the proto-Baltic people, but although their comparative geographical remoteness might suggest a certain isolation from the rest of the continent, this was by no means the case. Lacking any copper, tin or gold deposits in their lands, the proto-Balts were dependent on other cultures for these metals. Those in the western region—an area roughly corresponding to east Prussia, northern and central Poland, Latvia and Lithuania—traded with the metal-producing peoples of central Europe. The proto-Balts inhabiting the forest areas of eastern Latvia and Lithuania—extending to the Dniepr and upper Volga—came in contact with another set of cultures: Finno-Ugrians, Cimmerians, proto-Scythians and early Slavs,

Map 1. Maximum extent of the Baltic culture from c.2000 BC and during the Bronze Age, according to Marija Gimbutas and J. P. Mallory.

whose development depended on access to the metal riches of the Caucasus and southern Urals.

Fortunately the proto-Balts possessed a substance that was only found in their lands and was desired by all peoples—amber, the sun-stone, 'the gold of the north'. Since Stone Age times, when it had been traded by the Narva for flint, amber had been highly prized, not only for its beauty but because it was believed to be the substance of the sun itself and so must possess magical and protective properties. Although amber occurs in many parts of the world, the only known source in antiquity was the Baltic. Distinct from the ambers and fossilised resins found elsewhere, Baltic amber (or *succinite*) contains a high percentage of succinic acid, which makes it readily identifiable. This in turn means it is particularly useful to archaeologists, for unlike pottery and metal work (whose provenance can be uncertain and affected by other factors such as migration, common motifs and smithing techniques) amber with a significant percentage of succinic acid originates only in the Baltic and its presence is indisputable evidence of trading contact. The importance and extent of the trade in Baltic amber in Mesolithic, Neolithic and Bronze Age times can hardly be exaggerated. Baltic amber has been found throughout Europe and as far south as Egypt and the Near East.[4] And as we enter the Bronze Age and early historical times, it is the trade in amber with the Mediterranean world that is the most important source for our knowledge about the early Baltic tribes—the ancestors of the Old Prussians, Lithuanians and Latvians.

The Ancient Balts

Our understanding of pre-historic Europe, then, depends both on archaeological excavations and on theories about the development of the Indo-European languages. As the pattern of timeless moments which is pre-history slowly gives way to recorded history, more evidence emerges to link the Baltic peoples with the central European culture and that of Mycenaean Greece, and a significant amount of that data concerns the amber trade. Hoards of bronze and gold have been found concentrated on the Baltic coast and along the river systems that carried amber to the pre-classical Mediterranean world. Maritime trade, too, expanded dramatically in this period, driven by the need for the tin essential for the production of bronze. The Phoenicians and proto-Etruscans forged into the North Atlantic, bringing back precious metals from Britain and amber from the Baltic. By river, land and sea, the sun-stone reached Bronze Age Greece, Crete, the Near East and Egypt and in its turn brought bronze artefacts and precious metals north to enrich the Baltic culture.[5]

1. Amber Solar Disc, third millennium BC (reproduced by kind permission of the Amber Museum, Palanga, Lithuania)

The ancient Greeks were fascinated by amber, which they called *electron* (from whence our word 'electricity'), and many legends were told about its origin and the mysterious people of the north who gathered it. Perhaps the best known is that of Phaeton, the mortal son of the sun god Helios. Unable to control the fiery steeds of his father's chariot, his erratic flight threatened to destroy the cosmos, whereupon Zeus felled him with a thunderbolt. His sisters, the Heliades, weeping for their brother's death, were changed into poplar trees and their tears into amber. Like many myths, this too contains a kernel of truth: amber is indeed a kind of tree resin and its appearance in pre-historic times was generally associated with rivers. In the *Odyssey* Homer mentions amber necklaces 'that shone like the sun', and although he was recounting events that had occurred several centuries before his time, archaeological excavations and scientific dating methods have increasingly vindicated such oral traditions.[6] Written evidence begins to appear in the later Bronze Age: a cuneiform text from ninth-century Nineveh notes that the Assyrian King Ashur-nasir-apal secured amber from the distant seas where the North Star rises; amber is cited in the epic of Gilgamesh and in the Old Testament too.

The first historical reference to a specific Baltic people, however, does not appear until the work of the Greek historian Herodotus, who flourished in the fifth century BC. In Book IV of the *History* he considers the Scythians, a nomadic people who had reached the northern shores of the Black Sea by 700 BC and displaced the earlier Cimmerians, mentioned by Homer in the *Iliad*. Their territory eventually stretched in a vast crescent from the Danube and Dniestr in the west to the Don in the east and north along the Dniepr to what would one day be Kiev. Beyond that, however, 'dwell the Neuri', a people distinct from the Scythians:

> [T]he Ister [Danube] is one of the rivers of Scythia. But the next after it is the Tyras [Dniestr], which ariseth in a great lake in the north which is the border between Scythia and the land of the Neuri.

Although the Dniestr does not originate from a lake, only just to the north lie the extensive Pripet marshes (in Belarus) which may be the 'great lake' identified by Herodotus, since historically the marshes do in fact roughly divide the Slavic lands from those of the Baltic.

That the Neuri were a Baltic people is confirmed by modern excavations of hill forts and grave sites from the first millennium BC in that geographical area. There is important linguistic evidence too, for over a thousand river names, whose etymology and morphology are indisputably Baltic, survive in the upper Daugava and Dniepr regions. And river names, as linguists have cogently demonstrated, are still one of the best ways of establishing the ancient geographical distribution of a people.[7] Little else about the history and customs of these people has come down to us, though some can be inferred from their graves—like their love of horses which were given rich burials in separate cemeteries—and from oral tradition.[8] Herodotus himself is silent, only noting that the Neuri had adopted some Scythian customs but had refused to be drawn into the Scythian–Persian wars. Centuries later Roman historical accounts also mention the Neuri and locate their lands where Herodotus had placed them, observing in addition that the Dniepr and the Daugava rivers both arise in the Valdai hills (Russia).

In the first and second centuries AD, the Baltic coast and the names of some of its inhabitants appear in the work of several Greek and Roman historians—Strabo, Pomponius Mela, Pliny the Elder, Tacitus, Pliny the Younger—some of whom refer to still earlier explorations of the area. Thus, in his *Natural History* Pliny the Elder cites Pytheas, whose legendary voyage to Britain and the realms of the Northern Ocean took place c.320 BC.[9] Pytheas had described a people who lived a day's sail from the Germanic lands, on the 'Isle of Abalus', where amber was sold to the 'Teutones'. Pliny adds that the local name for amber is '*glesum*, hence the Romans call these northern isles *Glaesaria*, though to the barbarians known as *Austravia*'.[10] Although the precise location of the isles is conjectural and remains the subject of considerable debate, the etymology of the words is Baltic.[11]

That '*glesum*', 'the gold of the north', was gathered and bartered by a people distinct from both the Germanic and Scandinavian tribes is also confirmed a little later by Tacitus. In *De Germania*

(98), he describes the location of the Baltic 'Aestii': 'On the coast to the right of the Suevian ocean', where they gather amber, 'in their language called *Glesum*'. Hitherto it has been assumed that '*glesum*' must be an early form of Germanic *glaes* (glass), but amber in its natural state is rarely transparent and Tacitus clearly states that the term is native to the 'Aestii'. Intriguingly in Latgallian—the most archaic Latvian dialect—amber is indeed called *glēze*, while the Latvian word for fragile (and amber easily fractures) is *glezns*. Tacitus affirms that these non-Germanic folk had similar clothing and customs to the Suoni (the Swedes) but were far more diligent in the cultivation of crops than their Teutonic neighbours.[12] It is an open question whether he was referring to the amber-collecting Balts in general or specifically to the tribe living around the Frisches Haff, east of the Vistula estuary, who were the ancestors of the Old Prussians. However, other early historical records seem to indicate that Aestii was a generic name for the Baltic tribes as a whole and covered a broader geographical area. In the sixth century the Gothic chronicler Jordanus refers to them as 'a wholly peaceful people' living to the east of the Vistula. In the ninth century the Anglo-Saxon Wulfstan calls this area 'Eystmere' while Einhard's *Vita Caroli Magni* locates the Aestii along the whole eastern coast of the Baltic, and states that their neighbours were Slavs. This broader designation, that is from the Gulf of Gdansk to the Bay of Rīga—the heart of the amber lands—is preserved today: the Estonians still call themselves 'Eesti' while in Lithuanian the Frisches Haff is called 'Aismere'.

Tacitus mentions other non-Germanic tribes living on the Baltic whose names have also survived over the centuries. The Galindians and Sudeoni, ancestors of the Old Prussians, appear in later historical accounts as the Galinda and Sudova.[13] In any case, hundreds of Roman coins dating from the first to the fourth centuries have been found along the Baltic coast as well as in settlements on the Daugava river as far east as Daugavpils, near the Russian border. These findings clearly identify important Baltic coastal trading centres and the arteries of river commerce in the Baltic domains and in what would one day become Latvia.

Proof of the growing geographical knowledge of the Baltic and the importance of trading links with the Mediterranean is confirmed in Pliny's account of a famous expedition to the Baltic coast which had taken place a generation earlier.

> Amber is imported by the Germans into Pannonia [...]. From Carnuntum in Pannonia, to the coasts of Germany from which the amber is brought, is a distance of about six hundred miles, a fact which has only recently been ascertained; and there is still living a member of the equestrian order, who was sent thither by Julianus, the manager of the gladiatorial exhibitions for the Emperor Nero, to procure a supply of this article. Traversing the coasts of that country and visiting the various markets there, he brought back amber, in such vast quantities, as to admit of the nets, which were used for protecting the podium against the wild beasts, being studded with amber.[14]

The route, beginning at Carnuntum (near Vienna) and following the river valleys of the Morava and Vistula to the Gulf of Gdansk, was actually measured using one of the Roman milometers which discharged pebbles at calibrated intervals.

Another intriguing record of a precise Baltic place name occurs in the legend of Jason and the Golden Fleece, a myth which underwent several mutations over the centuries.[15] In the earliest versions, the *Argo* returned to Greece simply by retracing its route through the Hellespont. But over time accounts of that return voyage chart an ever more sophisticated journey, undoubtedly reflecting the vigorous nautical explorations of the Bronze and Iron Ages and the ever growing knowledge of the world. In the first century BC Diodorus of Sicily, quoting the still earlier author Timeaus of Tauremenium (who flourished in the fourth century BC) affirmed that finding the Hellespont closed against them by King Aeëtes of Colchis, the Argonauts sailed to the north coast of the Black Sea and then up a northern river—either the Tanais (Don) or the Borysthenes (Dniepr)—as far as its source. They then hauled their ship overland to join a west-flowing river (this can only be the Daugava) which they followed to Ocean. Then, sailing west and keeping land on their left, they eventually reached Gadeira (Cadiz) and entered the Mediterranean again. By the third century AD the point at which the *Argo* leaves the river and enters the northern Ocean is clearly named: 'They who dwell beyond the

North call it the "Cronian Water".'[16] 'Cronian' is 'Curonian', the realm of the Curs/Kurs who appear only a few centuries later in the Scandinavian sagas and Anglo-Saxon chronicles. The 'Cronian Water' is the Gulf of Rīga, into which the Daugava discharges; subsequently it was also known as the Kurisches Haff, that is 'the Gulf of the Kurs'. Even today the Curonian Spit in western Lithuania, where archaeological excavations have confirmed that a distinctively Baltic people inhabited the area in the first millennium BC, preserves the name, which resonates throughout Latvia's history (see chapter 3 below on the Duchy of Courland) and is still the name of its western region Kurzeme.

Certainly the Baltic coast and its peoples were known to the greatest of all cartographers in antiquity, Claudius Ptolomaeus, whose *Geographia* (compiled by 180 AD) would not be surpassed until the map-makers of the Renaissance. No contemporary copy of this magnificent work survives and although it was known to Arabic cartographers, it was lost to Western knowledge for a thousand years. Not until the thirteenth century and the travels of Marco Polo would the lands and seas known to the Romans be rediscovered and Ptolemy's mathematical system of latitude and longitude reinstated. It is an open question how faithful to the original the later Renaissance versions of his map were. Doubtless details were added, incorporating contemporary nautical information about important European trading centres, but the later versions are similar in essentials: they reproduce Ptolemy's commentary and place names, repeated in the details of his charts, and his lines of latitude and longitude. As regards the Baltic coast, Ptolemy's knowledge is undeniably sketchy—this was after all 'the seashore of the last known country', as he called it—but he clearly identifies the Danish peninsula with a scattering of its islands and he names four large continental rivers, roughly equidistant from each other, which enter the Baltic Sea: these are the Vistula, the Chronos (the Nemunas, which flows into the Curonian lagoon), the Rhodanus (possibly the Venta in western Latvia) and the Turuntes (the Daugava). The last is also correctly shown to have its source in an eastern mountain range (the Valdai hills) and all four rivers are drawn at approximately correct latitudes. In addition, the Vistula and the Turuntes are specifically named in the commentary so it is unlikely that they were added by later map-makers.

Ptolemy lists a great number of proper names, citing geographical features, tribes and their domains, and although at this temporal distance identifying their referents is a bit like Chinese whispers, a few words have echoed down the centuries to suggest possible links to the originals. For example, in classical antiquity the northern realm from which amber came was variously called Abalus—Basileia—Baunonia—Balcia. It is at least suggestive that Latvia is still sometimes called 'Baltia' and that the word itself derives from the Indo-European 'balt' (in Latvian 'balts') which means 'white', perhaps a reference to the pale, ice-rimmed waters of the northern seas. Only a few centuries later Wulfstan, Alfred the Great's chronicler, would refer to the Baltic domains as 'Whitland'.

Regardless of such speculation, however, by the first millennium AD a Baltic cultural group still flourished in roughly the same geographical area it had occupied since Neolithic times. Secure in the remote north-east, it was largely unaffected by the waves of expansion by the Scythians and other peoples that had swept through Europe in the preceding millennium, and had preserved the distinctive characteristics of its culture. Through the monopoly on amber, the tribes of this cultural area maintained vigorous trading networks with the Roman Empire and Free Germany to the south, the Finno-Ugrians to the north, and the Slavs to the east. Archaeological finds bear witness to the extent and richness of that trade and to the growing expertise in metal-working which enabled this people to evolve an individual Baltic style in jewellery, ornamentation, weaponry and horse gear. Indeed, it can be said that: 'The Balts [...] became the most important transmitters of the metal culture to the north and east, and their zone of influence was geographically the largest in Europe outside of the Roman Empire.'[17]

A Golden Age

The considerable material prosperity of the Baltic peoples in the first half of the first millennium AD, then, was founded on their

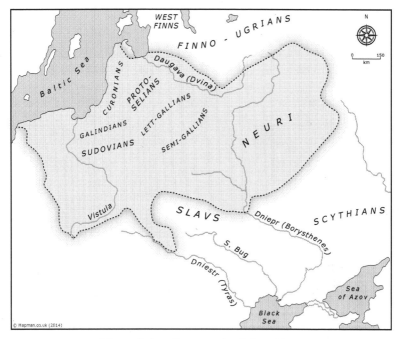

Map 2. Baltic Groups c.500 BC and later

advantageous trading connections, which linked the amber and fur producing regions of the north with European cultural areas to the south, west and east and with the provinces of the Roman Empire. Their territories remained little changed from previous millennia and excavations of settlements and cemeteries reveal a period of continual occupation, of increasing prosperity and of steady population growth. Central to the stability of these settlements were the fortified hill-top villages—or castle hills—typically situated on the highest river banks and on promontories of lake shores, which earned for the domains of the early Latvian and Lithuanian tribes the sobriquet 'the land of hill forts'. Fortified with ramparts and ditches, each consisted of about ten houses; some settlements were of great antiquity, dating from Chalcolithic and Bronze Age times. Their appearance in clusters, ranging in number from five to ten, with each hill-top fortification within sight of at least one or two others,

15

suggests that these clusters may have formed early tribal units or districts. Their continuity of occupation, like the continuity of burial rites revealed by the cemeteries, confirms a period of long occupation undisturbed by migration, invasion or population shifts.

From the first century onwards, however, the growth in population led to a gradual change in the nature of these hill forts as the small settlements expanded to form larger units. While the hill forts, prototypes of feudal castles, remained for protection, the surrounding farmsteads gradually coalesced to form the nuclei of the towns that would grow up around the hill. Where more densely populated areas gave rise to larger villages, new fortifications were also erected. Deep trenches and earthworks built of massive timber stakes covered with earth and stones rose 5 metres high and could be up to 20 metres thick; these were often surmounted by additional wooden palisades and ramparts. It was a period that also saw the rapid growth in, and development of, domestic metallurgy. Many villages had their own smithies which produced the iron axes, hoes, scythes, sickles and ploughshares essential for advances in agriculture and, by the fifth century, steel for high quality weaponry. The production of bronze, silver and gold increased dramatically as well and all forms of metal-working achieved a distinctive Baltic style. Baltic smiths and craftsmen readily adopted foreign techniques (such as enamel inlaying, which was imported from the Danubian province of the Roman Empire) and created ornaments whose intricate workmanship and refined style were highly prized. Not only fine weaponry but Baltic jewellery—fibulae, brooches, rings, pendants, necklaces and neck-rings, bracelets, head-dresses, and ornamental plates—were exported all over north-eastern Europe—to Estonia, Finland, Sweden—and east to Kiev, the Ukraine, and central Russia as far as the Urals.

With the progress in agriculture and metallurgy, the vigorous trading system and the general increase in prosperity came more clearly marked social distinctions within the tribal communities. Large cemeteries containing hundreds of graves now reveal striking differences between the graves of the well-to-do and the poor. Wealthy women were buried with vast quantities of jewellery;

wealthy men with iron axes, weapons, drinking horns, horse gear and rich personal ornaments. Burials of princely magnificence become more common, suggesting the existence of a feudal system led by a principal chieftain, a pattern familiar elsewhere on the continent. These aspects of the Baltic economy, habitation patterns, artistic achievements and social differences would develop still further in the centuries to come.

By the middle of the first millennium AD the Baltic tribes had coalesced into more clearly defined groups and territories, with the Old Prussians centred on the lower Vistula area and the Lithuanian tribes still occupying their traditional lands, which extended into northern Poland and east as far as the Pripet marshes. Of the Latvian tribes, the Kurs continued to dominate the western region, roughly corresponding to the area that would one day be Kurzeme and south as far as the Vistula, while the Latgallians (Lettgallians) slowly expanded over northern Latvia into territories which had been occupied previously by Finno-Ugric peoples; only a small enclave of the indigenous Liv tribe remained on the eastern side of the Gulf of Rīga, co-existing more or less peacefully with their Baltic neighbours. South of the river Daugava lay the lands of the early Latvian Semigallians and Selonians (see Map 3). The fortunes of all the Baltic tribes, however, were to be dramatically affected by two major European events which began in the middle centuries of the first millennium: the Slavic expansion into the territory of the eastern Balts, which began around 400 and would drive them from the lands they had inhabited since Mesolithic times; and the impact of Viking incursions along the east Baltic coast, which commenced around 650.

Excavations of the hill forts and hill-top villages throughout the eastern and southern Baltic territories indicate that many were destroyed—some by fire—and abandoned in the middle centuries AD when the Baltic tribes were displaced by successive waves of Slavic peoples, who were themselves responding to pressure from the migrations and invasions of Goths, Visigoths and Celts. The Slavic migrations from the south into the middle and upper Dniepr areas did not wipe out the eastern Balts entirely however; the latter survived in smaller enclaves for several centuries, as the existence of both Slavic and Baltic cemeteries in the same territories, some as late as the twelfth century, indicate. But as the poorer grave goods reveal, their material prosperity declined significantly and over time the Baltic domains contracted to an area more closely resembling the present-day geographical position of Latvia, Lithuania and northern Poland. The invasion of one such Slavic tribe, the Krivichi, drove many of the Latgallians westwards, an event which sank deep into the collective folk memory: to this day the Latvian word for 'Russians' is 'Krievi'.[18] Like the period after the fall of the Roman Empire, such migrations also disrupted established trade routes, though over time new ones took their place. Thus the Gothic historian Jordanus records that between 523 and 526 envoys from the 'Aestii' brought gifts of amber to the Ostrogothic King Theodoric in Ravenna and that he reciprocated, sending a letter and gold coins to the 'King of the Hellespont' at the town of Daugmale on the Daugava river, not far from where Rīga would be built.[19]

In the west the activities of the Vikings had a different impact. They had comparatively little effect on the geographical holdings of the Old Prussians, Lithuanians and Kurs, all of whom successfully resisted Scandinavian conquest. Apart from a few Viking colonies and short-lived local conquests in the two centuries from about 650 to 850, the Baltic tribes continued to occupy their ancestral lands. The types of graves and burial customs reveal that the differentiation into distinctive tribal units seen in the first centuries AD remained fairly stable while the immense increase in the quantity of silver, bronze and iron in the grave goods indicate a dramatic rise in material prosperity. However, faced with the continuing threat of invasion and piracy from 'the sea-wolves of the north', those same graves reveal a marked increase in weaponry and armaments as well as horse-harness, signalling the growing military importance of a well-equipped cavalry.

The hill forts and fortified villages of the Kurs, Semigallians, Latgallians and Lithuanians, then, continued to grow and prosper and were described in the ninth century chronicles as substantial 'towns'. Alfred the Great's chronicler Wulfstan, who visited the

Old Prussian lands between 880 and 890, bore witness to the many towns there, each with its leader or king, confirmation of a well-established feudal system. In his biography (876) of Bishop Anskar, the Bremen historian Bishop Rimbert included a detailed account of the strife between Scandinavians and Kurs (Curonians) in the mid-ninth century and a summary: 'a tribe, called Chori, living far from them [Swedes] was earlier subdued by the Swedes, but it was a long time ago, when they revolted and liberated themselves from the yoke'. He also noted the existence of five 'states' (*civitates*) in Kurland which owed allegiance to a high lord or king, and in his account of the battles between Vikings and the Kurs in 855 he named two towns of considerable size, stating that Saeborg ('Seeburg', probably Grobiņa not far from modern Liepāja) and Apulia (Apule) were able to muster 7,000 and 15,000 warriors, respectively, to repel the Viking attacks.[20] Given the frequency of the raids it is no wonder that many of the principal settlements in Kurland were situated between 5 and 25 kilometres from the coast.[21]

Relations between the Viking peoples and the Old Prussians, Kurs and Latgallians fluctuated between vigorous and mutually profitable trade, and piracy, accompanied by sporadic but in the end unsuccessful attempts by the Vikings to colonise the east Baltic coast. The Kurs were a fiercely independent people, fine warriors and intrepid seafarers who traded throughout the Baltic and North Sea and were perfectly capable of repelling Scandinavian attacks and of mounting retaliatory raids. In his *Gesta Danorum* the Danish historian Saxo Grammaticus relates how in the ninth century King Loker of Kurland captured the Danish prince Hadinga and held him for ransom, at the same time praising the Kurs as brave fighters and noting that a century earlier they had been allies of the Danes against the Swedes. Hadinga, however, later returned to Kurland and attacked Andvan, the 'King of the Hellespont' and lord of the stronghold of Düna (either Rīga or Daugmale). Andvan was captured and subsequently ransomed, but some years later Hadinga's son Frothi also assembled a fleet and attacked Andvan. Entering the fortress disguised as a woman, he opened the gates to the attacking host and the city fell. When Frothi demanded that Andvan hand over his daughter, the King replied with dignity:

a victor should take care not to be corrupted by his success and so become haughty. Rather he should spare the vanquished, respect their overthrown splendour and learn to value the former prosperity of those whose fortunes had dwindled. He should be cautious, not seize the empire where he sought kinship and, if he desired to honour someone through marriage, should not at the same time sully him with mean degradation, for in his greed he was liable to taint the dignity of the union. By the good-breeding of his words he simultaneously made the conqueror his son-in-law and preserved the freedom of his realm. This astute speech so impressed Frothi that he married Andvan's daughter. [22]

The Kurs and other Baltic tribes continued to enjoy a remarkable enrichment of their material wealth from the ninth century onwards, thus attracting further piratical raids from Sweden, Denmark and even Iceland; in return the Kurs plundered their coasts. By all accounts these maritime powers were fairly evenly matched. One such early tenth century raid is recorded in the Icelandic *Egils Saga*, a valuable source of information for its detailed descriptions of a typically wealthy Kurland household. The saga relates how Egil and his companion Thorolf were captured by the Kurs after fierce fighting, but eventually managed to escape, taking with them silver, weapons and other booty. The chieftain's holding consisted of several houses and barns built of great timber logs and protected by ramparts. The main house had large chambers on the ground floor, including a hall where the lord and his retainers feasted, with stairs leading to the upper floor where the beds were made up by serving men. Here too were stored the weapons as well as wooden chests full of silver and other treasure. Once Egil and Thorolf had freed themselves, they discovered some Danish prisoners who affirmed that they had been well-treated on the whole and had been set to look after the livestock, but after an abortive escape attempt had been confined to the cellar where Egil found them. *Egils Saga* also states that during a later raid on England Egil 'had at his side the sword he called Adder. He had got that sword in Kurland and it was the best of weapons.'[23]

Such accounts of the wealth and fine weaponry of Kurland are substantiated by the archaeological excavations of local Kur graves which are rich in silver, bronze, gold, and amber jewellery, leather gear studded with precious metals and amber, decorated horse harness and fine weaponry, confirmation that the treasure chests kept in the domains of chieftains and lords were indeed a temptation to Viking raiders. The Kurs were more than capable of holding their own, however, and their raids on the Danish and Swedish kingdoms are well documented in Scandinavian chronicles such as the *Heimskringla* and *Ynglinga Saga* where Snorre Sturleson mentions that so successful were the Kur attacks that a special prayer was introduced in Danish churches during the reign of Harald Hardrada (1045–66): '*För Kurerna beväre oss, milde Herre Gudi*'—'Deliver us from the Kurs, gentle Lord God'.[24]

From the middle of the ninth century onwards, however, the Viking presence in the eastern Baltic was driven by an even more important factor than piracy: the need to secure safe trade routes along the inland waterways. In Latvia the Lielupe river gave access to the Lithuanian lands to the south, while the Gauja was navigable north as far as Estonia, from whence the Vikings could proceed via Pskov and Lake Ladoga to the great markets of Novgorod. Here they met merchants from Persia, Byzantium and central Asia who had come up by way of the Volga river—some continued south to visit other Baltic trading centres. It is for this reason that Arabic geographers were able to describe the flourishing northern Latvian kingdom of Tholova (Tālava).[25] Most important of all was the river Daugava, the start of the great *Austrwaegr*, the 'East Way', to fabled Byzantium. Each spring convoys of Viking ships would gather at Visby on the island of Gotland, traverse the Gulf of Rīga to the trading post that would one day become Rīga, negotiate safe passage with the lord of Düna and then proceed up the Daugava.

2. Sword from Kurland, early thirteenth century (photograph © Museum of the History of Rīga and Navigation)

Their journey can be charted with some precision, for it was marked by fortresses, controlled by local lords and chieftains, a day's journey apart (the distance determined by the time it would take to sail upstream against the current).

One such prominent stronghold on the upper Daugava was Jersika, whose name is thought to derive from 'Guersike', meaning 'a trader with the Greeks'. It was here that goods were unloaded in order to bypass the dangerous river rapids and then re-loaded on the other side of the town. Here, as elsewhere, it would have been essential for the Vikings to have negotiated safe passage with the lord of the realm. The impressive extent of ancient Jersika can be seen even today: the site is still dominated by two fortress-crowned mounds, one on either side of the river, and excavations have uncovered a settlement of 18,000 square metres, protected by strong wooden stockades and earthen ramparts as well as by a moat on one side and a stream on the other. It would have been a formidable stronghold, well able to dominate river traffic and to levy tolls. Archaeologists have also unearthed evidence of flourishing domestic crafts: crucibles, moulds for metal work, bronze pincers and iron tongs, well-made iron locks and keys. There were kilns and the remains of what was clearly a successful pottery industry (Latgale is still famous for the quality of its ceramics). Below street level the cellars have yielded the remains of barley, wheat, rye, oats and, significantly, salt and rare spices, indicating an unusually sophisticated standard of living.

Viking convoys would continue beyond Jersika and the town of Daugavpils further east to Vitebsk (in modern Belarus), make a portage across to the upper Dniepr at Gdeznovo near Smolensk (Russia), and then proceed down the Dniepr with its hazardous cataracts and hostile tribes to the Black Sea and finally to Byzantium. The Vitebsk–Smolensk area is particularly rich in Latgallian and Viking burial mounds dating from the ninth and tenth centuries, when trade along the *Austrwaegr* was at its height. Some three thousand have been located, though only a thousand excavated to date. They confirm well-established and extensive Baltic communities in the area and indicate that the Scandinavian Vikings and the Balts must have co-existed peacefully.

The Daugava–Dniepr river route was immensely profitable for both peoples. In 860 the Scandinavian Rus gained control of Kiev and by 882 had added Smolensk and Vitebsk, thus consolidating the north–south route between the trading cities of the Baltic and the unimaginable riches of the Byzantine Empire. From the north came mink, sable, marten and ermine furs, black fox and beaver pelts; high quality slaves seized in Baltic and North Sea raids; honey and wax (always in demand for Byzantine palaces, churches and grand private residences); and barrels of precious amber. On the return voyage the Viking Rus brought back light-weight luxury goods, including Byzantine silk (whose fine quality and prestige were immense) and the refinements of medieval life: spices, gems, gold coins, glass, porcelain and *objets d'art*. Some of these would have gone to pay the Daugava river tolls and enriched the local communities; others may have been purchased by wealthy chieftains. All along the Daugava, Byzantine gold coins and silver coins struck in Baghdad, Damascus, Basra, Kufa and Isfahan as well as Anglo-Saxon silver pence, Swedish and Danish coins, silver necklaces and Baltic silver bars have been found. An impressive hoard was unearthed at the important river port of Daugmale, 14 miles south of Rīga. With so favourable a trading network, the early Latvian tribes and their chieftains became a significant power in the economic activities between Europe, Scandinavia, Kievan Rus and the realms of Byzantium and the East.

Along with the ever-widening sphere of commercial activity, accompanied by a growth in population and towns, the earlier system of bartering goods slowly gave way to the use of currency (until the tenth century foreign coins had been valued as ornaments for jewellery rather than used as monetary units of exchange). In the Baltic, slim silver bars weighing 100 and 200 grams appear in the graves of the rich, along with tiny folding scales. Lithuanian in origin, these bars continued in use until the fifteenth century. Large hoards of them as well as of the familiar Baltic and Kievan Rus silver ornaments, Viking swords and Arab, Byzantine, Danish, Swedish, German and Anglo-Saxon coins have been found along the principal river and coastal trade routes. The Baltic tribes also adopted the

Swedish system of weights and measures and the accounting system that had been established at Birka in Sweden, the central depot for the Viking trade with the East. Even today the Latvian word for money remains *nauda*, from the Old Swedish *naut*.

Lacking their own written language, the Baltic tribes enter the pages of history entirely through foreign eyes and accounts—whether Greek, Latin, Scandinavian, German, Slav—and what can be learned of them from archaeological evidence. It is clear that by the eleventh century their domains had contracted as a result of Slav, German and Scandinavian pressure to about a sixth of the territory they had occupied in archaic times, that is to an area roughly corresponding to modern Latvia and Lithuania.[26] The various tribes, distinguished one from another by different burial customs and types of grave goods if not always by recorded names, had slowly coalesced into larger groups, the four principal ones being the Kurs/Curonians, Semigallians, Latgallians/Lettgallians and Selonians, though the last gradually merged with the other three and do not appear in later history as a separate tribe.[27] In the absence of any indigenous writings, therefore, what is known of the customs, religion, language, social organisation and character of these peoples must come from archaeological evidence and from the few external written references. Nevertheless, a picture can be built up bridging the gap between pre-history and later accounts of the Balts, not only through the aforementioned sources but also through an exceptionally extensive body of oral literature, which survived centuries of occupation to offer us a glimpse into the nature and beliefs of these far distant peoples.

Map 3. Principal Baltic tribes c. 1000–1200 AD

2

A CONQUERED PEOPLE

'Land Under Sun': pre-Christian Baltic Society

From the surviving fragments of antiquity, later chronicles and sagas, and the more extensive written records of the early medieval period, a picture slowly emerges of the character, culture and social organisation of the Baltic tribes. Writing four centuries before the birth of Christ, Herodotus had distinguished the Neuri from the Scythians, noting that the former had adopted Scythian customs such as the equality of men and women and the paramount importance of the horse. The high esteem in which the horse was held is witnessed by the extensive and richly furnished burials devoted solely to that animal in both cultures. In the first century AD Tacitus had maintained that the Aestii, the amber-gatherers, were far more diligent in cultivating crops and the fruits of the earth than their Germanic neighbours, and in the sixth century the gothic writer Jordanus praised the Aestii as a wholly peaceful people. Then Bishop Rimbert, writing of Kur–Viking relations in the years 853–4, mentioned the considerable size of two towns, Apulia and Seeburg, but it was to the Anglo-Saxon chronicler Wulfstan that we owe the first detailed account of the customs of the Aestii in the late ninth century. After noting that they had many fortified settlements, each ruled by its king, he states:

There is a great deal of honey and fishing. The king and the most powerful men drink mare's milk, the poor men and the slaves drink mead. There is very much strife among them. There is no ale brewed among the *Este* but there is plenty of mead. There is a custom among the *Este* that after a man's death he lies indoors uncremated among his relatives and friends for a month, sometimes two. The kings and other high-ranking men remain uncremated sometimes for half a year—the more wealth they have the longer they lie above ground in their houses. [...] On the very day on which they intend to carry the dead man to the pyre, they divide his property—whatever is left of it after the drinking and gaming—into five or six portions, sometimes more, depending on how much there is. They place the biggest portion about a mile from the settlement, then the second, then the third, until it is all distributed within the mile, so that the smallest portion is closest to the place where the dead man lies. All the men who have the swiftest horses in the country are assembled at a point about five or six miles from the property, and then they all gallop towards it. The man who has the fastest horse comes to the first portion (which is also the largest) and then one after another until it has all been taken. He has the smallest portion who gets from his ride the one nearest to the settlement. Then each of them rides on his way with the property and is allowed to keep it all. For this reason good horses are extremely valuable there. When the man's treasures have all been spent in this way, then he is carried out and burned up with his weapons and clothes. They use up most of the dead man's wealth with what they spend during the long period of his lying in the house, and with what they put by the wayside which strangers ride up to and take. It is the custom among the *Este* that the men of each tribe are cremated, and if one bone is found not completely burned, heavy compensation must be paid.

There is a tribe among the *Este* that knows how to cause cold, and this is why the dead men there lie so long and do not rot, because they keep them cold.[1]

Such cremation practices—which included the deceased's horses, weapons, clothes and ornaments—persisted well into the fourteenth century, despite strong opposition from the Christian church. Indeed, in some parts of Kurland cremation rituals in sacred groves continued into the fifteenth century.[2]

It is from early church records of the eleventh and twelfth centuries, however, that the clearest picture of early Baltic beliefs and customs emerges. Around 1075 Adam of Bremen had described the Old Prussians of Samland as:

a most humane people, who go out to help those who are in peril at sea or who are attacked by pirates. Gold and silver they hold in very slight esteem.

They have an abundance of strange furs, the odour of which has inoculated our world with the deadly poison of pride. But these furs they regard, indeed, as dung, to our shame, I believe, for right or wrong we hanker after a martenskin robe as much as for supreme happiness. [...] Many praiseworthy things could be said about these peoples with respect to their morals, if only they had the faith of Christ whose missionaries they cruelly persecute. [...] Although they share everything else with our people, they prohibit only, to this very day indeed, access to their groves and springs which, they aver, are polluted by the entry of Christians.[3]

3. Bronze Necklace and Brooch (*sakta*), early thirteenth century (photograph © Museum of the History of Rīga and Navigation)

He also names Kurland, referring to Bishop Anskar's designation of the inhabitants as 'Chori', and notes that it 'takes eight days to traverse' this land.

> Gold is very plentiful there, the horses are of the best; all the houses are full of pagan soothsayers, diviners and necromancers, who are even arrayed in a monastic habit. Oracular responses are sought there from all parts of the world, especially by Spaniards and Greeks.[4]

To the consternation of early Christian missionaries to the Baltic in the eleventh and twelfth centuries, the inhabitants fiercely resisted attempts to convert them and stubbornly continued to observe their cremation rites, belief in reincarnation, worship of gods and spirits, reverence for sacred groves, trees, fields and waters, and their respect for diviners and soothsayers of both sexes. Even after the Teutonic Knights had conquered the Baltic lands in the thirteenth century, imposing baptism on the local populations and forbidding pagan rituals, villagers and country folk preserved their traditional beliefs and customs—the Old Prussians remained resolutely pagan until their extermination in the seventeenth century.[5] The comparatively recent advent of Christianity, then, was a stratum that lay very lightly on the ancient belief systems of the Balts, which survived in folklore, song and art and indeed still permeate Baltic culture today. Although a modern sensibility may consider details of that pagan religion of limited importance, the customs and beliefs—like the folk art that arose from them—offer an invaluable insight into an archaic world view which reaches back to the very beginnings of Western culture. This makes them intensely interesting and is as important for an informed understanding of Baltic history as are archaeological remains or as Latvian and Lithuanian are for the reconstruction of the ancient Indo-European mother-tongue.

Passages in church records of the thirteenth and fourteenth centuries refer to pagan religious buildings (*domos sacros, sacras villas*) which, being constructed of wood as was common throughout northern Europe, have not survived. However, archaeological excavations have uncovered the remains of distinctive round and oval temples on hill-top sanctuaries, some dating from as early as the fifth century BC. Many such ancient sites were subsequently built over with Christian churches and chapels. Adam of Bremen, cited above, mentions the prevalence of pagan priests, diviners and magicians (*sancti viri, auguri, sacerdotes, nigromantici*) and as recently as the sixteenth century written sources noted that such personages still commanded immense respect. Political power, however, was always vested in secular figures—chieftains, lords and kings. The pagan religion was universal throughout the Baltic, informing life at every level and it remained astonishingly resistant to efforts to destroy it.

The most fruitful source for reconstructing the pagan world view of the early Latvians is the immense body of oral folklore that has survived and in particular the *dainas*, which are short lyric songs (usually four lines). Over a million texts and their variants have been catalogued along with some 30,000 melodies, making this one of the richest oral repositories on earth. They are remarkable for the details they give not only of a long-vanished traditional way of life but also for transmitting its principles of existence, its deeply religious view of the cosmos and of humanity's place in the scheme of things. Some of the *dainas* are clearly of great antiquity, reaching back to that archaic period when the Indo-European tribes flowed into the Baltic lands, bringing their gods with them. They reveal that the patriarchal newcomers must have reached an accommodation with the indigenous Narva people and their female deities, for (rare among the European pagan religions) the Baltic peoples absorbed the Indo-European pantheon yet also preserved the old order of things. Thus the great natural powers that govern and shape the world remained female, with a corresponding sense of nurturing and benevolence. The Sun (*Saule*) who drives her horses across the sky is also the matron of a vast cosmic household. The world itself is called *pasaule*, the land under the sun. The earth is *Zemes māte*, the sea is ruled by *Jūras māte*, the forests are presided over by *Meža māte*, and although the four winds are masculine, they are governed by their mother, *Vējas māte*. The goddess of living things is *Māra*, and her sister deity *Laima*, often equated with Fate or Necessity, can bring riches and blessing.

Laima decrees my life
As linden leaf, as apple tree;
May I grow like the linden leaf,
May I blossom like the apple tree.[6]

These and other female powers survived from that ancient matricentric belief system once thought to have been universal throughout Europe and the Near East.

The Indo-European newcomers and their masculine deities—the shining sky-god *Dievs* (later conflated with the Christian God) who rode on horseback through the heavens, *Pērkons* (god of thunder who smote evil-doers), *Mēness* the moon (shepherd of the stars who taught mankind mathematics) and others—shared the power and worship of the older female deities. In short, the ancient Baltic religion embraced a concern for the well-being of the land and the heavens and fostered a sense of kinship and reciprocity between humanity, the natural world and the realm of the spirit. In that archaic view of the cosmos the whole of nature was sacred and humankind an integral link in the great chain of being, as the *dainas* record:

Māra's room is filled
With tiny, balanced swings;
If you move one,
All the rest sing.

In the thirteenth century Cardinal Oliver Scholasticus wrote of these Baltic heathens:

They honour forest nymphs, forest goddesses, mountain spirits, low-lands, waters, field spirits and forest spirits. They expected divine assistance from virgin forests, wherein they worshipped springs and trees, mounds and hills, steep stones and mountain slopes—all of which presumably endowed mankind with strength and power.[7]

The *dainas* also transmit a distant folk memory of the pastoralist Indo-European custom of interring the dead in large barrows or mounds;[8] Baltic folk poetry is redolent with references to the 'white hill' of the dead.

How should I fear to sleep
Beneath the white sands of the hill,

When past it walked the pied cattle,
And past it the shepherds sing still.

In the ancient conception of life and death, the souls (*dvēseles*) leave the visible world to cluster at the white sandy hill before continuing to the realm of eternal light 'beyond the sun'.[9] The dead maintain a link with the physical world, however, for in addition to the soul (comparable to the Greek *psyche*) which departs this life, there are also spirits or ghosts, the *veļi*, which remain on earth,[10] as well as a life-force (akin to the Roman *anima* or the Greek *pneuma*) which at the moment of death flows into trees, flowers, birds and animals.

The *dainas* re-create a world in which people saw themselves as 'the sons of god' (*Dievs*) and 'the daughters of the sun' (*Saule*), the division itself exemplifying the merging of the masculine and feminine pantheons of old. Throughout the Baltic this shared heritage and reverence for the natural environment transcended tribal divisions and fostered that sense of community which would one day become the foundation of a nation. Every season of the year with its attendant tasks, from sowing to harvest and the details of animal husbandry in each month, had its appropriate *dainas*; every stage of human life from birth to death was celebrated in song. The *dainas* transmit the traditions governing the old tribal communities: details of family relations, courtship and marriage rituals; the conventions of warfare; the dangers and rewards of commerce on the Daugava and the seas; the lamentations sung at times of illness, misfortune or bereavement. The *dainas* are voices that sing from the other side of a dense forest of time, a rich legacy that still infuses the art, literature and music of both Latvia and Lithuania.

Although the ancestors of today's Latvians and Lithuanians developed no epic poetry, there was an extensive body of folklore which included the types of universal hero-figures whose stories reveal much about life in early feudal societies. Chief among these was *Lāčplēsis*, or Bear-slayer, who became the archetype of the wise ruler. According to legend it was he who established the laws and created administrative systems.[11] He was supported by a group of loyal retainers, the *draudze* (companions) and advised by a council of the wise, the *burtnieki* (that is, those who could read and write—from *burts*, meaning 'letter') who were the guardians of the common law. Throughout the early Latvian kingdoms tribunals composed of the *burtnieki* would have implemented the laws, resolved local disputes and overseen the system of monetary fines. From the sixth century onwards, as with the exchange of letters and gifts between the 'King of the Hellespont' and the gothic King Theodoric, they helped to negotiate treaties between friendly tribal chiefs as well as with hostile powers.

The social organisation of the early Latvian tribes was not unlike that found elsewhere in early medieval Europe. The basic unit was the extended family, the *saeime;* several *saeimes* constituted a clan (*gints*) whose lands together formed an administrative unit (*pagasts*) and the territory of several clans was known as a *novads*, referred to in church chronicles as *terra*.[12] Overall authority rested with the *kungs*, the lord or seigneur, with his household of *draugi* (friends). In times of danger a particularly powerful *kungs* would assume control over several such territories and become a *Lielkungs* (great lord or overlord); such personages were cited in Latin texts as, variously, *dux, princeps, rex*. The land ruled by each tribal lord or king was called the *valsts* (from *vald*, meaning 'to rule') and the root word resonates in the names of several early Latvian kings: *Visvaldis* (All-Ruler), *Tālivaldis* (Far-Ruler), *Vienvaldis* (One Ruler). These feudal monarchs required military service from their chieftains and yeomen for the defence of the realm; with the help of the *burtnieki* they would have levied taxes and tolls, administered justice in their lands, sent forth diplomatic missions and agreed treaties with other powers. Written records from the medieval period also indicate that the principle of hereditary rule was accepted in the Baltic.[13]

At the beginning of the second millennium AD, the territory that would one day become Latvia was composed of five tribal kingdoms: Tālava and Latgale (Lettgallia), both north of the Daugava river; Kurland (Courland/Curonia), the kingdom of the Selonians, and that of the Semigallians south of the river. It is possible that these loosely allied kingdoms would have formed a federation over time and been united under some particularly able king, such as the powerful and charismatic Visvaldis of Latgale, renowned for the successful defence of his realm against Russian and Lithuanian incursions. But this natural coalescence, achieved in neighbouring countries such as Poland under the Piasts and Lithuania under Mindaugas, was short-circuited by two aggressive powers, each supported by a militant Christian church: the very rapid expansion and consolidation of German mercantile activity in the Baltic, and the arrival of the Teutonic Knights.

The eastern Baltic was rich in natural resources which were eagerly sought by the north German merchants: amber, oak and pine; rye, linseed, flax; foodstuffs such as fish and meats, cheese and honey; the beeswax needed for both church and state; manufactured staples such as hemp rope and sailcloth made by the Kurs. The same merchants recognised that if they were to achieve control of the eastern Baltic and its ports to gain direct access to the riches of the Slav and Russian hinterland, they would need to eliminate Scandinavian competition. As early as the tenth and eleventh centuries, merchants from Bremen sought to displace Swedish and Danish influence in the strategically placed port of Visby on the island of Gotland, some eighty miles from the coast of Kurland. With the founding of Lübeck in 1158,[14] the control of Visby achieved by 1163, and a number of favourable commercial treaties—such as that with Novgorod in 1195—concluded, the merchant princes of the north German Hanseatic towns succeeded in supplanting both Scandinavian and Slav competition, and the economic exploitation and colonisation of the lands of the Old Prussian, Lithuanian, Latvian and Estonian tribes began.

In that commercial conquest and the territorial one that followed, the German merchants initially sought the support of the Finno-Ugric Livs, a small enclave of whom had settled between the Daugava estuary on the Gulf of Rīga and the Salaca river in northern Latvia. Recognising that the minority Livs might welcome additional support in their disputes with the neighbouring Latgallians—and that the Liv settlements conveniently separated the southern from the northern Latvian tribes—the Hanseatic merchants signed treaties with the Livs. They then approached the independent Latvian kingdoms one by one, and by setting tribe against tribe came to dominate the economy of the area, securing the trade routes north along the Gauja river to Estonia—and hence to Pskov and Novgorod—and east to the Slavic principalities of Polotzk and Smolensk. Thus it came about that although the Livs occupied only a comparatively small coastal area,[15] the Germans gave their name to the entire territory inhabited by the Latvian and Estronian peoples, a name that would endure for centuries—Livonia.

That commercial conquest was paralleled by the increasingly vigorous efforts of the Christian church to abolish the pagan religion of the Baltic tribes. Earlier attempts by Danish, Swedish and German missionaries to bring Christianity to the eastern Balts had met with firm resistance and only sporadic success, though a number of crosses do appear in eleventh and twelfth-century graves. Indeed, as early as the ninth century merchants in an expedition against the Kurs launched by Olaf of Sweden had sought to introduce the new religion. In 1045 the Danish king Sweyn Astrittson subsidised the building of a chapel at Domesnaes on the Kurland coast, though that was soon destroyed, and in 1161 the Danish prince Abel appointed his chaplain Ernemordus Bishop of Kurland and sent him to baptise the Kurs of Palanga (near Klaipēda, Lithuania).[16] From the east Greek Orthodox missionaries accompanied by armed escorts proselytised among the tribes of Latgallians and Tālavians, taking advantage of tribal disputes and promising military aid from the Prince of Polotzk. The complex and shifting alliances this engendered between the various tribal kingdoms and emissaries from both Roman and Orthodox churches will be discussed later, but although local rulers generally tolerated the new religion, few accepted baptism and those who did as often as not returned to the old faith.

The reasons for that remarkably sustained resistance to Christianity will remain a matter of debate, but it must have been founded on three key aspects of Baltic culture. Firstly, the power of a religion which saw humanity as part of a benign order of things must have made the austerity of Christianity with its emphasis on sin, guilt and redemption temperamentally uncongenial. Secondly, the Balts' sense of themselves as a people was founded on their oral history, transmitted by the *dainas*, which integrated religious sensibility, customs, traditions and social structure, as well as preserving these in a language of immense antiquity. And thirdly, the scattered and fiercely independent tribal communities had successfully defended their lands from foreign incursions for centuries through the strategic positioning of their castle mounds and forts, dating from the Iron and Bronze Ages. It was this very independence however and the reluctance—or inability—to forge permanent and mutually sustaining local alliances, that was to prove their undoing.

Northern Livonia

Christianity, then, came late to Latvia. It was not until 1186 that an Augustinian canon, Meinhard of Holstein, attempted to found a bishopric in Rīga, supported by the promises of armed protection from German, Danish and Norwegian merchants. Faced with an intransigent population, however, he and his armed escort moved to a site several miles up the Daugava river to the village of Uexküll (Ikšķile) where he founded a church and promised to build a stone fortress, provided the villagers convert to Christianity. The fort was built, whereupon those who had been baptised relapsed, while others simply refused baptism altogether. It was to prove a common pattern in the decades to come.[17]

Meinhard died in 1196 and was followed by Bishop Berthold of Hannover, who proved equally unsuccessful and soon perished in his crusade against the 'treacherous Livs'. In a far different mould was Albert, nephew of the influential Archbishop of Bremen. He was consecrated Bishop of Livonia and with the blessing of the pope—who proclaimed 'The Baltic Crusade' equal in importance to the Fourth Crusade to recapture Jerusalem—arrived in March 1200 with twenty-three ships and an army of 500 crusaders. As well as his church title he was also a prince of the Holy Roman Empire.

Unlike his predecessors, Albert possessed the qualities of astute diplomacy and ruthless expediency in equal measure. Distrusting the local Livs and Latgallians, he relocated the church from Uexküll to Rīga and invited the principal dignitaries of the city to a banquet (taking care to surround the house with his German soldiers) where he forced the city Elders to surrender thirty of their sons as hostages.

Albert then built a town adjacent to the existing one 'in a spacious green field, next to which there was a potential harbour for ships'.[18] With the help of imported masons he erected the cathedral, houses for himself and his priests, barracks for the military and new warehouses, and surrounded the whole stronghold with a wall and a moat, part of which is still the city canal. Although there had been an important trading port and town here since pre-historic times, it was Albert's city that would become known as Rīga. The origins of that name are still uncertain: one chronicler affirms that 'the Livonians showed the bishop the site of the city which they call Riga. They call it Riga […] from Lake Riga next to the site.'[19] This supports the view that there was originally a river Rīga and indeed the name appears in 1154 on the famous map of the Baltic by the Arab traveller and geographer Idrisi, who also calls the coast *ard al magus*, 'land of the idolaters'.[20] Equally plausible is the explanation that traders had stored their goods for centuries in the local warehouses or *riji* ('barn' in Latvian) and that over time the 'j' hardened to 'g', though as late as 1589 Hakluyt still calls the city 'Rie' in his *Principal Navigations*. In any case, the diocese of Livonia was formally proclaimed in 1206 and in 1207 Rīga became the capital of the Livonian principality, seat of the bishopric under papal suzerainty.

To consolidate his position, Bishop Albert persuaded Pope Innocent III in 1201 to sanction the establishment of a crusading Order to subdue the natives; the pope duly consecrated this Order and gave it statutes similar to the Knights Templar. Variously known as the Order of the Livonian Templars and, with devastating irony, the Knights of the Sword, after the insignia of both red cross and sword on the shoulders of their white cloaks, this Order merged with the Teutonic Knights in 1237. Thereafter it was known as the

4. City Seal of Rīga, 1225–6

Order of the Teutonic Knights in Livonia, or the Livonian Order for short. However, whatever their title, these German knights swept through the countryside with swift brutality. The same crusaders who had sacked and looted Constantinople in 1204 proved equally adept and rapacious here in the north and their depredations of the Baltic lands became a perpetual reason for local rebellion and a source of conflict with the church. In an effort to curb their power various measures were taken, all of them ineffectual. Pope Innocent III attempted to do so in 1215 by formally pro-claiming the new Livonian bishopric *Terra Mariana*, to emphasise the interest of the Holy See.[21] Pope Honorius III also issued a bull in 1225 which took all the Christian peoples of the Baltic lands under papal protection, at the same time granting Rīga the rights of a *civitas*, a free city of the Holy Roman Empire. This gave it a considerable degree of self-government and the power to mint its own coins. Notwithstanding these measures, the Order defied both bishop and pope, as well as the burghers and merchants of the city with whom they had treaties. For the next two hundred years a

39

state of almost continual armed conflict would exist between Rīga and the Order.

The conquest of Livonia was justified on the grounds that these vast and rich domains were sparsely inhabited by an unregenerate and heathen people 'without a history', and it proceeded in carefully planned stages through a series of masterly strategies devised by Bishop Albert, supported by the papacy, the German merchants, the Knights of the Sword and the magnates of the Holy Roman Empire. Having firmly established his position in Rīga, Albert obtained a papal bull authorising the blockade of Daugmale, the important Semigallian port on the Daugava river some 16 miles to the south-east, perceived as a threat to German commercial interests in Rīga. Both town and port were completely destroyed. Between 1204 and 1206 Albert directed the Knights of the Sword to occupy strategic sites throughout the Liv domains.[22] After repelling an abortive raid on Rīga by the Lithuanians in 1205, and having secured his southern borders by signing a treaty with King Viesturs of Semigallia, Bishop Albert turned his attention eastwards and sent his forces to subdue the next important river settlement, Koknese, which owed allegiance to the king of Latgale. The lord of Koknese fled in 1207 and the town and surrounding lands became part of the Livonian bishopric, with the Knights of the Sword firmly in possession. Albert then sent them to occupy the Selonian stronghold of Sēlspils (Selburg), a strategically important fortress that controlled a ford in the middle Daugava. Thus by 1208 Bishop Albert was in control of the two most important strongholds on the Daugava and had actually extended his power into the kingdom of Latgale. In the same year, the northern kingdom of Tālava asked for military aid against the Estonians and Russians of Pskov and Novgorod. This Albert readily provided, with an eye to the future conquest of the north. The following year, 1209, he again moved his forces east, this time openly against King Visvaldis of Latgale, who had accepted the Greek Orthodox faith and who was temporarily absent from his domains. The bishop's knights sacked the capital Jersika and took the queen hostage. Faced with this *fait accompli* King Visvaldis had little choice but to convert to

Roman Catholicism and become a vassal of the bishop, though he was permitted to keep his lands intact for the time being.

Thus, as so often happens in the history of imperialism and colonialism, commerce and Christianity went hand in hand in the conquest of the Baltic. Albert, who now dominated the entire length of the Daugava river as far as the Russian border, turned his attention once more to the northern kingdom of Tālava, his aim being to secure control of the Gauja river which provided access to the rich markets of Pskov and Novgorod. By exploiting the mutual distrust of the tribal chieftains he conquered the smaller domains of Tālava one by one. His policy was simple: to promise military aid in return for two-thirds of the land, leaving one third for the sustenance of the local lord, but for that lord's lifetime only. The result was that the hitherto independent chieftains and their sons first became vassals and then mere yeomen living on small-holdings. The policy proved equally effective in 1214 when King Tālivaldis of Tālava himself was captured in a Lithuanian raid. His people asked Albert for help, which he granted on condition that the king convert to Roman Catholicism, become his vassal, pay tithes and tribute, and cede two-thirds of the kingdom to the Rīga bishopric. In the same year Albert directed the Order to attack Jersika again, accusing King Visvaldis of Latgale of conspiring against him with the Samogithians of the south and the Novgorod Slavs of the north. This time Jersika was looted and utterly destroyed. It was never rebuilt.

Albert proved equally adept at diplomacy, balancing the respective authorities of the pope and of the Holy Roman emperor to give himself as much autonomy as possible. He used Rome's plan to establish a strong papal state to act as a buffer against the Greek Orthodox Slavs to his advantage: in 1210 he secured the right to appoint and consecrate bishops who in turn had the power to adjudicate both civil and criminal cases.[23] Then in 1213 he negotiated a significant shift in the chain of authority: henceforth the Rīga bishopric would be answerable directly to the pope and not, as before, to the archbishop of Bremen. However, in order to consolidate his power in the north Albert attempted another alliance which was to prove a tactical error. In 1218 he offered feudal homage to the Danish King Valdemar II in return for military assistance in the north and to confirm the appointment of his own brother as bishop of Estonia. The reasoning behind the decision was understandable. Valdemar had recently captured Reval,[24] the second most important port on the Livonian coast, and had successfully kept the Russians at bay. His notional support did indeed profit Albert temporarily but bypassing the authority of the pope and the Holy Roman emperor was to prove a costly mistake. Both the Rīga elders (baptised Livs and Latgallians) and the influential cathedral chapter of powerful German burghers and merchants—second in authority only to the bishop—opposed the alliance with the Danish king, preferring to remain under the protection of the Holy See and the Holy Roman Empire. Albert's offer of homage to Denmark had been contingent on their agreement and his failure was to fuel future tensions with the Danes. He also had to re-affirm his allegiance to the emperor, while having ignored the pope undoubtedly cost him the expected elevation to the rank of archbishop.

Yet the temporary support of the Danes did enable Albert to direct his forces south in an attempt to conquer independent Semigallia. In 1218 Albert appointed a titular bishop of Selonia for that still unconquered area and in the same year he visited Germany and brought back a strong contingent of military troops, many of them supplied by the Duke of Saxony and Anhalt. An opportunity to invade Semigallia came the next year when a delegation from the important Semigallian fortress of Mežotne appealed for aid against an expected attack from Lithuania. Albert now felt strong enough to come south himself, baptise the local population *en masse*, and leave behind a strong German garrison. However, he under-estimated King Viesturs, who rightly averred that Albert had broken the treaty of 1205. Viesturs attacked Mežotne himself, regained the stronghold and ousted the German garrison. The bishop's subsequent incursions into Viesturs' realm in 1220 were vigorously repelled by the inhabitants, who had allied themselves with the Kurs, and when Viesturs died in 1229 he was still king of a free Semigallia.

It will be clear that the rapid German conquest and colonisation of the Baltic littoral and hinterlands was achieved by the combined forces of bishop, pope and crusading Order, aided by supplies and soldiers from the princes and nobility of the Holy Roman Empire, and that it was in the interests of both church and secular authorities to support the German merchants and burghers. The latter's refusal to sanction Albert's proposal to the Danish king earned them the gratitude of both the pope and the Holy Roman emperor.

Then Frederick II issued a Manifesto in 1224 condemning the molestation of the converted inhabitants of Prussia, Samblandia (an area between Prussia and Samogithia), Semigallia, Livonia and Estonia, confirming their status as free citizens of the Holy Roman Empire and affirming his protection. Frederick II's son Henry next issued another decree in 1225 uniting the Livonian and Estonian lands conquered by Bishop Albert into a Livonian Mark, or frontier province, with the bishop as its prince. In the same year Pope Honorius III issued a papal bull which also confirmed that full rights of citizenship in the Holy Roman Empire had been given to all the converted peoples of Livonia. Furthermore the pope agreed to send a papal legate to arbitrate in the dispute that had arisen with the Danes over the boundaries of Estonia and Livonia and to resolve the increasingly acrimonious relations with King Viesturs of Semigallia.

The appointed legate, Bishop William of Modena, persuaded King Viesturs to permit Christianity to be preached throughout his domains while accepting the king's steadfast refusal to become Albert's vassal. Viesturs' distrust was well-founded for, notwithstanding treaties and agreements, the Knights of the Sword continued to harass the Semigallians, though they failed to make significant inroads during the lifetime of Viesturs himself. Then in the north an accommodation was also reached with the Danes: it was agreed that they would control northern Estonia, while southern Estonia and the old kingdom of Tālava would remain under the aegis of the Rīga bishopric and be administered by the Knights of the Sword who, in theory at least, owed obedience to Bishop Albert. William of Modena's arrival had another important result. It was at his request that the earliest formal history of the Baltic domains was compiled by Henry of Livonia (Henricus de Lettis), whose comprehensive *Chronicle* is the most valuable source we have about the coming of Christianity to, and the conquest of, these lands.[25]

Albert died in 1229, the same year as King Viesturs of Semigallia, the ruler of a vast principality, having failed only to assimilate the southern kingdom of Semigallia. The acquisition of that kingdom was necessary in order to join Livonia and Estonia to the realm of the Old Prussians further south, which was in the process of being conquered by another military Order, that of the Teutonic Knights. Only the independent kingdoms of Semigallia and Lithuanian Samogithia stood in the way of creating that united Roman Catholic and German state along the Baltic littoral that had been envisaged by the papacy as an essential buffer against the Greek Orthodox Slavs. In geographical terms, the realm established by Albert was composed of Rīga, the Liv territories and the tribal kingdoms of Tālava, Koknese and Latgale—that is, nearly all the territory north of the Daugava that would one day become Latvia. He had consolidated German control over the immensely lucrative trade routes to the Slav principalities of Polotzk and Smolensk in the east and to Pskov and Novgorod in the north. Moreover by strengthening the authority of the cathedral chapter of Rīga and the position of the German burghers and merchants in the city, he had created a force which would one day be able to defy the Knights of the Sword. Although, as we have seen, this military Order owed obedience to the bishop, Albert had been unable to control its rapacity. The Order's greed for land and wealth, its disregard for the law and the rights of the native population and its unchecked brutality dismayed church and state alike. In his attempts to curb the Order's excesses, Albert had appealed to both pope and Holy Roman emperor, re-affirming the allegiance of the Livonian bishopric in the hope of restraining the knights. That hope was to prove illusory. The atrocities continued unpunished and the ensuing decades of the century were to witness a systematic brutality that would crush the last sparks of freedom in the native Baltic peoples.

A CONQUERED PEOPLE

Southern Livonia

Upon the death of Bishop Albert, Pope Gregory IX, who had succeeded Honorius III in 1227, confirmed the Rīga cathedral chapter's choice of successor and also appointed a new papal legate, Bishop Baldwin of Aune, to consecrate the new bishop and to press ahead with the papacy's vision of a single Prussian–Livonian state. To achieve the last it was essential to hasten the conquest of Prussia and the conversion to Christianity of the still recalcitrant Kurs, Semigallians and Lithuanian Samogithians. Accordingly, the domain of the Old Prussians, centred on the area between the Nieman and Vistula rivers, was invaded by another crusading power, the Teutonic Order,[26] which had been directed to convert the pagan inhabitants by force. However, subduing this area proved particularly difficult, for the lagoons, dunes and marshlands made large military campaigns and the use of heavy cavalry impractical; furthermore the Old Prussians had formed an alliance with their close kin to the north, the Kurs. The Teutonic Order had been given a large tract of land at Thorn (Torun) by the Polish Duke Konrad in 1225 (a gift ratified by the emperor the following year) to be a base for their operations against the pagan Prussians and Lithuanians and to protect the duchy from their raids. The next year, in an act of breath-taking arrogance, Emperor Frederick II also gave the Master of the Order sovereignty over all the domains of the as yet unconquered Old Prussians. This both strengthened the Order's standing and dramatically increased its recruitment from the younger sons of the German nobility eager to acquire land of their own.

Although the statutes of such military and church Orders demanded vows of obedience, chastity and poverty and forbade individuals to own land and goods, each Order itself had great collective wealth, was not subject to secular authority or law, and its members lived in richly endowed castles. The forced conversion of the Baltic pagan population by these Orders all too often meant simply dispossessing them of their lands and property. In practice individual knights could do as they pleased—and did. The power of the Teutonic Order was further increased by its union in 1237

45

with the Livonian Knights of the Sword, though it would take their combined forces six more decades of bloody conflict to complete the conquest of Old Prussia, Semigallia and Samogithia.

Unlike the subjugation of northern Livonia—which had proceeded piecemeal by exploiting the mutual distrust of Livs, Latgallians and Tālavians and by offering military assistance to repel Estonian and Slav raids—the conquest of the south would prove far more difficult. The depredations of the Knights of the Sword in Livonia and of the Teutonic Order in Prussia had made it abundantly clear to the Semigallians that if they wished their kingdom to survive they would need to ally themselves with the Samogithians as well as to cultivate closer ties with the Kurs. Resistance to the Teutonic Order was also fuelled by reports of their brutality and treachery. A typical example was the treatment of King Lamikis of Kurland who had signed a peace treaty with Pope Gregory IX in 1230 in order to save his realm from both the Knights of the Sword and the Danes. He agreed to be baptised, to permit the establishment of a bishopric in Kurland, and to become a feudal vassal of the papacy. In return he would be able to retain the title of king and his kingdom. The treaty was ignored by the Knights of the Sword, who marched into Kurland, attacked stronghold after stronghold, looted each, and massacred the defenders. One by one the castles of Kurland fell.[27] The few Kur lords who survived were forced to surrender, sign away their lands, and submit unconditionally to the Order. They appealed to the papal legate Bishop Baldwin and to Pope Gregory IX, who responded by censuring the Master of the Order for the invasion of Kurland and by recalling Bishop Baldwin. In 1234 he despatched William of Modena for a second term as papal legate and also consecrated him the first Bishop of Kurland, but nothing else was done to limit the depredations of the Knights of the Sword.

Meanwhile some of the Semigallians and Samogithians, outraged by reports of what had happened in Kurland, put aside their feuds and in 1236 agreed to combine their forces. They trapped the main army of the Knights of the Sword, which was returning north after a particularly successful raid in Samogithian lands. At Saule the united tribes attacked and the Knights, hampered by their spoils and unable to manoeuvre their heavy horses in the marshy terrain, were annihilated.[28] The Samogithian captives—men, women and children—were freed and sent home, while the superior steel weaponry, armour and horses were appropriated by the victors. The power and reputation of the Knights had suffered a crushing blow. At this point the future of the Baltic lands was poised on the proverbial knife-edge: had a strong leader emerged to unite Kurs, Semigallians and Samogithians, the victors of Saule might have gained control of their realms, marched on Rīga and liberated northern Livonia. But no such leader emerged and the Order's defeat at Saule, coupled with the successful resistance of the Old Prussians, so alarmed Pope Gregory that he hastened the proposed merger of the Knights of the Sword with the Teutonic Order.[29] Thus the former became the Order of the Teutonic Knights in Livonia, or the Livonian Order for short. In theory it was subordinate to the Teutonic Order, whose statutes it adopted, and whose provincial Master was appointed by the Grand Master. In practice however the new Livonian Order retained a considerable degree of autonomy. It also adopted the white cloak and black cross of the Teutonic Order but kept the traditional black tunic, which had earned its members the soubriquet the 'Black Knights'.[30] The merger ensured the survival of both Orders, enabled them to consolidate and add to their existing holdings in the Baltic and to lay the firm foundations for a German Prussian state. However, at the same time both branches of the enlarged Teutonic Order were hard pressed by hostile forces. The Livonian branch had to counter a serious threat from the Russians and Estonians in the north as well as continued unrest in Kurland and Semigallia;[31] the parent Teutonic Order was encountering determined resistance in Prussia, an unexpected attack from the Duke of Slavic Pomerania, and also facing the threat of Mongol invasion from the east.

It was at this juncture that another power arose in the Baltic: a leader of both vision and political shrewdness had appeared in Lithuania—Mindaugas. In 1240 he succeeded in uniting the Lithuanian tribes and emerged as a potential champion of Baltic resistance. To both church and secular powers, however, the Lithuanian leader was perceived as a useful buffer against the ever-present threat of invasion by the Tatars, who had already reached Muscovy. Accordingly, in 1250 Mindaugas was persuaded to sign a treaty with the Order accepting baptism, permitting the establishment of a bishopric in his domains and ceding the northern part of Samogithia to the Order, who in return recognised his claim to rule all of Lithuania. In 1252 he was crowned Grand Duke of Lithuania and in 1260 he ceded his last remaining lands in Samogithia and Kurland, along with a small disputed area in Selonia (south of the river Daugava), to the Teutonic Order. Nevertheless the Order still had to pacify the inhabitants of Kurland, Semigallia and Samogithia, who continued to resist the invaders and their religion.

During the 1250s both Kurland and Semigallia temporarily succeeded in expelling the hated Teutonic Order. Indeed, aided by a large Samogithian force in 1261 they marched north into Livonia and defeated the Order in a battle at Lielvārde on the Daugava. Also in both Samogithia and greater Lithuania a strong pagan reaction had set in against Christianity. At one point it even seemed that Mindaugas might be persuaded to revolt against the Teutonic Order, but he was killed in 1262. Meanwhile the Teutonic Knights had concluded a binding peace treaty with the Russians, which left them free to turn their attention to the final subjugation of Prussia and southern Livonia. The strongholds of Piltene, Aizpute and the capital Kuldīga—all of which had been freed in the previous decade—fell once more to the Order, and the defeated Kurs were compelled to sign a peace treaty in 1269. This left only the independent kingdom of Semigallia to resist the Order. King Nameitis was successful in defending his realm and in 1280 even marched into Rīga, capturing the marshal of the Order. The Livonian Knights then offered a peace treaty but with the death of the king in 1281 resumed their campaign. They repeatedly besieged Tērvete, the principal fortress of Semigallia, but were unable to take it and in 1287 the master of their Order was killed. In retaliation the Knights resorted to scorched-earth tactics: they devastated Semigallia, systematically burning farms and fields of crops and massacring the inhabitants. The surviving Semigallians, starving and desperate, resolved to destroy their remaining strongholds rather than have them fall into enemy hands, and abandoned their kingdom. It is estimated that 100,000 souls—most of the population—fled south into Samogithia in 1290 where they were joined by what remained of the Old Prussians. Semigallia lay waste and empty; the Livonian Order had to re-populate the entire region with farmers and peasants brought in from northern Livonia.

The exiled Semigallians joined the Samogithians and continued the war against the Teutonic Order, a war that lasted well into the fourteenth century. In 1323 Prince Gediminas of Lithuania claimed the title of duke of Semigallia (there is some evidence that he may have been a grandson of King Nameitis) and in 1345 his son Algirdas again invaded Semigallia, regaining Tērvete and several other strategic castles. He then marched into Rīga and even reached Cēsis in the heart of northern Livonia, though he failed to take it. His gains were short-lived,[32] but other forays and raids against the Order continued as late as 1372. In any case the casualties inflicted on the Order were massive: for example in 1351 its master acknowledged that he had lost 117,000 men in the preceding decade. Ten years later there was another uprising in Prussia which took the better part of a decade to suppress, but eventually 'the Prussians were wiped off the face of the earth'.[33]

It will be apparent even from this highly condensed summary that the conquest of southern Livonia was prolonged and bloody and that the original aim of creating a sovereign papal state with a population that embraced Christianity had failed, not least because of the Teutonic Order's uncontrolled rapacity. In 1255 Pope Innocent IV had united the dioceses of northern and southern Livonia, raised the status of Rīga to an archbishopric, and appointed the Prince-Archbishop Albert Suerbeer titular ruler of these Baltic domains. Like the bishops before them, the archbishops actively supported the influential burghers of Rīga in their disputes with the Livonian Order but the papacy was fast losing interest in, and control of, this distant northern region. The Order consistently ignored papal edicts and continued to harass and defy the Rīga archbishops, one of whom excommunicated the entire Order in 1325. In 1302 Archbishop Iscarus had been forced to flee the city and nearly all his successors chose to reside at Avignon until 1410, when a Lithuanian–Polish army decisively defeated the Teutonic Order at the battle of Tannenberg (Grünwald).

When the papacy had agreed to the creation of a crusading Order to bring these northern lands into the arms of the church, it had failed to imagine that such a military body, composed almost entirely of landless Germans, would one day turn against church authority in order to secure fiefdoms for itself. What had once been envisaged as *Terra Mariana*, to be ruled by clerics under a relatively benign system in which the rights of a converted native population would be respected and defended, became a lawless realm in which the dispossessed inhabitants, entirely subservient to their foreign overlords, would rapidly decline into mere labourers servicing the Order's fiefdoms. Thus, while feudalism gradually waned throughout the rest of Europe, in the Baltic it became entrenched as a caste system that would endure for centuries.

This came about slowly but inexorably, helped by the fact that there were two distinct feudal domains in Livonia, governed by the church and by the Teutonic Order. These domains were not in territorial blocks, however, but formed a complex geographical mosaic, with the church controlling about a third and the Teutonic Order about two-thirds of the Baltic provinces. This was accompanied by the tensions and disputes that inevitably arise under such a patchwork dispensation. How had this come about? In 1224 Bishop Albert had granted the Knights of the Sword a third of Livonia, at that time only northern Latvia; in 1234 the Order was given nominal charge of two-thirds of Kurland and in 1251 half of Semigallia, and in fact all of the latter would be in its hands by the end of the century. Then in the north, after a failed revolt in 1343 in which 10,000 Estonians had laid siege to Reval (Tallinn), the grand master of the Livonian Order purchased the rest of Estonia from King Valdemar IV of Denmark in 1346 and so consolidated the Order's northern realm. To be sure the archbishop of Rīga was both temporal and spiritual lord over the whole of Livonia, and technically the Teutonic Order owed him obedience, but the archbishops had no military power at their command to enforce either their decrees or those of the papacy. The only allies they had were the burghers of Rīga and the great merchant houses of the Hanseatic League. In any case the result of these two parallel land systems was that the Latvians and Estonians of Livonia were caught in a process which would progressively reduce them to the status of helots in their own domains.

That reduction proceeded through several stages. Initially the vassals were of two types, theoretically equal in standing and both equally subject to Roman and canon law: the land-hungry German barons and knights (some of whom had left the Order), and the indigenous lords of Kurland, Semigallia, Latgale and Tālava who had surrendered their hereditary rights and lands to receive them back as fiefs. Those vassals who owed fealty to the prince-archbishop of Rīga had their rights upheld and received delegated judicial powers to administer their lands. This meant that they were able to preserve a degree of independence for themselves and their people using the traditional councils, *pagasts*, whose elders upheld and implemented the common law. While the conquest of Livonia was still incomplete, the same system operated for vassals under the Livonian Order as well. But once that conquest had been achieved—and given the Order's increasing disregard of archiepiscopal authority—the native lords had their rights and freedoms progressively eroded. The Teutonic Order imposed its own bureaucracy: each of the Order's estates was ruled by a castle commander who was assisted by an administrative agent, a landmaster, and both were directly responsible only to the master of the Order. This meant that the large number of independent farmers on each estate, who owed tithe, tax and labour duty to the overlord, were simply subject to the dictates of that lord. It was this manorial system that slowly abolished the rights of the native population.

In theory the prince-archbishop of Rīga was the final authority and judge for all Livonia but as the power of the Order and its

German vassal lords grew, the latter established their own feudal courts to resolve disputes, with the lord of the manor as both judge and jury. The feudal principle of trial by one's peers, which had given the native farmers and yeomenry their own rural courts, was ignored. So was the authority of the local council, the *pagasts*, whose elders had applied traditional common law. Thus when a farm or smallholding became vacant, it was no longer disposed of by the *pagasts* or distributed among members of the community, but reverted to the overlord. Also the German seigneurs issued their own dictates and ignored both Roman and canon law whenever it was in their interests to do so. One such alteration in accepted practice was the increase in feudal labour dues: whereas it had been the custom to work for a week or two on estate lands, that duty labour was increased to as much as five days a week. The result was inevitable. Unable to cultivate their own lands, still less recover after a season of poor harvests, the independent farmers fell into debt to the local lord without hope of extricating themselves. Then in 1403 the Livonian Order was officially emancipated from the archbishop's jurisdiction, legalising what in fact had been widely practised in the previous century. By the end of the next century farmers were actually forbidden to leave their properties or to dispose of them without the permission of their lord—in effect they were serfs. Little wonder that in Latvian folklore the hated German landlord was equated with the Devil himself.

The increase in the system of feudal dues and the erosion of the native population's rights was more gradual in the great estates which owed allegiance to the church, but it proceeded there as well. Slowly the lords and farmers of Kurland, Semigallia and Latgale lost their lands and their descendants were reduced to serfdom.[34] Henceforth an unbridgeable chasm would divide the Baltic peoples from their invaders. Whether the foreign power spoke Latin or German (or in the following centuries Polish, Swedish or Russian), on one side stood the conqueror, on the other the native Latvians, Lithuanians and Estonians, who clung with ever-increasing tenacity to the one thing the invader could not destroy—their ancient languages.

Map 4. The Baltic Littoral: Period of the Teutonic Knights

3

THE POLITICS OF SURVIVAL

The Livonian Confederation: Hanseatic League and Teutonic Order

> Five stags trod the sea,
> Another five the Daugava;
> Rīga's lords walked in front
> Counting money by the sack.[1]

By the fourteenth century the whole of what would one day become Latvia and Estonia was controlled either by the Teutonic Order or the church, with the exception of a small enclave adjoining Rīga which was administered by the Rīga Municipal Council (see map 5). Rīga had been granted a high degree of autonomy as a *civitas* of the Holy Roman Empire in 1225 and thereafter had governed itself through an elected council, a burgomaster and a chief justice, though the appointment of the last was subject to the approval of the bishop (later archbishop) of the city. It had also been given a tract of land to the west wherein farmers were allowed a considerable degree of independence: in return for the usual taxes and labour duty, they were permitted to own and manage their properties. Then, too, in 1290 Rīga had adopted the city statutes of Hamburg, at the time considered among the most liberal in Europe, which confirmed the city council as the highest court of appeal. Under Bishop Albert and his immediate successors there had been no distinction drawn between Liv, Latgallian, Kur or

German burghers; their craftsmen and traders established guilds and ran their own affairs in accordance with the city statutes. These liberal measures, however, were to change with the rise of the third great power in the Baltic littoral—the Hansa.

The rise of the Hansa—that economic alliance of German towns and merchant guilds that came to dominate the trade and economy

Map 5. Livonian territories (fourteenth to mid-sixteenth centuries) belonging to:

  A—Archbishop of Rīga
  K—Kurland Bishopric
  D—Dorpat Bishopric
  O—Oesel and Wiek Bishopric
  R—Rīga Muncipal Council

of northern Europe—began in the twelfth century and grew with remarkable rapidity throughout the thirteenth. Although its origins can be traced to the eleventh century when German traders had established a presence in Visby and Novgorod, it is generally agreed to date the creation of the Hansa from the founding of Lübeck in 1159. The purpose of the alliance was to protect the commercial interests of its members by negotiating favourable trading rights with the cities of the North and Baltic Sea littorals. Lübeck, which had achieved the status of a free imperial city in 1227, quickly rose to become the centre of Hansa interests. It allied itself with Hamburg in 1241, with Köln in 1260, and then with many key coastal as well as inland towns. The members of the Hansa agreed to cooperate in trading matters, to be bound by a single legal system, and to come to each other's defence. The language of its commerce was Middle Low German.[2]

The impact of the Hansa on the eastern Baltic cannot be over-estimated. The Livonian cities joined in rapid succession: Rīga in 1282, Reval (Tallinn) in 1285 and Dorpat (Tartu) soon after, along with several towns which had strong Hansa communities and which, though not granted full membership, were deemed associates. In Estonia those included Fellin (Viljandi), Narva and Pernau (Pärnu); in Latvia Goldingen (Kuldīga), Kokenhusen (Koknese), Lemsal (Limbaži), Roop (Straupe), Wenden (Cēsis), Windau (Ventspils) and Wolmar (Valmiera). The main trade routes of the Hanseatic League stretched from London to Novgorod,[3] and the other pre-eminent cities along it were Bruges, Köln, Hamburg, Lübeck, Danzig, Visby and Rīga. Like other members of the League, the Livonian towns had their own Hanseatic parliament, or *diet*, and the right of appeal to the Lübeck council. Moreover the free cities of the League owed allegiance not to local authority but to the Holy Roman emperor and it was this independence that enabled the Rīga burghers and Hansa merchants to resist the Teutonic Order.[4]

The uneasy balance of power between church, Order and Hansa was delicate and ever-shifting. The Order, which had been given permission to engage in trade by Pope Urban IV in 1263, depended on the Hanseatic League to trans-ship the produce of its fiefdoms: timber, wheat and rye, wax, furs and amber. But when the price of grain rose, the Order—which had secured a monopoly on its production and sale in its Prussian domains—also began trading in its own right, and this brought it into conflict with the Hansa. For its part the Hansa needed the protection of the Order for its town communities as well as its shipping—piracy on the high seas was still rife and the Danes were an ever-present threat.[5] There were other reciprocal benefits which prevented the outbreak of overt hostility and modified the rivalry between League and Order. For example, after conquering the eastern Baltic, the Teutonic Order had secured a monopoly on any amber found on the seashore or excavated along its banks. By the fourteenth century it was a crime punishable by hanging for anyone in the east Baltic littoral to possess raw amber, which had to be surrendered to the Order's steward who paid for it in salt. So valuable was this resource that the amber revenues alone paid for the entire annual running costs of the Teutonic Order. The amber thus collected was sent to the Order's headquarters at Marienburg (Malbork) castle near Danzig, from whence it was shipped to the guilds of the Hansa cities of Lübeck, Bruges and, later, Königsberg, which shared the monopoly on the production of amber artefacts for nearly three centuries. But that monopoly also meant that henceforth there would be no native craftsmen left on the Baltic coast: a whole tradition dating back millennia before the birth of Christ was simply wiped out.

The entry of Rīga into the Hansa raised the city's status and generated considerable wealth, but also had negative implications for the native population. Under Hansa rules, wholesale merchants had to belong to one of the great guilds whose membership was restricted to Germans, thus excluding Kurs, Livs, Latgallians and Semigallians.[6] Native Rīgan burghers were barred from holding administrative posts; trade guilds were closed to them; the city militia would accept only Germans for its cavalry—indigenous citizens had to serve as foot-soldiers. By 1469 native Rīgans were even forbidden to own property in the city. However, Hansa towns could also provide refuge for farmers and craftsmen who had fled the fiefdoms of their oppressive German lords, whether they owed fealty to the church or to the Teutonic Order. As elsewhere in Europe, a year in the 'free air' of a chartered town meant a 'free man'.

Disputes with the Teutonic Order by archbishop, city burghers and Hansa merchants were bitter and prolonged, fuelled by the jostling for dominance in both commercial and political matters, the Order's disregard for the law and its vow of obedience to the archbishop, and exacerbated by the growing tendency of vassals of both church and Order to change their allegiance whenever they could gain by it.[7] In 1297 matters came to a head when the Rīga burghers sought to build a bridge across the Daugava not far from the Order's castle of St George. The Order deemed this a hostile action, seized the archbishop and proclaimed the city's independence at an end. Rīga's appeals to Lübeck, the papacy and the Danes went unheeded.[8] In desperation the burghers turned to Lithuania and in 1298 a combined force of Rīgans and Lithuanians defeated the Order and killed the Master at the Battle of Treiden. The Livonian Order then summoned reinforcements from its Prussian brethren and again engaged the city's forces. The pope intervened, declared a truce and ordered the release of the archbishop. However, as part of its continued tactics to intimidate the city, the Order signed a treaty with the Danish king in 1304 and the following year built a fortress at the mouth of the Daugava, thus compromising Rīga's access to the sea.

In 1312 the archbishop of Rīga appealed to Pope Clement V, submitting 230 articles of complaint against the Livonian Order; the pope responded the following year by excommunicating the Order but this had little effect, nor did a subsequent excommunication in 1325. The Order continued its feud with Rīga, laid siege to the city in 1330 and after six months the starving citizenry surrendered. The city council was forced to swear fealty to the Master of the Livonian Order and in 1332 Emperor Louis IV confirmed the Order's supremacy, though the city continued to affirm that these decrees had no judicial validity. The disputes continued until 1356 when the 'Golden Bull' issued by Emperor Charles IV stated that princes in their domains held sovereign judicial rights but were also enjoined to consult their vassals. This strengthened the position of the Rīga archbishopric, though it took another ten years—and another threat of excommunication, this time from Pope Urban V—for the Order to relinquish sovereignty to the archbishop. Such shifts in power and allegiance continued to bedevil Livonia for the better part of another century and a half.

Meanwhile the composition of the Teutonic Order itself had been changing, with implications that would eventually contribute to its downfall. Although it continued to grow with ever larger numbers of vassals, administrative officials and mercenaries, the aristocratic membership was rapidly declining. By the fourteenth century there were fewer than 300 knights,[9] barely sufficient to man the Order's castles, and numbers continued to drop. Notwithstanding this decline, the Teutonic Order remained the ruling power in Livonia and Prussia. In the north, Russian incursions had almost ceased, owing to the Tatar threat from the east, and the Danes were occupied in feuding with the Hansa. However, to the south lay Lithuania, still independent, still mostly pagan, with powerful military resources and alliances at its command—a formidable opponent to German hegemony. With shrewd foresight Grand Duke Gediminas of Lithuania had re-affirmed his people's commitment to convert to Christianity. He also concluded a treaty in 1323 with representatives from the archbishop of Rīga, the Livonian bishops, the Livonian Order itself and their Danish vassals in Estonia. Alarmed by this accord, which would destroy the Teutonic Order's hopes of gaining Lithuanian territory to create a corridor uniting their domains of Prussia and Livonia, the Grand Master directed his Prussian bishops to reprimand their Livonian brethren. The latter complied, promptly withdrawing from the treaty, whereupon the Order resumed its raids into Samogithia.[10]

At this point the history of the Baltic had once again reached a turning point: the Lithuanian army may well have had the power to drive the Teutonic Order and its vassals from the whole Baltic littoral, but after repelling Tatar incursions from the east the Slavic lands were a far more tempting prospect and the successors to Gediminas created a Polish–Lithuanian empire that stretched from the Baltic to the Black Sea.[11] Meanwhile the resistance of the Samogithian tribes to the Teutonic Order continued. Furthermore the Order's continual depredations, their power-base in Danzig (acquired in the previous century) and their successful monopoly of the Prussian grain trade so alarmed Poland and Lithuania that their leaders resolved to move against the Order.[12] In July 1410, between the villages of Tannenberg and Grünwald, their combined army inflicted a crushing defeat on the Order from which it never recovered. Although it continued for over another century, its power and prestige were severely shaken. After Tannenberg the Livonian and Prussian branches also drifted further apart. The Grand Master's authority to appoint the Master of the Livonian branch gradually weakened and another defeat inflicted on the Prussian branch in 1435 by the Polish army effectively signalled the severance of the Livonian Order from its partner.

By the middle of the fifteenth century the Livonian Order was also in some difficulty, numbering fewer than 200 knights. Nonetheless it still had considerable military resources at its disposal: over 1,000 mercenaries, several hundred cavalry and 40,000 foot-soldiers supplied by its vassals. By comparison the Rīga archbishopric could muster only 2,000 militia and the city of Rīga 5,000. Antagonism and further bloodshed between the Order and the city and archbishop continued, not helped by a weak papacy and the decree of Emperor Frederick III in 1481 conferring sovereign rights over the Livonian bishops and over the archbishop himself to the Master of the Livonian Order. This did not end the struggle for power of course, but in 1491 the Order inflicted a resounding defeat on the city, imposed humiliating terms and perpetuated the division of interests, thus further undermining any possibility of rapprochement among the disputing parties.

The end of the fifteenth century also marked the coming dissolution of the 'Livonian Confederation'. This had been created earlier in the century by Archbishop John VI, a distinguished jurist who had taken up office in 1418. In an effort to end the disputes, he had succeeded in bringing the various parties to the negotiating table and had drafted a 'Constitution of the Livonian Diet' which proposed a loose confederation of the five Baltic bishoprics (Rīga, Kurzeme, Dorpat, Oesel-Wiek and Reval), the Livonian Order, the Hanseatic cities of Rīga, Dorpat and Reval, and the many semi-independent noble vassals of both Livonia and Estonia. Each party was entitled to send as many delegates as it wished, though each 'estate' would only possess a single, representative vote. In theory this seemed an equitable procedure. The first Diet, convened in 1419, agreed that henceforth it should have legislative powers over all the parties present, citing as its authority the Golden Bull of 1356, and that it would meet annually. However, mutual distrust and suspicion undermined the effectiveness of the Diet, which came to be dominated by the Order and German landed interests to the detriment of the clergy and the burghers. The rights of the native population were eroded still further.[13]

Such internal dissensions notwithstanding, Livonia and the experimental Confederation remained firmly in German hands during the fifteenth century. However, the second half of that century—and the opening decades of the sixteenth—were to witness far-reaching changes, precipitated by four key external events: the secularisation of the Teutonic Order, the Protestant Reformation, the decline of the Hanseatic League, and the increasingly aggressive territorial ambitions of Muscovy, Sweden and Poland–Lithuania.

In 1454 the Teutonic Order's Prussian vassals and the city of Danzig revolted against its rule and after a decade of strife successfully defeated the Order with the aid of Poland. The Order was forced to sign a treaty in 1466 which transformed its membership: henceforth half would be Polish and the Grand Master himself a vassal of the King of Poland. Immense changes were to follow. In 1524, after a meeting with Martin Luther, the Grand Master Albert of Brandenburg became a Protestant. He then renewed his allegiance to Sigismund I of Poland, whereupon the king made Prussia an hereditary dukedom with Albert as its first duke. Next, Duke Albert negotiated a politically convenient marriage to the daughter of the Danish king and his knights followed his example, accepting the Protestant faith and making advantageous marriages to become hereditary landed nobles in the new political dispensation.[14]

The waning might and authority of the Teutonic Order after Tannenberg also meant that it was less able to support the Hanseatic towns. When the Hanseatic League announced in 1447 that it now possessed a complete trade monopoly in the Baltic, the proclamation met with a storm of protest and outrage, especially from English and Flemish towns which immediately closed the League's local depots (*komtors*). The Netherlands then proclaimed a general boycott of the Hansa. In the naval skirmishes that followed, the Hansa, lacking the protection of the Teutonic Order and with few other allies, was defeated. It was forced to rescind its decree and re-open its ports to English and Flemish traders. German control over land and sea in the Baltic was challenged by other powers as well. Sweden, which had become emancipated from Danish and Hanseatic control through the able efforts of its ruling Vasa dynasty, took over part of the lucrative Baltic grain trade and grew progressively more important in the trade with Muscovy. Poland had gained control of Danzig, the Vistula river and the east Prussian Hanseatic towns. Then to the north Muscovy, which had hitherto been dependent on the Hansa cities of Rīga, Narva and Reval and on the merchants of the independent principalities of Pskov and Novgorod for access to Western markets, became increasingly aggressive. In the last quarter of the fifteenth century Russia resumed raiding Livonia and under the leadership of Ivan III, Grand Prince of Muscovy, plans were made to bypass the Hansa. In 1482 he built a fortress opposite Narva to deflect trade from that Hanseatic port to the nearby Swedish port of Viborg, thus securing direct routes to Western markets. In 1484 he also closed the Hansa *komtor* in Novgorod, which in effect had become part of his Russian domain, though it was not formally annexed until the following century.

Meanwhile, mutual distrust continued to undermine the Livonian Confederation, now reduced to little more than a loose association of warring interests. Rīga remained alienated, the church and Order locked in conflict, while German plans to secure Samogithia to the south remained unfulfilled. At this juncture, however, Livonia's fortunes briefly changed for the better and postponed her coming dissolution. This came about with the arrival of a new Master of the Livonian Order, Walter von Plettenberg, a man of outstanding diplomatic skills and vision who ruled the Order from 1494 to 1531. Although Rīga had declared itself Lutheran in 1524, von Plettenberg refused to leave the Catholic church or to turn Livonia into an hereditary duchy. His vigorous efforts to resolve the acrimonious disputes were remarkably successful, undoubtedly helped by the arrival of a new archbishop, Casper Linde, by all accounts an eminently humane and intelligent individual. The two established a close rapport and under their joint aegis Rīga and Livonia flourished as never before. Von Plettenberg also concluded a binding peace treaty with Muscovy in 1531 that lasted for more than two decades.

At the beginning of the sixteenth century, then, the position of Rīga and Livonia was a promising one. While it would be difficult in the absence of reliable written evidence to quantify the wealth of the city, still less its distribution among the ethnically diverse population, there must have been a cultural as well as an economic

5. Earliest woodcut of the Rīga skyline, c. 1547

florescence. Its legacy can still be seen today in the great churches, the Dom (cathedral) of St Mary's, the castle of the Livonian Order, the magnificent guildhalls and other architectural monuments of the time. As historians have pointed out, the architecture of cities and towns signals more than material affluence. By their very nature towns change social patterns and ways of thinking; they attract artisans and craftsmen, encourage greater numeracy and literacy, and stimulate the rural economy. In all this the native Rīgans as well as incoming Kurs, Latgallians and Semigallians must have profited.

It was otherwise in the countryside. Elsewhere in Europe the German presence was better integrated into the infrastructure of the region so that gradually artisans, minor clergy, prosperous farmers, traders and merchants emerged to form a middle class, but in the Baltic the Teutonic overlords remained an isolated—and hated—elite. The coming partition of Livonia would do little to alter this, for whichever international power ruled the Baltic, it was the German barons who still owned the land. They made an accommodation with each succeeding authority—and the peasants remained in bondage. The Latvian countryside today is a living diagram of that past and remains a feudal landscape, dotted with castles, manor houses, church spires and villages, but lacking those lively provincial university towns common throughout the continent.

Naturally as the prosperity of Rīga grew, and with it the demand for agricultural produce, the countryside also benefited. Increased production of wheat, rye and barley flourished throughout northern Europe, the result of innovations such as better ploughs, the use of the scythe (rather than the sickle) and crop rotation. Throughout the continent serf labour was also slowly giving way to wage labour. This in turn weakened the feudal manorial structure and over time would change the rigid social hierarchies of the past. In short, greater prosperity usually enabled a greater degree of social mobility. The sixteenth century would also witness an unprecedented rise in the price of goods by an estimated fourfold, which also resulted in new opportunities for peasants and labourers. But it was otherwise in Livonia where the new wealth remained in German hands. The lord of the manor merely increased tithes and taxes, placing an ever greater burden on the peasantry who remained locked in a feudal system with no hope of betterment. Their economy remained at a subsistence level: the staple diet was rye bread (even today the dense black bread of Latvia is called *rupjā maize*, literally 'coarse bread') supplemented by garden produce. Meat was a rarity as was fish, for both forests and rivers were the preserve of the local lord. Nevertheless, under von Plettenberg Livonia as a whole was more peaceful and secure than it had been since the invasion of the Teutonic Knights in 1201. On his death in 1535 he left his successors a stable Livonian Confederation, a rich capital city and a pacified countryside. Under his followers, however, that Confederation would disintegrate and Livonia would be partitioned among the great powers of Poland, Sweden and Russia.

The Partition of Livonia

One of the most extraordinary achievements in Renaissance cartography must be the great *Carta Marina* of Olaus Magnus, made by this Swedish cleric in Danzig and published in Rome in 1539. It was the first detailed map of Scandinavia and the Baltic and today it hangs in the University Library of Uppsala, Sweden.[15] Not only are the geographical features minutely drawn—mountain ranges, rivers, plains, woodlands, seas, lakes, ice-floes, islands, cities and towns—but also tiny icons of the people, produce or animals most characteristic of each region. The Baltic coast near the Vistula river is designated *ripa succini* (the amber bank) and accompanied by a picture of several large barrels of amber, indicating its continued importance in Baltic trade, for only the key product or characteristic of each region merits a picture in the *Carta*. The icons defining Lithuania are equally suggestive: a burning forest (referring to the wholesale destruction of sacred groves ordered by the church), an altar with fire, a grove of trees, a serpent on a plinth.[16] Here is contemporary proof of the survival of pagan belief systems over three hundred years after the papacy had sent missionaries to convert the heathens to Christianity.

The emblem for Livonia is equally telling: a troop of spear-bearing mounted knights along with three great cannon look eastwards; across a thin dividing line of trees another group of armed warriors on horseback face them, poised to invade Livonia from Muscovy.[17] The Livonian Wars, however, need to be seen in the general context of Muscovy's history. After the Mongols had captured Kiev in 1240, Russia had had to pay tribute to the Tatars of the Golden Horde, while to the west German expansion throughout the Baltic and central Europe had created a new racial, economic and cultural map, as we have seen. The great empire that resulted from the union of Lithuania and Poland in 1386 was perceived as yet another threat to Muscovy and to Orthodox Christianity.[18] To the north-west the sea powers of Denmark and Sweden curtailed Russian territorial ambitions on the Baltic, while to the east the Ottoman Empire was expanding its sphere of influence. The fall of Constantinople (1453), which resonated throughout Europe and re-configured its political and religious map, also signalled the opportunity to acquire new territories. It was at this juncture that Ivan III ('The Great') came to the throne of Muscovy and began to create a unified Russian state. He rapidly conquered Pskov and Novgorod, repelled a Tatar attack on Moscow in 1481, repeatedly invaded Lithuania and by 1503 had added much of what is today Ukraine and Belarus to his empire.

In Livonia, however, he met his match. In 1502 Walter von Plettenberg, Master of the Livonian Order, defeated a vast Russian army with a comparatively small force. He later negotiated a treaty (1531) with Tsar Ivan IV ('the Terrible'), which was to last for more than two decades. Local raids and skirmishes would have continued of course, but it was not until 1558 that Ivan IV resumed his ambition to add the Baltic littoral to his empire. Styling himself 'Heir of Livonia', on the slender grounds that an ancestor had once ruled Dorpat (Tartu), he attacked and conquered Narva, thus securing a foothold on the Baltic, though subsequent campaigns were to yield little in the way of permanent territorial gains. The Tsar then demanded that the whole of Livonia north of the Daugava river be ceded to him. Not surprisingly this was vigorously rejected by the Livonian Confederation as well as by Lithuania and Poland, but the ever-present threat of invasion from Russia was to shape the policies and the future of Latvia, Lithuania, Estonia and Poland for centuries to come.[19] It is perhaps from this period, too, that one might date the historical enmity between Germany, Poland and Russia.

The decades after von Plettenberg's death in 1535 saw Livonia descend into chaos, for he was succeeded by several weak masters and church prelates whose diplomatic ineptness progressively alienated the German emperor and the Duke of Prussia, while failing to gain any meaningful support from Poland–Lithuania. Livonia stood isolated and vulnerable, beset on all sides by powers eager to annex her lands and defended only by German lords who had lost what military skills their forebears had had and who barricaded themselves in their castles, preferring to send out poorly paid and unreliable mercenaries to repel the raiders. The native inhabitants were left virtually defenceless, and as the incursions became more frequent, Livonia became a byword for general lawlessness.[20] However, in 1558 the Livonian Order appointed as its new master the energetic, shrewd and ambitious Gotthard Kettler. Faced with the prospect of Livonia's imminent dissolution, he rapidly concluded a series of treaties to ward off Russia and to secure his borders. In return for money, arms and diplomatic support, he sacrificed nine of the southern border districts and part of Latgallia north of the Daugava to Duke Sigismund II of Lithuania, the island of Oesel and three enclaves in Kurland to Denmark, and promised to cede Reval to Sweden. He also pledged part of Semigallia to the Duke of Prussia in return for military aid and persuaded the Livonian Diet to pass a law making every third adult male a soldier.

Kettler's ambition was to create a Duchy of Livonia similar to that of Prussia with himself as its first duke. To that end he persuaded the influential and well-connected William of Brandenburg, at the time Archbishop of Rīga, as well as the principal Livonian vassals and the city burghers (though not the Rīga city council) to join him in swearing fealty to the King of Poland. This was an astute political move, for it meant that Livonia now had powerful protection yet would continue to acknowledge the Holy Roman emperor as overall liege-lord and so ensure that it retained a measure of independence; had the oath been made to the Duke of Lithuania, Livonia might have been incorporated into the duchy as another province. Although Kettler's hope of securing the whole of Livonia for his dukedom with Rīga as its capital was not to be realised,[21] he was created Duke of Courland and Semigallia in 1562, with additional administrative responsibility for part of Latgallia. The duchy was to be held as an hereditary fiefdom with the proviso that should the ducal line fail through lack of a male heir it would escheat to the King of Poland. Duke Kettler's realm consisted of just over forty per cent of Livonia; the rest was ceded to the Polish crown, which at the time had a treaty of non-aggression with Muscovy. It was thus hoped to deflect further Russian invasions, though that hope was to prove misguided.

Another significant factor in the creation of the duchy was the king's undertaking to ratify the holdings of the German vassals, who held eighty per cent of the manors as fiefs of the archbishop or the Livonian Order,[22] and to uphold the rights, liberties and privileges of all Livonians regardless of estate in both secular and ecclesiastical law. This strengthened the principle of legality and was to prove useful to the native Latvians in the next century. Duke Kettler, then, had preserved southern Livonia more or less intact, ceded northern Livonia to a power theoretically capable of defending it, and established a dukedom that was to become an embryonic nation-state in its own right and a significant presence in, and contributor to, the political canvas of the Baltic for the next two hundred years (see below).

In northern Livonia, however, the last decades of the sixteenth century witnessed a bewildering series of changes as one great power after another sought to erode Poland's authority. King Sigismund II's vision of a strong buffer state composed of northern Livonia, Estonia and Finland was short-circuited by further attacks from Muscovy and by increasingly powerful diplomatic pressures from Sweden and Denmark. The temporary gains and reversals of these powers in Livonia, during a period generally known as the Muscovite wars, are too detailed and numerous to itemise here but

Sigismund II's attempt to create stability by allowing Russia to keep Narva and the territory around Dorpat on condition the Tsar relinquish claims to the rest of Estonia and Livonia gained him only a temporary respite. That ended when he ceded Estonia to his brother-in-law, the King of Sweden, in 1570. This alarmed Muscovy and initiated several more years of warfare during which Russia temporarily gained Estonia (only Reval remained to Sweden) and occupied Livonia north of Rīga and the Daugava. The Tsar set up a puppet monarch, Duke Magnus III, lord of Danish Oesel and Piltene (in Courland) as 'King of Livonia'.[23] Magnus' reign, however, was short-lived, for in 1571 Sigismund II died without a male heir, thus leaving the Polish crown elective. Although it was not until 1576 that a successor agreeable to all factions was crowned, the choice was a shrewd one—the warrior-prince of Transylvania, Stephen Bagory. He rapidly moved into Livonia and expelled the Russian forces the following year; 'King' Magnus III abdicated and placed himself under the protection of the Polish monarch. King Stephen had also forged a close alliance with Sweden which promptly sent an army into northern Livonia, regained Narva and Dorpat, and decisively routed the Muscovite forces. Tsar Ivan IV was forced to recognise Poland's rights in Livonia, conclude a treaty with King Stephen in 1582, and relinquish Estonia to Sweden the following year. Russian efforts to secure the Baltic had failed.

Under Polish suzerainty Livonia was divided into four districts, each of which had its own court and representatives to send to the Polish parliament. These semi-autonomous provinces were governed by the German nobles of course, whose existing manorial lands and rights over the local population had been confirmed, and the language of the courts and administration continued to be German. However, King Stephen's reign was to prove comparatively enlightened. He appointed a Land Commission in 1582 to examine the title deeds of the German nobility and upon its findings reduced the number of properties and manors that had been illegally acquired, as in the Muscovite wars when deserted properties had simply been annexed by the local lord. He also lessened the exorbitant taxes and labour service owed by farmers and peasants and passed new laws, such as replacing corporal punishment and imprisonment with a system of monetary fines. Had he lived, these and other measures would have substantially alleviated the wretchedness of the native population, but Stephen died in 1587 and his successor had little interest in implementing his reforms.

However, before his death Stephen had also persuaded Rīga, hitherto a free imperial city owing allegiance only to the emperor, to throw in its lot with Poland–Lithuania. In 1581 the city acknowledged King Stephen as its sovereign lord on condition that he guarantee its existing rights and privileges. These included the right to acquire landed property, to coin money and issue passports, to grant freedom to anyone who had lived within the city limits for two years, to govern itself through a council which had the power to judge its citizens and foreigners alike, and to control the Daugava waterway. Indeed, Stephen even offered the city the opportunity to found a university but the Council declined, fearing the expense this would entail. Rīga also received guarantees that its policy of religious toleration would be respected, a particularly important consideration given that the city was Lutheran and Poland–Lithuania of course Roman Catholic. The Lutheran church had brought a measure of educational humanism to the city and to the larger towns in Livonia and though the language of instruction remained German, both Livs and Latvians were vigorous participants in the new faith and some gained the right to preach the gospel in Latvian. The cultural life of the city flourished and in 1587 the first printing press was set up by a Dutchman, one Nicolas Mollyn, who produced texts in Latin and German and, later, a few in Latvian.[24]

Rīga was to enjoy twenty years of comparative peace and prosperity, though given the inequitable distribution of wealth and lack of fair representation, the city was also riven by internal dissension. This was largely fuelled by the rivalry between the powerful city council and the three 'estates': these were the equally powerful Great Guild, composed of wealthy and influential German merchants and members of the professional classes from whom the council drew most of its members; the Little Guild of German

71

artisans and lesser merchants; and the third group composed of indigenous Livs and Latvians who had no voice on the council nor any way of participating in the running of the city. The inequalities between the guilds, themselves composed of a German minority, and the majority native population, who were gradually achieving greater material prosperity and education, would continue to foment dissatisfaction.

Despite the temporary liberalisation Livonia had enjoyed under King Stephen, the countryside remained locked in a backward agrarian system and feudal infrastructure, certainly when compared to the rest of Europe. Stephen's successor, Sigismund III Vasa (of Sweden), passed a series of reactionary laws which cancelled the liberal measures his predecessor had introduced. In 1589 he decreed that all key administrative posts in Livonia must be held by Roman Catholic Lithuanian and Polish nobles, and he relaxed the restrictions that had curbed the rapacity of the German landowners. In 1599 the Code of Livonian Serfdom still further reduced the number of independent farmers to a condition of virtual slavery. This was achieved through new punitive measures such as a fresh military tax and the requirement that taxes be paid in coin rather than with produce, as heretofore.[25] Farmers who had no means of obtaining such coinage were declared defaulters, their lands appropriated and they themselves degraded to serfdom. Moreover, taxes were no longer paid through the local councils, the *pagasti*, but directly to the lord of the manor, and many did not scruple to bend the laws to their own ends, punishing defaulters for their own aggrandisement. By creating a situation in which farmers became perpetual debtors through the taxes imposed on them, the rural population as a whole rapidly sank to a condition of permanent serfdom.[26] In such a state of wretchedness and oppression, with no redress in law, the survival of the country's folk culture and ancient language was nothing less than miraculous.

The accord of Poland and Sweden under a single ruler of the Vasa dynasty, however, was short-lived. Sigismund III Vasa had been elected as the Polish monarch and was also heir to the Swedish throne, but he was a staunch Roman Catholic and cherished the misguided ambition of bringing Protestant Sweden as well as Orthodox Muscovy into the fold of the Catholic church. Not surprisingly he met with outraged resistance. The Swedish parliament deposed him in 1599 and elected his uncle Charles Vasa (Charles IX) instead. Charles IX promptly invaded Livonia and over-ran the country, though he failed to take Rīga. Nearly three decades of warfare with Poland followed. In 1613 his successor Gustavus Adolphus persuaded the Russian Tsar Michael Romanov to recognise Sweden's rights in Livonia and in return ceded Novgorod and Pskov to Muscovy. In the context of European politics Sweden could count on support from the Protestant countries, especially England and the Netherlands, while Catholic Poland had the backing of the papacy, the Hapsburg Empire and Spain. The Polish–Swedish wars which raged throughout Livonia were part of the European-wide Thirty Years' War (1618–48) which devastated so much of the continent. It was not until 1629 that the Truce of Altmark ratified Sweden's dominion over Livonia, Estonia and Ingria as well as a large part of the Prussian coast north of Königsberg and brought a measure of stability to these lands; Poland was left with the small and largely Catholic province of Latgallia which bordered Muscovy.

Both Gustavus Adolphus of Sweden and Sigismund III of Poland died in 1632 and the status quo agreed at Altmark generally remained in place for some three decades despite sporadic efforts on both sides to extend their territories. At this point in history Sweden possessed a powerful army and an equally powerful navy and was eminently capable of defending her territorial gains.[27] The Peace of Westphalia, which concluded the Thirty Years' War in 1648, recognised those gains which now included Finland, Ingria, Estonia, Livonia, Courland, Prussia and Pomerania. By comparison Poland's prestige and holdings had suffered a drastic decline and the country found itself unable to counter attacks from both Sweden and Muscovy, who also repeatedly engaged each other's forces in Livonia. Not until the Treaty of Oliva in 1660 would the competing interests of Sweden, Poland, Russia, Denmark and the Duchy of Courland be resolved. Poland was forced to re-affirm

Sweden's dominion over Estonia and Livonia and to renounce all claims of the Vasa dynasty to the Swedish crown; east Prussia became independent, governed by the Elector of Brandenburg; and the following year Sweden and Denmark declared an end to their hostilities, while Muscovy retreated from Latgallia, which it had devastated, though bitter warfare between Poland and Russia over the partition of Ukraine would continue for another six years.[28]

Even from this compressed summary it will be clear that so incessant a state of warfare between the last decades of the sixteenth century and the first three of the seventeenth had a disastrous effect on Livonia and would have decimated her population. Armies raged across the land burning crops, laying waste towns, villages and churches, and slaughtering the inhabitants. Some indication of the magnitude of the destruction can be gleaned from contemporary sources: for example in the formerly flourishing Hanseatic town of Limbaži only eight people survived; in others fewer, or none.[29] The emergence of Sweden as the principal power in the Baltic littoral, however, did initiate an era of peace with humane and far-reaching reforms that have been respectfully acknowledged by Estonian and Latvian historians. But the process of reconstructing these devastated and impoverished lands was formidable. Of the 5,151 farmsteads recorded at the end of the sixteenth century, only 2,416 remained in 1624. Farms lay deserted; cattle, livestock and horses had virtually disappeared; and those peasants who had survived had no recourse but to harness themselves and their families to the plough.[30]

Gustavus Adolphus of Sweden acted promptly, dispatching his administrators to reform the courts and granting manors to his nobles throughout Estonia and Livonia. He honoured his undertaking to establish schools, hospitals and poorhouses, and to support the Lutheran church: whereas in 1623 there had been only five parish priests in Rīga, by 1630 there were forty-eight, and Latvian sacristans were appointed to keep records and to create hymnals in the vernacular. His efforts to reform land management were equally vigorous. Under his aegis representation in the local courts changed: henceforth only two members would come from the gentry whereas three would be appointed from the local farmers. For the first time parishes were required to provide primary schools and by 1634 compulsory education had been introduced, ending centuries of illiteracy and ignorance. In his *Historia Lettica* (1649) pastor Paul Einhorn of Courland poignantly summarised the centuries-old intellectual deprivation of the indigenous inhabitants:

> Most of the Germans look upon the establishment of schools as inadvisable [...] For they say, if the Latvians should be allowed to attend schools, and obtain the right to move around freely, and to reach the stage where they might be able to read and understand the chronicles of their land, and to discover that in ancient times the country belonged to them, and that they were the masters therein, and that the Germans had seized it from them, and had pressed them into serfdom and slavery [...] then they would relentlessly strive to free themselves from this serfdom and to regain their land and their former status.[31]

Indeed, he goes on to cite an occasion when some sympathetic Germans, having translated a few pages of the chronicles into Latvian, explained how the land had once been theirs and they subsequently reduced to serfdom.

> They listened carefully and then, thinking that no one could overhear them, considered what they should do. They decided to inform other Latvians about what they had learned so that they might gather together throughout the land, attack the Germans, and drive them out of the country.[32]

The lot of the peasant farmers improved significantly as a result of Swedish reforms, though implementing them proved to be a slow process. German (and sometimes Swedish) landowners often refused to pay the parish pastors, repair churches or open schools. At the same time the king had to treat the nobility with some caution for he needed their support in the continuing disputes with Muscovy and Poland. Nevertheless, radical changes in the legal system made reform inevitable. This process was hastened by the efforts of an unusually able and energetic administrator, Johan Scytte (a pupil of Hugo Grotius and the king's former tutor), who was appointed governor of Livonia in 1629. With the king's backing he abolished the right of landlords—whether German or Swedish— to sit in judgment over their peasants; henceforth all cases had to be heard in one of the three district courts of Rīga, Wenden (Cēsis) and Koknese. At one stroke Scytte had begun the process that would dissolve the powerbase on which the entire feudal system in Livonia had rested for centuries.

The reforms continued under Charles XI, who in 1681 presented the Livonian Diet with a set of proposals which were to transform the lives of Livonians beyond recognition. The first of these provided for a reduction of estates; that is, landed properties which had been in the hands of the nobles since the time of the Teutonic Order would now become Crown domains with the landholders as tenants of the state. Secondly, all properties would be measured and assessed according to a system that had been introduced in Sweden in the 1530s. Thirdly, serfdom—which had never existed in Sweden— was summarily abolished. Although it took several years for the reforms to take full effect, nonetheless the lot of the small farmer saw an immediate improvement. The fresh assessment of property value ensured a far more equitable taxation process, for the new system took into account not merely the size of the property but its fertility. This in turn meant that those whose farms included infertile land or land unsuited to agriculture had their tax burden substantially reduced. Once the new tax duties had been calculated and recorded in five large volumes known as the Great Livonian Cadaster, it was illegal to levy more or to demand additional labour service from the farmer. In addition the new code provided an incentive to farmers to better themselves, for it also granted exemption from tax and labour duty upon payment of a lump sum. In some districts a significant number of farmers were able to do this,[33] but in all cases—and for the first time in three centuries— small farmers were able to raise and sell surplus produce for their own benefit. They were also entitled to use common meadows and pastures for the raising of cattle and horses and to have free access to the forests. The economic emancipation was accompanied by further judicial reforms: tenants of Crown lands—which in practice meant most of Livonia—were not only forbidden to expel their peasants but required to reduce taxes in times of famine and hardship and even to grant loans. Peasants now held their lands by right of inheritance and were free to dispose of their personal property instead of having it sequestered. Under such favourable and humane terms, with farmers no longer struggling to survive at bare subsistence level, agriculture and the rural economy flourished and in time some farmers amassed considerable wealth.

Charles XI of Sweden became known as the 'Peasant King'. He had recognised the fundamental importance of a healthy peasantry

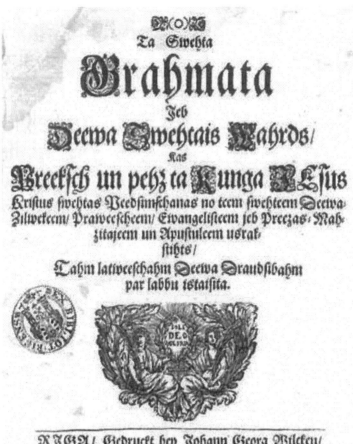

6. The first Bible in the Latvian language, 1689

to the state and although both Swedish and German nobles sought to check his legal and agricultural reforms through their representation on the Livonian Diet they were unsuccessful. In 1684 the king curtailed the power of the Diet; henceforth it would serve only as a consultative body to the governor. He also decreed that no governor of Livonia could exercise separate judicial power over the inhabitants. In 1696 the right of landlords to flog their tenants was abolished and all disputes, whether by landlord or farmer, had to be submitted for arbitration to the rural court, with the right to carry the case to the district court and even as far as the Royal Court in Stockholm. These economic, judicial and political reforms, which abolished feudalism in Livonia, had far-reaching social and cultural benefits as well. Schools had been established in all parishes by 1687; the Bible had been translated into Latvian (the New Testament in 1685, the Old Testament in 1689); grammars and lexicons were printed in the vernacular; and pastors and teachers of Latvian origin were appointed—many had graduated from the University of Dorpat (founded in 1644).

Naturally Rīga was always a case apart, but here too there were beneficial reforms. Earlier in the century Gustavus Adolphus had won the trust of the city burghers by granting them participation in the Swedish Diet in Stockholm. Rīga reaped the benefits of Sweden's declaration that the Baltic must be free to the shipping and trade of all nations (as distinct from the Hanseatic League's attempts to monopolise trade) and not only became the premier port for the 'Baltic Granary' but also vital for the trans-shipment of goods from Muscovy to the West. It rapidly grew to become the largest city in the Swedish dominions and by 1648 was home to over a thousand wealthy merchants. The city successfully repelled a Muscovite attack in 1656, after which Charles X added a crown to Rīga's coat-of-arms. The city's historic right to self-governance was respected and although power remained primarily in German hands, Sweden initiated enlightened schemes for the city's cultural and educational life. From 1621 onwards Gustavus Adolphus had encouraged the admission of Latvians to the cathedral school; 1632 saw the publication of the first newspaper, the *Ahwises* (in modern

Latvian *Avīse*); the new Royal Printing Office included religious tracts and other texts in the vernacular among its publications. In short, with political and economic stability and the considerable rise in prosperity, a sense of optimism and self-confidence blossomed and Rīga grew to become one of the liveliest cultural and intellectual centres on the Baltic.

Sweden's benevolent hegemony came to an end with the Great Northern War of 1700–21, when Estonia and Livonia were lost to Peter the Great to become Russian dominions for the next two hundred years. But before turning to that period of European history it is essential to consider the extraordinary phenomenon of the Duchy of Courland, which for a time became a nation-state in its own right and was to become an important model for, and focal point of, the National Awakening movement of the Latvian people in the nineteenth century.

The Duchy of Courland

> Blow gentle breeze, drive the little boat,
> Send me to Kurzeme;
> A Kurzeme lady promised me her daughter,
> She who mills the corn.[34]

It is a truism, though no less appropriate for that, that no nation is small which lives by the seaside. Since antiquity the western part of Latvia south of the river Daugava had been known as the land of the Curonians–Chori–Kurs and in centuries past, as we have seen, their domains had stretched from the Bay of Rīga southwards as far as the Vistula river. The Curonian Spit, that long peninsula whose beauty von Humboldt, Thomas Mann and many others were to admire and which today divides Lithuania from Kaliningrad, still bears their name, as does the westernmost of Latvia's four regions, Kurzeme (*zeme* means 'land'). When Gotthard Kettler became the first Duke of Courland his realm consisted of slightly more than forty per cent of Livonia. Although he had not succeeded in making Rīga his capital—that position went first to Kuldīga and then to Mitau (Jelgava)—he possessed the large ice-free port of

Map 6. The partition of Livonia: sixteenth to eighteenth centuries

Estonia	1565 to Sweden; 1721 to Russia
Oesel	1559–1645 to Denmark; then to Sweden; 1721 to Russia
Livonia	1561 to Poland; 1629 to Sweden; 1721 to Russia
Latgallia	1559–1772 to Poland; thereafter to Russia
Courland and Semigallia	1561–1795 a Duchy (in fief to Poland); thereafter to Russia
Piltene (Kurland)	1559–85 to Denmark then to Kurland until 1795
Lithuania	1386 dynastic union with Poland; 1795 to Russia

Ventspils and controlled much of the Daugava, as well as the Lielupe and Venta river systems, which gave him trading access to Lithuania's interior.[35] With such natural advantages he was able to lay the foundations for an economically viable realm which, though it technically owed fealty to the Kingdom of Poland, was in practice an independent state for over two hundred years. The fortunes of the Duchy of Courland, therefore, comprise a history within a history of the lands that would one day become Latvia.

Upon gaining his dukedom, Gotthard Kettler set about founding a dynasty. He married the German princess Anna of Mecklenburg and later allied his family with several powerful German and Lithuanian houses: he affianced his eldest son Frederick to Princess Elisabeth of Brunswick, his second son William to Princess Sophie of Prussia and married his daughter Anna to Prince Radziwill, Duke of Olyka. His shrewd understanding of international affairs enabled him to hold aloof from the conflicts of the neighbouring powers, and through a combination of astute political alliances and diplomatic measures he succeeded in defending the autonomy of his principality. Mindful of the need to stabilise the dukedom's internal structure and administration, he also reached an accommodation with the disaffected Curonian nobles. The *Privilegium Gothardianum* of 1570 set out the rights and duties of the landowners and of the state. The duke undertook to protect Lutheranism; to establish schools and hospitals; to formalise the statutes of Courland and its judicial system in consultation with the nobles; and to confirm the existing class privileges and holdings of the gentry, the nobles and the Bishop of Courland. At this time, Courland was composed of over four hundred fiefs held as personal property, of which half belonged to the duke, a third to the nobles and the remaining sixth to towns and townsmen.[36]

However, conditions in these land divisions differed substantially. In order to win the loyalty of the nobles—and to pre-empt action by his most disaffected subjects, the German landowners—Duke Gotthard undertook to honour their traditional rights. These included the right to judge cases on their lands and to determine punishments without appeal. Moreover peasants and their goods were deemed the personal property of the nobles and so could not leave their farms, sell their produce abroad, hunt, or even brew their own ale. Corporal punishment was routine and even a free farmer could be condemned to serfdom by a lord's *fiat*. By contrast, farmers and peasants on the ducal manors enjoyed far more liberal conditions: taxes and labour duty were fixed; a number of trades and clerical positions as well as military service were open to them; the estate stewards were enjoined to promote the welfare of the inhabitants; and farmers could appeal to the duke himself.[37]

Under Duke Kettler's comparatively benevolent despotism the ambitions of the Curonian nobles were held in check, but the duke died in 1587 and the duchy was apportioned between his two sons: Frederick became Duke of Zemgale, William Duke of Courland. This divided authority gave the Curonian nobles the opportunity to act at last. Duke William however refused to bow to their new demands, dismissed the Diet in 1615 and executed some of the conspirators against his reign. The nobles accused the duke of murder and, eager to obtain the even more favourable privileges enjoyed by the Polish nobility, petitioned King Sigismund III and the Polish Diet to remove Duke William and his heir Jacob. This was in Poland's interests of course: given that Frederick was without issue, Courland would escheat to the Polish monarchy on his death and become a Crown province. Duke William repeatedly refused to agree to a trial by the Polish Diet and he and his son fled to one of the German principalities. The heirless Frederick was declared duke of a re-united Courland and Zemgale in the expectation that he would support Polish interests and policies. However, like his father Duke Frederick proved adept at conciliating the nobility and balancing various domestic and international demands. He kept Courland neutral during the Polish–Swedish conflicts and defended the duchy's Lutheranism against Catholic pressure from Poland. Although he agreed to a new constitution, the *Formula Regiminis*, which provided for a new Diet with some enhanced powers for the nobility, the new constitution did not differ significantly from the earlier *Privilegium*—for example it had no authority to determine foreign policy and could only advise on economic and social matters.[38]

Both Duke Frederick and his deposed brother William also used their powerful family connections with several German princely houses and with the kings of France, Denmark and England—King James I of England was godfather to the young Jacob—to diplomatic advantage. When Charles I came to the throne he too recognised the economic and political importance of an independent and Protestant Courland friendly to English shipping in the Baltic. In 1638, after decades of dispute about the future of the duchy, the new English envoy to the Polish court Sir Thomas Roe, aided by the French ambassador, succeeded in persuading the Polish Diet to recognise Jacob as Duke Frederick's heir. Frederick died in 1639 and the following year Jacob returned from exile. In 1642 he began his spectacular forty-year reign which was to establish the Duchy of Courland as an economic and political power in the Baltic.

Duke Jacob's long exile had made him resilient, resourceful and keenly aware of the need to secure and maintain strong international alliances. In 1645 he was created a prince of the Holy Roman Empire and in 1654 he married Princess Louisa Charlotte, sister to the powerful Elector of Brandenburg. A highly educated man with degrees from German universities and also the Rector of Leipzig University, he understood modern economic theory and the importance of free trade. He greatly expanded the ambitious programme of shipbuilding begun by his father, supported mercantile activities in general and succeeded in transforming the duchy into a considerable maritime power.[39] Although he had supported the Royalist cause during the English Civil War by providing both ships and artillery, he later established friendly diplomatic relations with Cromwell and the Commonwealth as well as negotiating advantageous treaties with western Europe's principal maritime nations—Denmark, France, Holland, Portugal, Spain and Sweden. In domestic matters he turned his formidable energies to fostering local industries, setting up new sawmills, wool and linen mills, factories and refineries for the manufacture of saltpetre and tar for export, as well as limekilns, glassworks, brickworks and paper mills. Courland has some of the most fertile land in the Baltic littoral so agriculture also flourished, especially on the duke's manors where the prosperity of the farmers improved dramatically.

With a buoyant and growing economy, a peaceful domestic scene and a powerful navy at his disposal, Duke Jacob turned his attention to acquiring colonies abroad, an endeavour which was to prove rather less than successful. He purchased the Caribbean island of Tobago in 1645, with the consent of Charles I of England, and despatched ships and Curonian families to set up a colony—even today there is still a 'Little Courland Bay' on the island. But the initiative was doomed to failure. Neither the Dutch nor the French welcomed the presence of another maritime power in their sphere of colonial activity and English privateers did not scruple to raid the colony. In 1665 England resumed possession of the island. Duke Jacob's second colonial venture proved equally short-lived. Despite the fact that Courland was Protestant, he succeeded in persuading the Holy See to fund an expedition to West Africa. He purchased the island of St Andrews at the mouth of the Gambia river from a native chieftain and built Fort Jacob. This, however, brought him into conflict with the Dutch. Then on the restoration of Charles II to the English throne relations with that kingdom cooled and in 1660 a small fleet of English ships arrived, laid siege to Fort Jacob and took possession of the island. The West African experiment, like the Caribbean one, had proved to be a costly mistake.

Duke Jacob was more successful in the realm of diplomacy, although he was hard-pressed to preserve Courland's neutrality in the wars between Poland and Sweden. When Sweden, which now controlled Livonia, invited him to renounce his allegiance to Poland in its favour, the duke declined. But mindful of the need to conciliate his powerful neighbour he sent Charles X a loan of 50,000 thalers, prompting the Swedish monarch's memorable quip that Duke Jacob was too rich for a duke, too poor for a king. The duchy's relations with Sweden continued to be strained and in 1658 Swedish forces invaded Courland, captured the capital Mitau and took the duke and duchess prisoner. Only after intensive negotiations and international pressure did Sweden agree to retreat in return for the strategically important island of Rüno in the Bay of Rīga and some territory on the Daugava estuary. Duke Jacob was released and restored to his principality. However, his misfortunes continued, for shortly afterwards a devastating plague killed an estimated third of the population. For the next twenty years, until his death in 1682, he concentrated on restoring the country's prosperity.

Notwithstanding some of the reversals experienced in Duke Jacob's reign, conditions as a whole improved significantly for the population. The burgeoning economy offered new opportunities for enrichment and advancement, while the provision of schools and the printed word advanced literacy and culture. Although the language of both court and commerce continued to be German, some of the German pastors had begun to translate German and Latin texts into the vernacular. One such was Paul Einhorn, responsible for church administration throughout Courland, who wrote a guide for clergymen (published in Rīga, 1630) which is also a testament to the vigorous survival of pagan beliefs among the country folk.

> Even today they invoke their gods and goddesses; he who doubts it should listen to what they say, especially when going to work in the forest, fields or gardens, or when setting out on a journey; listen how they invoke and worship forest gods and goddesses, the Mother of the Fields, the Mother or Goddess of Gardens, the Goddess of the Road; one should listen to the songs they sing to their gods in the way real hymns are sung.[40]

While he deplored such rituals, he also sympathetically compared the Curonian and Livonian myths to those of the classical world in his *Historia Lettica* (1644).

The German pastor Mancelius, who became Duke Jacob's court chaplain, also criticised his flock's stubborn adherence to pagan rituals. Referring to the midsummerfestival of *Jāņu Nakts* (St John's Eve), he exhorted his parishioners in a sermon:

> Now my good friends, let us, with God's aid, begin the Jāņi-day. Let us not be as yesterday when men and women made merry, gathering various flowers and herbs in the forests and fields, coming home and adorning gates and all buildings inside and outside with oak leaves and flowers, believing that thereby they could chase away wizards and witches. They fastened special flowers to the wall as a token of luck: if the flower withers during the night, the owner of the house will die during the year, and if the flower remains fresh

and blossoms he will live. Having done such rich work, they light a big Midsummer fire, and dance around it, drinking the whole night as if at a wedding.[41]

Another German pastor, one Fürecker, translated hymns into Latvian and published them in 1672. He also produced a Latvian dictionary and grammar (1685). But the greatest single contribution to the preservation of the vernacular was the fine translation of the New Testament (1685) and the Old Testament (1689) by Ernst Glück, which was to have as great an impact on the spoken and written language as the King James Bible of 1611 had on English.[42] At what point the regional variations of the vernacular would have flowed into one another is difficult to judge, though undoubtedly the advance of printing would have hastened the standardisation process. At the same time one must not lose sight of the enduring strength and beauty of the oral tradition. The *dainas* had preserved the history, customs and beliefs of the people as well as their archaic language. This sense of a shared heritage in turn would have fostered the view of the Kurs, Semigallians, Livonians and Latgallians that they were a distinct people set apart from their conquerors.

Duke Jacob died in 1682 and was succeeded by Ferdinand Cassimir, an urbane and polished individual who had lived abroad and cherished the notion of bringing European culture to Courland. He was devoted to the arts and during his reign Mitau became a centre for music, opera and ballet. These cultural activities came at a cost, however, and more than once the duke had to resort to the unpleasant contemporary custom of selling his peasants as soldiers to friendly neighbouring powers such as Brandenburg. But his extravagance was to pay off when he invited Peter the Great in 1697 to break his journey at Mitau while en route to Königsberg. The tsar had received a rather cool reception in Rīga where apparently the Swedish governor had treated him with disdain. The contrast of the welcome at Mitau could not have been greater. The feasts, fetes, gala performances in his honour as well as the rich gifts made a lasting impression on the tsar and when he subsequently invaded Livonia, devastating towns and farmsteads alike, he spared Courland and indeed took an active part in preserving its sovereignty.

Duke Cassimir died in 1698, leaving his infant son Frederick William to succeed him. In the interim his brother Ferdinand was to become regent, but Ferdinand compromised Courland's carefully balanced neutrality by joining a Polish–Saxon–Danish–Muscovite coalition against Charles XII of Sweden in 1700. He was defeated and fled, sending the young Frederick William to Berlin for safety. Charles XII promptly took over Courland and immediately began to implement the reforms that had been so successful in Livonia. In the war with Russia, however, Swedish forces were ousted from Courland in 1709 and Rīga fell in 1710, though it would take another ten years to complete Sweden's defeat. The Russian victory was to prove beneficial to Courland in the short term, for Peter the Great and Frederick II of Prussia agreed to restore the exiled Frederick William to his dukedom. Furthermore they arranged a dazzling alliance—marriage to the tsar's niece, Grand Duchess Anna (who would be offered the throne of Russia in 1730). The marriage was celebrated in St Petersburg, but on the journey back to Mitau the young duke fell ill and died. The Kettler dynasty had failed and Courland was left a vulnerable pawn in the wider political upheavals that were taking place throughout the Baltic littoral.

After Sweden's final defeat in 1721 Russia acquired eastern Finland, Estonia and Livonia while Sweden retained western Finland and the promise of free passage throughout the Baltic for her ships.[43] Peter the Great had secured his 'window on the west' and Russia was now the dominant power in the Baltic. The fortunes of Livonia and Latgale under Russian dominion will be considered in the next chapter, but meanwhile in Courland the nobles were waiting to see if the widowed Duchess Anna would produce a posthumous heir. When that hope failed, the Curonian Diet proposed several candidates, none of whom met with Peter the Great's approval. However, after his death in 1725 Catherine I of Russia, Augustus II of Poland and the Curonian Diet agreed on a compromise figure: this was Count Maurice de Saxe, a natural son of Augustus II, who had served in the Russian army against Sweden with some distinction. The choice proved a disastrous one. Scandalised by reports of the count's womanising adventures, the duchess refused to countenance marriage to such a man and in 1726 the Polish parliament deposed the new duke and recalled the former regent of Courland, the ageing Ferdinand. He became duke and ruled the duchy until his death in 1737.

International events now intervened to ensure that Courland would remain independent. First, Peter the Great's niece, Grand Duchess Anna, became empress of Russia in 1730. Then in 1733 Augustus III of Poland, who had succeeded his father and was anxious to obtain the goodwill of the new Russian empress, agreed that the Curonian Diet could elect a new duke after the death of Ferdinand, thus guaranteeing the duchy's continued autonomy, notwithstanding the end of the Kettler dynasty. At this point history takes on the guise of romantic fiction. During her years as a widow in Mitau, Anna had fallen under the spell of a remarkable man, Ernst Johann Biron. Apparently he was a native of Courland, the son of a forestry official in the ducal administration. By all accounts Biron was an extraordinary individual, energetic, highly intelligent, possessing great charm of manner and considerable personal magnetism. His talents earned him the position of steward on one of the ducal manors and it was at this juncture that he met the widowed Duchess Anna. Under her patronage his rise was nothing less than meteoric; he served first as her secretary, was ennobled by her and then made a Count of the Holy Roman Empire. When she became empress he was elevated to the rank of Chamberlain in the Russian court and finally Minister of State. It was to this charismatic man that Anna offered the Duchy of Courland, and on Ferdinand's death in 1737 Biron became its duke and proceeded to found a new dynasty.

Whether Anna and Biron had become lovers while she was in Mitau remains an open question, as does the unsubstantiated rumour that she bore him a son. In any case after her accession to the Russian throne she married Biron to one of her ladies-in-waiting and stood godmother to Biron's son Peter, on whom she bestowed the titles of Royal Highness and Duke of Russia. Furthermore she planned to marry the boy to her niece, thus placing Biron's son in a position to inherit the Russian throne. The plan came to nothing. Without going into the complicated details of the intrigues in the tsarist court, it was actually the young son of Catherine I's niece who was to inherit the throne, albeit briefly, as Ivan VI. The empress then decreed that Duke Biron would be regent during his infancy, thus making him the most powerful official in Russia. On her death in 1740, however, a palace coup was to deprive Biron of both regency and dukedom and he and his son would be deported to Siberia.

Although he had preferred to live in St Petersburg, Biron had turned his energies to modernising Courland and increasing its prosperity. One of his first edicts had been to retrieve the 150 estates belonging to the Kettler dynasty which had been illegally appropriated by the nobles. He implemented laws reducing and regularising taxes and labour duty to alleviate the burden on farmers and peasants. Most importantly he extended and improved the ports of Liepāja and Ventspils, encouraged shipping and trade and supported local industries. Courland flourished as never before, recalling the heady days of Duke Jacob's reign. Biron also embarked on an ambitious building programme. Even before his elevation to the rank of duke he had commissioned the Italian architect Bartolomeo Rastrelli—the same who had designed the great Winter Palace in St Petersburg—to begin constructing an imposing palace in Mitau. Although that project was perforce halted when he was sent into exile, it was resumed when Biron returned.

After the death of Empress Anna, the Russian court was riven by intrigues and successive palace coups which are beyond the scope of this chapter to summarise, but suffice it to observe that in 1741 the Grand Duchess Elisabeth (daughter of Peter the Great) ascended the throne. On her death in 1762 she was succeeded by her nephew Peter III. The new tsar, remembering the kindness and hospitality Biron had shown him in his younger days, recalled the exiled duke and reinstated him. In the interim years, the duchy had been governed by the Curonian Diet and, for the short period between 1758 and the return of Biron in 1763, by a son of Augustus III. When Biron arrived in Mitau he resumed the projects he had begun over a quarter of a century earlier. He endowed schools and hospitals and once more engaged Rastrelli as well as the noted architect Giacomo Quarenchi to design palaces and fine public buildings throughout the realm.[44] In 1769 Biron abdicated in favour of his son Peter and retired to Prussia where his second son, Karl Ernst, was also to found a dynasty. The duke died in 1792 but his heir carried on his plans for Courland, developing and strengthening the economy still further, embellishing the capital and endowing an academy which he presented with an excellent library.

Events beyond the control of Duke Peter were to end this ducal line as well. In 1763 Augustus III of Poland died and although his successor Stanislaw Poniatowski had been put forward by Catherine II ('the Great'), Poland soon faced fresh territorial demands from Russia. The Polish monarch then made a catastrophic error of judgment: in desperation he turned to Russia's great enemy, the Turkish Porte, for aid. This undoubtedly hastened the final partition of the country, a partition which was agreed in a secret treaty by Russia, Austria and Prussia in 1772. In 1773 the Polish king was forced to cede several territories to Russia including Latgale, which had been part of the Polish Commonwealth since the sixteenth century, enjoying a degree of self-government with a Diet in Dvinsk (Daugavpils) and the right to send delegates to the Polish parliament. Alarmed by these and other concessions to the Russian empress, Duke Peter purchased another dukedom in Silesia in 1786, thus hoping to secure the added protection of Prussia but unaware that his relative Frederick II had already agreed that Courland would be given to Catherine the Great's favourite, Prince Potemkin, though this scheme was pre-empted by Potemkin's untimely death.

Early in 1794 an insurrection in Lithuania spread into Courland, where it was eagerly supported by the farmers and townspeople, and swept northwards, taking control of Rīga and gaining support throughout Livonia before being suppressed. The terrified nobles of the Curonian Diet promptly appealed to Russia for troops. In the words of the French ambassador to the Prussian Court: 'the Kuronian nobles are […] shamefully engaged in selling out this beautiful and unfortunate province to Russia'.[45] In March 1795, recognising that Poland's days as a sovereign state were numbered,[46] the Curonian Diet passed a resolution to secede from Poland and sent a delegate to St Petersburg armed with a petition requesting that the duchy be annexed by Russia. Catherine the Great removed Duke Peter, bestowing on him two million roubles and an annuity as compensation for the loss of his dukedom, and the deposed duke retired to his property in Prussia where he died in 1800. Courland became a Russian province, to be ruled by a governor-general and subject to Russian law and the Russian taxation system. Its 230 years of autonomy had ended.

4

UNDER RUSSIAN RULE

A Time of Revolutions

The appearance of Russia as a European power in the early modern period was driven by the economic and administrative reforms of Peter the Great, who ruled that vast territory of many nations, languages and peoples from 1682 to 1725. His principal aims were to expand and consolidate Russia's territory, to bring Western science and technology to what was still a backward agrarian economy, to transform a stagnant state bureaucracy into an efficient one based on merit, and to secure access to the Baltic while eliminating any threat from Sweden. He achieved this last, as we have seen, in the Great Northern War of 1700–21 when he added Estonia and Livonia to his domains. He built St Petersburg, set up technical schools and an academy of science, encouraged the growth of an intellectual elite, and began the process of industrialisation that would one day transform Russia into an international power. But in the huge expanses of his realm, the educated elite were a tiny island of culture; the masses remained illiterate and the provincial nobles reactionary and resistant to reform. The basis of the economy continued to be serf labour, and indeed Russia would be the last country in Europe to abolish serfdom.

The Peace of Nystadt signed between Russia and Sweden in 1721 did more than transfer Baltic territory into Russian hands. It also halted the decades of economic, social and cultural progress achieved under Swedish rule. The landowning German–Balt nobility, which had collectively supported Russia, succeeded in negotiating extraordinarily favourable terms for itself. Notwithstanding Peter the Great's assurances that the rights and privileges which all classes had enjoyed under the Swedish monarchs would be respected, Swedish reforms were summarily abolished. The schools that had been established by Charles XI in 1687 were closed and Crown lands quickly appropriated by the German nobles. The tsar's Land Commissions, set up to look into land restitution and reform, accepted a simple oath from a noble as proof of land ownership—no documentary evidence was required. Moreover landownership would henceforth be restricted to the nobility; other classes could hold land only under lease or tenancy agreements, and land owned by burghers could be, and was, redeemed. In short, Livonia was forced to revert to a primitive and repressive feudal system; and once again, as so often in the unhappy history of the Baltic, it was the native peoples who suffered, dispossessed of their lands, their goods, and their freedom. Under Russian rule peasants once more became the property of their masters and their conditions were among the most wretched in Europe. Livonia was ruled by a succession of governors, nearly all of them German, who continued to pass ever more repressive laws restricting the movements and rights of the population: the right of the landlord to recapture serfs was re-introduced and the burden of taxes and labour duty increased at will. It is not hard to imagine the sense of defeat and crippling misery that engulfed the native inhabitants after decades of relative prosperity, personal independence and self-respect during what came to be called 'the good old Swedish days', nor to understand why their grievances would fuel unremitting strife and bitterness between them and their landlords.

In general the political state of Russia in the eighteenth century did not differ significantly from other absolute monarchies on the continent. Although the ideals of the Enlightenment resulted in a number of practical reforms, some of which were humanitarian, few were liberal in the political sense. The accession of Catherine the Great is a signal example, for although she founded schools and was an enthusiastic patron of the arts and sciences, she also upheld and reinforced the privileges of the nobles, recognising that her power depended on their loyalty. Thus she abolished the right of serfs to petition against their masters, rescinded the requirement that nobles provide military service, and granted the latter immensely lucrative monopolies to set up factories and mines. During her rule (1763–96) she extended the empire, acquiring Ukraine and the Crimea which secured her access to the Black Sea, and halted the menace of Ottoman invasion.

In the first year of her reign Catherine the Great visited Estonia and Livonia. Shocked by the degradation, wretchedness and drunkenness of the inhabitants, she ordered her Livonian governor Count Browne to devise a scheme for relieving the condition of the peasants. He immediately ordered the re-opening of parish schools throughout Livonia in the same year and in 1765 forced the Livonian Diet to accept a number of reforms. These included: restoring to farmers the right to hold personal property and to inherit land tenure or tenancy; fixing the taxes and labour duty; and curtailing corporal punishment. But there were no measures passed to monitor, still less enforce, these new regulations and so abuses continued, including the indiscriminate sale of human beings. In 1777 one Protestant pastor recorded:

A man servant can be bought in Livonia for thirty to fifty rubles silver; an artisan, cook or weaver for anything up to one hundred rubles; the same price is asked for a whole family, a maidservant rarely costing more than ten rubles, while children can be bought for four rubles each. Agricultural workers and their children are sold or bartered for horses, dogs, pipes, etc.[1]

Conditions in the towns were rather better for local traders, merchants and burghers, and there was some relaxation of the social and political restrictions after 1783 when the Livonian Diet was persuaded to permit wider access to membership of city and town councils. But the introduction of the Russian poll tax the following year was greeted with universal outrage and sparked countrywide revolts, whereupon Russian troops marched into Livonia, quelled the rebellion and deported many of the insurgents to Siberia.

Rīga's autonomy, which had been preserved under both Polish and Swedish rule, had been abolished in 1710 when the city surrendered to Russian forces. The city militia had been disbanded and control of the city gates passed to the Russian military. In 1721 Peter the Great effectively removed authority for Rīga's governance from the councillors and elders by making the Russian governor-general of Livonia Comptroller of Rīga's finances and by installing a Russian chief of police. The end of the century, however, would witness a modest easing of social and political conditions. Responding to pressure from the native Rīgans to be admitted to membership of the Great Guild (hitherto exclusively German), a law was passed in 1785 dissolving that guild and replacing it with three merchant guilds whose membership would be open to all nationalities. Further liberalisation of the city's government came later in the same year when the electoral roll was extended to include all citizens over the age of twenty-five who paid taxes of at least 50 rubles. They were empowered to elect a lord mayor, two burgomasters and the twelve-strong city council, and although in practice the electoral roll was small and still overwhelmingly German, even this modest extension of the franchise was rescinded a decade later when the strongly pro-German and reactionary son of Catherine the Great, Tsar Paul I, ascended the throne. He summarily abolished his mother's reforms for both the countryside and the city.[2]

This oscillation between mild reform and repression was to characterise Russia's history—and therefore that of Livonia—throughout the next century. Paul I, whose five-year reign was reactionary, capricious and tyrannical, and who had been deeply alarmed by the French Revolution and its aftermath,[3] was assassinated in 1801. He was succeeded by his son, the idealistic Alexander I, who had been educated in accordance with Enlightenment principles and had gathered a coterie of young Russian liberals at court. The new tsar visited Livonia in 1802 after reading a French translation of Garlieb Merkel's influential pamphlet *Die Letten* (1796), denouncing the condition of serfdom in his native Livonia.[4] His proposals had found a sympathetic response in Count Friedrich von Sievers and in the Livonian governor of the day. The

Diet had been urged in 1797 to pass measures based on Merkel's recommendations, but approval had been blocked by Tsar Paul I. Alexander I, however, dismayed by the appalling conditions and bloodshed he had witnessed—his visit had coincided with a local uprising—instructed von Sievers to resurrect the proposals of 1797. This resulted in the Agrarian Reform Bill of 1804 which was passed despite vigorous opposition from the German–Balt nobility. It offered some alleviation of conditions in that it recognised the right of peasants to be hereditary leaseholders, prohibited the sale of a peasant apart from his land, once more fixed the amount of labour service and tithes, and halted the covert appropriation of common land by the manor lords. It also provided for the creation of rural courts with three justices to be drawn from the rural community, the *pagasts*.

However these measures were not introduced in the province of Kurland where conditions for the rural population steadily deteriorated, exacerbated by a series of disastrously poor harvests. Unrest was fuelled by rumours that Napoleon's proposed invasion of Russia through the Baltic lands would bring liberty to the native peoples. This hope sustained widespread rebellion, though of course the promise of freedom, like that for Poland, came to nothing. Napoleon invaded Lithuania and Kurland in June 1812 and the Russians fled, taking with them their possessions, peasants, horses and cattle, leaving the area completely denuded. Napoleon's Prussian allies moved into the Baltic to suppress any unrest and on 1 August two Frenchmen, De Chamboudois and De Montigny, were installed as regents of Semigallia and Kurland with orders to requisition supplies for Napoleon's army en route to Russia.

The Baltic littoral was a comparatively small pawn on the great chessboard of international events, though Rīga had been important for English shipping to bypass Napoleon's continental blockade. The end of 1812 witnessed Napoleon's defeat, and the disillusioned Kurlander peasantry continued their agitation and appealed to the tsar. In 1817, in order to quell the unrest, the Russian governor offered the Diet a choice between accepting the Livonian Agrarian Reform Act of 1804 or the Estonian Act of 1816. The latter included a provision to free the serfs but it gave them no entitlement to live and work on their ancestral lands. The argument in Estonia had been that if manor lords were to lose their serfs' labour and tithes, they must receive compensation; and this came in the form of ratifying the possession of the lands outright without any restrictions. In theory labourer and landlord would be free to negotiate the terms of a tenancy in accordance with free market principles, but in practice the peasants were worse off than before. The new enfranchisement was ironically termed *Vogelfreiheit* (as free as birds) but landlords had the advantages of education and of law enforcement powers as well as the support of the judiciary in drawing up contracts and so were in a position to ensure that the terms of new leases were in their favour. The system ended up creating a class of landless labourers who had nowhere to go, for industry was still in its infancy, while enabling the nobles to enlarge their manor holdings. Serf emancipation had simply become another form of expropriation. It was this system that the Diet of Kurland adopted in 1818.[5]

A catastrophic fall in grain prices in the 1820s brought further suffering to Kurland where the now unprofitable arable lands were converted to pasture, leaving large numbers of peasants destitute and landless. Under the repressive regime of Tsar Nicholas I (1826–55) conditions in both Kurland and Livonia worsened still further, and between 1835 and 1840 another series of poor harvests resulted in riots and uprisings. These were brutally suppressed by Russian troops. Given the conditions of degradation and starvation, it is hardly surprising that a fixed and ineradicable hatred for the German–Balt landlords burned in the hearts of the peasants. However, although Tsar Nicholas was autocratic and conservative in the extreme, he was aware that he had a large number of able, ambitious and loyal Germans who staffed a considerable percentage of the Russian government's administration and provided high-ranking officers for the military (an estimated 25 per cent of the former and 60 per cent of the latter). In view of the continuing unrest in the Baltic, he appointed a Committee on Baltic Affairs in 1846 to re-examine the agrarian laws of Livonia. The driving force behind this inquiry was the German Hamilcar von Völkersahm, who had lived in the United States of America and been deeply impressed by its liberal principles and governance. With the tsar's support he persuaded the Livonian Diet to adopt a number of measures on a six-year trial basis. The Bill of 1849 stipulated that although manor lords might keep their tithe-paying peasants, they would not be entitled to lease or sell their farms to any but members of the rural community. Furthermore the Bill decreed that peasants would pay for their leases with money rather than, as hitherto, through the crippling labour service and tithes in the form of produce, forms of taxation which were notoriously open to abuse by the landlord. In theory, it was felt, this should benefit the peasant and eventually create a class of independent smallholders, as indeed proved to be the case. Alarmed by the success of these measures and the emergence of a class of farmers outside the control of the nobility, the Diet attempted to rescind the Bill in 1856 after the trial period, but fortunately was over-ruled by the new tsar, Alexander II.

International events once more contributed to changing conditions for the better. Russia had lost the Crimean War (1854–6) and although the autocratic rule of Tsar Nicholas I (who died in 1855) had appeared to be immune from the revolutionary fervour that was sweeping throughout Europe, the continued insurrections, violence and disorder in the rural communities of the empire, coupled with the dawning recognition that modernisation of Russia's traditional institutions was essential to realise her vast potential, enabled his successor Alexander II (1856–81) to proceed with far-reaching reforms that would earn him the title of the 'Tsar Liberator'. In 1861 he freed the serfs and decreed that the Russian nobility must sell a portion of their lands to the newly emancipated peasantry. (These measures were also applied in the province of Latgale.)

In 1863 peasants obtained freedom of movement through a new passport system and in 1865 the Russian government decreed an end to all remaining labour-duty in the Baltic provinces and abolished corporal punishment of tenant farmers, though the manor lord could still inflict chastisement on the peasants of his own manor.

In 1866 the authority of the nobles was further limited when governance of the rural communities passed into the hands of the *pagasti*. The community assemblies now had the right freely to elect the rural court justices and to elect their own governing body as well as a presiding mayor. Banks were set up so that peasants could purchase lands and hold them in their own right, and a reformed judiciary was put in place throughout the Baltic littoral.[6]

Tsar Alexander II was killed by an anarchist's bomb in 1881 and his liberal reforms halted by his successor Alexander III (1881–94) who extended the dreaded secret political police, the *Ochrana*, to the Baltic provinces, initiating a new era of oppression and fear. But meanwhile, the ideas of the eighteenth-century Enlightenment had been disseminated throughout the Baltic littoral and gradually, as elsewhere among the small nations of Europe, a cultural revolution was taking place which found expression in a passionate national consciousness and political awakening. The following sections of this chapter will focus on the emerging phenomenon of nationality which united Livonia, Kurland and Latgale into the Latvian nation.

Awakening

In 1765 the Enlightenment thinker and philosopher Johann Gottfried Herder, who lived and taught in Rīga from 1764 to 1769, recorded his response to the lively midsummer celebration of *Jāņu Nakts* (St John's Eve) at Lake Jugla not far from the city.[7]

> Here I have had the opportunity of seeing living nations keep alive the ancient heritage of songs, rhythm and dance [...] nations whom our culture has been unable to deprive of their own language [...] and customs nor replace them with something much more debased.

Central to Herder's doctrines, which have deeply influenced Western thought since the eighteenth century, was the belief that the character and integrity of each culture is unique and can survive only if its people have the freedom to speak their own language and to follow their own line of historical development. To deny or seek to destroy that distinctiveness, he argued, is the most terrible of injustices for it impoverishes the whole of humankind. He recognised in the *līgo* songs of midsummer and in the *dainas* something more fundamental and creative than a mere nostalgia for a distant past; rather, these songs testified to the accumulated experience and collective wisdom of a unique community. Their spontaneous performance articulated and confirmed the nation's cultural identity, affirming its vision of the world and its own place in it: 'Their songs are the archives of the people, the treasury of their science and religion.'[8] He was fascinated by the historical development of human cultures and languages and made the first collection and translation of Latvian and Estonian folklore in *Stimmen der Völker in ihren Liedern* ('Voices of the People in their Songs', 1773). He persuaded the German printer Hartknoch to open a publishing house in Rīga, and indeed some of the great works of the century, for example Kant's *A Critique of Pure Reason* (1781), were first published there.

Herder believed that there was an intimate connection between the character and temperament of a people and their natural environment.[9] The *dainas*, which celebrate the richness and beauty of the natural world and humanity's place in it, also illuminate a sacred past, giving meaning to the present and hope for the future. As Simon Schama has cogently argued,[10] landscapes are constructs of the imagination, projected onto forests, waters, rocks and meadows; they can become so embedded in a people's collective consciousness and memory as to be inseparable from a nation's sense of itself. In chapter 2 this history offered a brief account of the ancient belief systems of the early Baltic peoples, which are remarkable for having survived centuries of oppression to validate a people's sense of belonging to the land itself, to a sacred landscape which no conqueror could possess. It was through such myths and metaphors, enshrined in a language of great antiquity as well as through native traditions, that a cultural nationalism evolved which was to develop into an articulate and sophisticated political consciousness in the following century.

The cascade of events sparked by the American Revolution of 1776 and the French Revolution of 1789 rippled across Europe as nations and peoples everywhere called for political reform and independence. It reached the Baltic in due course and fired one of Herder's young friends, Garlieb Merkel—the son of a Livonian pastor and an ardent disciple of Rousseau's ideas—to write his denunciation of conditions in Livonia, *Die Letten* (1796), which had so impressed Tsar Alexander I.[11] Subsequently pamphlets were written in the vernacular and distributed (about two-thirds of the peasantry were literate by the end of the eighteenth century) in anticipation of Napoleon's imminent arrival and the dizzying prospect of liberty. Although it was a hope that would prove illusory, there is no doubt that it stimulated the growth of a spirit of nationalism.

Earlier in the century, and despite reluctance by both the German nobility and Russian bureaucracy to foster education for the masses, a Protestant sect called the Moravian Brethren had arrived in 1732 to set up schools and a teacher's seminary to train preachers for communities that had no established churches. Although the movement was banned in 1743 for preaching such seditious ideas as equality, it went underground and continued its educational activities. In 1764 Catherine the Great allowed the Brethren to return officially and also decreed that parish schools be re-opened throughout Livonia. Psalters and religious works as well as calendars and almanacs were printed in the vernacular so that a language which had largely been confined to the home and to a few enlightened churches was now acknowledged in the wider public domain. The impact of this may be difficult for us to understand today, but it must have generated an extraordinary sense of liberation, coupled with a new self-respect in a people whose very humanity had been denied for so many centuries. Although it would not be until 1833 that the first official secondary school would open in Kurland—and 1839 in Livonia—opportunities for education had begun to grow earlier, supported by a few progressive German magnates who had sent the brightest abroad for further and higher education. The second half of the century saw the establishment of many secondary schools, specialist institutions for navigation as well as polytechnics, which produced teachers, skilled artisans and offered a range of other professional qualifications.

The gradual emergence of a middle class also stimulated the growth of publishing in the vernacular. Although the 1632 Latvian language shipping newsletter *Awihses* can claim to be one of the oldest newspapers in Europe, most periodicals and books in the eighteenth century were in German, with the exception of the Bible and various religious tracts. In 1761 the *Rigasche Anzeigen* ('Rīga Journal') appeared and in 1778 the *Rigasche Politische Zeitung* ('Rīga Political News'). However, in 1822 the first newspaper in the vernacular, *Latweeschu Awihses* ('Latvian Newspaper'),[12] was published in Jelgava (Mitau) under the editorship of a Scottish pastor who also founded the Latvian Literary Society in the same city in 1824. Other Latvian periodicals soon followed, witnessing the growth of a literate population, and the Rīga gazette *Tam Latweeschu Lauschu Draugam* ('Friend of the Latvian People') which appeared in 1832 became so influential that it was suppressed by order of the Russian government in 1846.

A decade later, however, the lively weekly paper *Mahjas Weesis* ('The House Guest') began publication in 1856 and gained popularity for its pro-Latvian articles written by a new generation eager to re-discover and disseminate their suppressed heritage. Among the contributors was Juris Alunāns, one of the first systematically to collect local folklore; his *Dziesmiņas* ('Little Songs') also appeared in 1856. The paper attracted contributions from several figures who were to become important in the National Awakening Movement: Krišjānis Barons, the great collector of the *dainas*, subsequently published in eight volumes;[13] the sociologist Atis Kronvalds; and the economist Krišjānis Valdemārs who, urging the importance of a strong maritime shipping industry, was instrumental in founding several schools of seamanship.[14] While residing in St Petersburg, Valdemārs had succeeded in persuading the Russian authorities to appoint him press censor for Latvian publications. This in turn enabled him to bring out the first Latvian political newspaper in 1863, the *Pēterburgas Awihses*, which achieved a wide circulation in Livonia and Kurland. It was closed down after only four months for its liberal political views—and several of its contributors were deported—but the paper later re-appeared under the editorship of

Krišjānis Barons on the condition that the contents were first approved by the governor of Rīga. That the paper was permitted to re-appear at all is remarkable, though initially it may have been considered in the tsarist government's interests because it carried a popular feature called '*Zobu gals*' ('Biting Satire') whose sketches were heralded by the caption: 'German Fritz says that peace means keeping quiet. Don't believe Fritz!' It would not have escaped readers that 'Ivan' could be substituted with equal relevance. The paper was deemed too subversive and was finally banned in 1865.

Nonetheless, the steady growth of a literate and increasingly politically aware public continued to generate a demand for the expression of its cultural and intellectual life. In 1868 Ansis Leitans, who had brought out the *Mahjas Weesis* in the previous decade, founded the *Rigas Latweeshu Beedriba* ('The Riga Latvian Fellowship') whose readers and contributors created a cultural network which was to become the nucleus of the later Latvian Association and the National Awakening Movement. Its members actively supported the publication of a Latvian encyclopedia, the foundation of a national theatre and opera, and it was under this paper's aegis that the first Latvian Song Festival was held in 1873.[15] This was followed by the first daily newspaper in Latvian, the *Rigas Lapa* ('The Riga Page') in 1877, and in 1878 *Balss* ('The Voice') rapidly became the most widely read journal in the country. Other specialist periodicals soon followed, like the *Baltija Semkopis* ('The Baltic Agriculturalist'), printed in Jelgava.

The growth of Baltic political consciousness was part of the great wave of nationalism that had spread across Europe in the aftermath of the near continent-wide revolutions of 1848, resulting in the unifications of Germany and of Italy and the formation of the Swiss Confederation. Everywhere the peoples of eastern Europe— Czech, Slovak, Romanian, Bulgarian, Serbian, Polish, Lithuanian, Latvian, Estonian among them—called for recognition of their national integrity. In Latvia these aspirations were summarised by the sociologist Atis Kronvalds, whose article '*Tautiskie centieni*' ('A Nation's Strivings') was published in *Nationale Bestrebungen* in Dorpat in 1872.

We are not merely men [...] we are also a nation, a community which has distinctive features such as language and customs, spiritual gifts and beliefs. We are members of a community and are called Latvians. We have the same rights as others to tend and maintain our traditions and we also have the right to exist, grow and prosper as Latvians as we live.[16]

Then came the assassination of Alexander II in 1881 followed by the reactionary rule of Alexander III (1881–94). The new tsar viewed both the growing spirit of national consciousness in the Baltic and the powerful German nobility—whether Baltic landowners or the administrative and military personnel in Russia—with equal suspicion; his reign initiated an era of political and cultural repression. The Baltic lands were re-named the 'Northwest Provinces' in an attempt to deprive them of their identity, and in 1885 a truly draconian programme of Russification was introduced, designed to extinguish nationalist aspirations in the native populations. The vernacular languages were banned and Russian was decreed the sole medium of instruction in schools and in administration throughout the Baltic. Teachers were given two years in which to learn the language and not surprisingly many German and overseas instructors simply left, to be replaced by poorly qualified Russians. Even the historic University of Dorpat in Estonia, which had been largely staffed by German trained academics and which had hitherto provided a sound tertiary education for native Balts, was transformed into a mediocre Russian institution. Its graduates were denied employment in their homelands and offered positions in remote Russian provinces; it is estimated that half had to leave the countries of their birth.[17] In local administration and management efficient German staff were replaced by a flood of poorly trained Russian officials whose incompetence and corruption became notorious.

In 1888 the Russian police system with its infamous network of surveillance and spies was imposed on the Baltic like an iron grid to crush even the most modest stirrings of political debate. Press censorship was rigorously enforced, accompanied by propaganda—'One Tsar, One Church, One Race'—and by the growing persecution of the local Jewish population which had been prominent in both the economy and the intellectual life of the

7. Rīga City Council Square, oil painting by K.T. Fechhelm, 1819 (photograph © Museum of the History of Rīga and Navigation)

Baltic. The Lutheran church came under attack and peasants were lured to join the Orthodox church with promises of exemption from military service and of land, though no one mentioned that the land allotment was in Siberia. These and other measures intended to eliminate opposition to, and criticism of, the tsar's government merely served to fuel the rising tide of anger in the Baltic communities against both German landowners and Russian authorities. The second half of the nineteenth century had witnessed the transformation of the Livonian and Kurlander peoples from a nation of serfs into one of independent landowning farmers, with an articulate, professional middle class actively engaged in commerce and education, and with an increasingly influential class of labourers who had migrated to the towns and cities to work in the rapidly growing industries. Their passionate sense of themselves as Latvians entitled to recognition and self-determination in their own historic homeland could not be held in check much longer. In 1886 the political organisation 'Jaunā strāva' ('The New Movement') had launched its publication *Dienas Lapa* ('The Daily Page') to provide a forum for debating issues such as the universal rights of man, the principles of democracy, the equality of men and women. It offered an opportunity to understand and compare the parliamentary systems of democracies like France, Switzerland and England, and although the leaders of Jaunā strāva and other nationalist organisations were arrested in 1897 and deported, they were soon replaced by others.

The closing decades of the nineteenth century also saw a blossoming of literature in the vernacular, influenced by continental schools of both Romanticism and Realism, which nurtured the National Awakening and defied Russification. The folk legend of the great hero *Lāčplēsis* ('Bear-slayer') was re-created in an immensely popular epic poem by Andrejs Pumpurs. Another influential poet of the period was K. M. Auseklis, whose *Gaismas Pils* ('Castle of Light') retold the ancient folk myth that Lāčplēsis would rise again from the great castle of truth and light (which had sunk beneath the waters of Lake Burtnieks after the hero's defeat by the Black Knight) to drive out the oppressor and restore his people's independence.[18] In prose the realist school found its finest expression in the work of the brothers Reinis and Matīss Kaudzītes, whose novel *Mērnieku laiki* ('The Time of the Land-Surveyors') addressed the life of the peasant in Vidzeme, 'The Middle Land', as Livonia north of the Daugava was re-named.[19] A host of other talented indigenous writers followed, most notably Rūdolfs Blaumanis, whose masterly novels of Vidzeme rural life in the late nineteenth century—*Purvju brīdejs* ('The Wader in the Marsh') and *Salna pavasarī* ('Hoar-frost in Spring')—can deservedly be compared to Hardy's Wessex novels.[20]

In music, arts and crafts, architecture and painting artists were also finding their distinctive styles, transmuting ancient motifs into contemporary forms. A nation of music-lovers was reaffirming its traditional folksongs and dances in festivals which celebrated its ancient instruments—horns, flutes, bagpipes and the zither-like wooden *kokle*—and its *dainas*. The composers of the National Awakening period may have studied at the St Petersburg conser-

8. The folk-hero Lāčplēsis fighting the Black Knight, from the epic poem by Andrejs Pumpurs

vatory but they wrote their music for their own people, and songs, symphonies, operas flowed into the public domain and were eagerly supported. Folk costumes, amber jewellery, ceramics, weaving, embroidery, wood carving in a proliferation of designs that had evolved in the nation's different regions since time immemorial became an intrinsic part of the national revival of arts and crafts; they were exhibited at the First Baltic Archaeological Congress held in Rīga in 1894. Individually and collectively they exemplify Rainer Maria Rilke's evocative lines: 'some simple thing, shaped for generation after generation/until it lives in our hands, in our eyes, and it is ours' (*Duino Elegies*). Architecture, hitherto largely German-influenced, began to develop its own national romantic style, incorporating traditional elements from vernacular buildings, but it also participated in the international Art Nouveau movement, and indeed Rīga still has some of the most extensive art nouveau buildings in all Europe. Then, too, a new generation of painters who had studied abroad in St Petersburg and Paris extolled the history and life of their nation through the visual arts. In every aspect of political, social and artistic activity this Awakening would inform and strengthen the rise of nationalism and the call for independence in the next century.

The metaphor of awakening, as from a centuries-long sleep to re-discover an ancient heritage, was not confined to the Baltic of course, but was characteristic of the growth of nationalism throughout nineteenth-century Europe. Moreover, as history has revealed, such growth depends less on the spread of specific political ideologies than on the validation of the languages and cultural systems that give each people its identity as a nation. It is no accident that the nineteenth century was also the great age of lexicography and philology, which classified vernacular dialects and saw the publication of dictionaries and grammars to standardise native languages. That standardisation in turn, along with the growth of literacy and the proliferation of newspapers and journals, enabled communities to articulate their powerful feelings of unity as a people with a right to self-determination. Equally the growing interest in folklore and anthropology, the cultural florescence of poetry, music, fiction, the visual arts and crafts, indicated something more important than growing leisure or material prosperity. By interpreting a common heritage and celebrating its continuity, art showed its relevance to the present and made sense of the sacrifices of the past, thus strengthening national consciousness still further. As many historians have pointed out, nothing so powerfully supports a people's sense of itself than the metaphors which evoke the most deeply held bonds between humanity and country, whether it is described as fatherland, motherland or homeland. In Latvia, as elsewhere in the Baltic as this history has sought to show, language and cultural heritage had proved astonishingly resistant to extirpation. The fresh validation of that language and the re-creation in a modern context of those archaic belief systems that had nourished the people over the centuries enabled the Latvians, Lithuanians and Estonians to mount a remarkably powerful resistance to the attempted Russification of the Baltic lands.

The Rise of a Nation and the Great War

By the end of the nineteenth century Russia's cumbersome administrative system, the slow pace of economic and social reform, and the out-dated autocratic mode of government had signally failed to contain growing unrest and violence throughout the empire. Attacks on bailiffs and landlords were widespread, as were the killings of tsarist officials. Revolutionary and anarchist movements proliferated and although these lacked cohesion and unity, they were symptoms of the powerful social unease that would explode in the revolutions of 1905 and 1917. Nicholas II (1894–1917) was unable to implement the radical political, economic and social reforms that might have preserved his realm and brought it intact into the twentieth century. There is no doubt that Russia had the potential to become a great economic power: although it had taken forty years after the emancipation of the serfs, there were signs that the independent peasant-farmers had at last broken out of the cycle of subsistence farming and periodic famines; industrial productivity was on the increase, supported by the creation of a vast railway network; a new class of businessmen and entrepreneurs was emerging. But these developments were frustratingly slow, hampered by bureaucracy and the increasingly repressive system of police surveillance. Then in 1905 Russia suffered a humiliating defeat in the costly war against Japan, followed by the atrocity of 'Bloody Sunday' when soldiers fired on a peaceful demonstration in St Petersburg. Public outrage was typified by the telling observation of one Western diplomat:

> I never knew the Russian public to be so united in their views in connection with the acts of the authorities in ordering the soldiers to shoot the work-men, their wives, children, and inoffensive spectators last Sunday in St

Petersburg. All classes condemn the authorities and more particularly the Emperor. The present ruler has lost absolutely the affection of the Russian people, and whatever the future may have in store for the dynasty, the present Czar will never again be safe in the midst of his people.[21]

Fuelled by decades of discontent and sparked by the massacre in St Petersburg, the 1905 Revolution erupted and spread rapidly across the immense territories of the Russian empire. The anger of the Russian people, however, was only one factor. As Hugh Seton-Watson has observed, the uprising was

> as much a revolution of non-Russians against Russification as it was a revolution of workers, peasants, and radical intellectuals against authority. The two revolts were of course connected: the social revolution was in fact most bitter in non-Russian regions, with Polish workers, Latvian peasants and Georgian peasants as protagonists.[22]

The revolution, then, had gained much of its energy from the growing nationalism of the empire's subject peoples, now threatened by Russification. Nations are imagined political communities which come into being through cultural systems that define their identities and give them purpose.[23] In the Baltic littoral, as we have seen, the phenomenon of nationality was particularly vigorous, fostered by ancient languages whose expression in poetry and song had preserved each people's distinctiveness and identity over centuries of helotry in their own lands. The ill-advised policy of Russification struck at the very heart of that identity, threatening entire cultures with extinction, so it was hardly surprising that it met with passionate resistance.

If the preservation of a nation's indigenous language and culture was the central factor in the growing demand for self-determination in Russia's subject states, there were others. Throughout their history the Latvians had had to be trilingual in order to mediate between themselves, their German landlords and whichever imperial power was in control. This had another consequence: the ability to master several languages gives access to the publications of other nations, in this case those of western Europe with its debates about civic and individual liberty, nationality, and modes of government. This in turn facilitated the development of a politically self-conscious population in Latvia which was able to articulate and focus the growing demand for reform and independence in the second half of the nineteenth century and the opening years of the twentieth.

At the same time the growth of industry in the Baltic and the influx into the cities of dispossessed peasants created an increasingly influential proletariat whose voice was joined to that of a generation of energetic young intellectuals for whom there was no professional employment in the Russian-controlled educational and administrative systems. The 1890s saw the formation in Latvia of a Social Democratic party which was supported by a liberal–radical newspaper, *Dienas Lapa* ('The Daily Page'). In 1898 a general strike in Rīga resulted in the abolition of this paper and the deportation of its editors along with 134 members of the Socialist party to Siberia. But its place was taken by the progressive *Mahjas Weesis* ('The House Guest') and joined in 1902 by the *Rīgas Ahwihses* ('The Rīga News'), a more conservative nationalist paper. Between them these two periodicals represented the political spectrum in Latvia. Both were equally committed to achieving independence, but the former adopted the tenets of the German Social Democratic party with its strong Marxist bias, while the latter tended to distance itself from the more radical aspects of the international labour movement.

The revolutionary activities of 1905 prompted some constitutional reforms in the Russian regime, in particular the establishment of the *Duma*, a consultative council, though the principle of autocracy remained unchanged. Violence and disorder continued throughout the empire. On the eve of the First World War and despite her growing economic power, vast army and modern weaponry, most of rural Russia was still sunk in abject poverty with an illiterate and ignorant population, and she was the only European power in which revolutionary and terrorist activities continued to grow. In the Baltic provinces discontent with Russification was exacerbated by the centuries-old resentment against the German–Balts, whose landed and industrial interests still dominated the city governments, and the Diets, in which the native populations had little representation. The Baltic Marxist-inspired labour movements that sprang up became increasingly nationalistic in character, which brought them into conflict both with the authorities and the Russian Workmen's Social Democratic party. The central committee of the latter had split into two factions in 1903: the Bolshevik, committed to revolutionary methods and dominated by Lenin; and the Menshevik, which also aimed to achieve radical reforms but insisted on working within a democratic constitution. A comparable division also characterised debate in the Baltic, though here the majority came to recognise that neither political autonomy nor full sovereignty would be supported by Lenin and his followers. Accordingly, a Baltic Congress was held in Bern at which representatives from Estonia, Finland, Latvia and Lithuania agreed to join in a common cause against both internal German control and external tsarist rule and issued a proclamation calling for independence and the right of their nations to establish constitutional assemblies with full sovereign powers.

The proclamation was ignored, but throughout 1905 the call for independence continued undiminished and violence escalated throughout the Baltic. German manor houses were looted and estates burned while in the towns the citizenry rose up and ousted the hated Russian police. By the autumn of that year the radical and conservative wings of the Latvian Social Democratic party set aside their differences to unite in their demand for autonomy; a principal figure in diplomatically resolving their disputes was Jānis Rainis, who was to become Latvia's national poet. Throughout the country locally elected revolutionary committees were set up, and by the end of the year they had effectively taken over governance of the country, announcing the restoration of civil liberties such as freedom of speech and of the press as well as the right of assembly; they also reinstated the Latvian language in schools and promised to implement a programme of land reform. The result was predictable. In 1906 Russia declared martial law in Estonia, Livonia and Kurland, and Russian troops, supported by the local German–Balts, marched into the Baltic and initiated a reign of reprisals and terror. They burned farms, shot or hanged civilians without benefit of trial and deported others to Siberia. Thousands fled the country and sought refuge abroad, especially in the United States and the United Kingdom.

Another consequence of the 1905 uprising was that it confirmed the German–Balts in their view that the Baltic littoral would be far safer in their hands than in those of Russia's inept tsar. Therefore, as they resumed control of their lands and commercial interests, they also embarked on a vigorous programme to forge more links with Berlin. Somehow they persuaded the tsarist government to modify the policy of Russification and to allow German once more as the medium of instruction in schools, administration and commerce. Next they set up *Kultur* unions in Estonia, Livonia and Kurland, designed to educate the local populations in the benefits of German culture and civilised government, at the same time implicitly decrying Russian incompetence. Neither the restored German overlordship with its propaganda nor the Russian military and police presence, however, could eradicate the memory of the brief period of independence in 1905. In Latvia secret societies sprang up and flourished, dedicated to fostering the Latvian language and to preserving the nation's history, literature and music.

Meanwhile the small number of Baltic representatives in the Russian *Duma* were powerless to press for meaningful reform, still less for autonomy. 'Russia indivisible' remained the official policy, though some provincial councils were allowed limited powers of self-governance. However, in the Baltic such budding liberal measures were undermined by a fresh onslaught of Russification in 1908–9. Once again the Latvian language was forbidden in schools and attempts were made to curtail the use of German in commerce and administration. Although the latter was largely unsuccessful, it spurred the German–Balt community to further strengthen its ties with Germany by two means: firstly, faced with an unreliable industrial labouring class and a disaffected peasantry no longer bound to the great estates, they planned to replace the native workforce in Kurland and Livonia with tens of thousands of peasants imported from Germany. This mass immigration would be achieved by the German squires ceding a third of their estates to immigrants (in compensation they would obtain large tracts of forest land) and by forcing each of the 25,000 independent Latvian farmers to sell half their land for re-settlement by German colonists.

Secondly, they would intensify efforts to consolidate German commercial dominance in the Baltic Sea.

It is no wonder that the Latvians felt they were caught between two equal, if different, evils and faced an impossible choice when war broke out in 1914: neither Germany nor Russia could be trusted, yet the embryonic nation-state could not possibly survive alone. In the hope that Russia's alliance with the Western powers might eventually result in some liberalisation and democratic reforms for her subject peoples, and faced with the unpalatable prospect of becoming once more a mere colony of Germany—a danger signalled by the recently announced policy of re-colonisation—the Latvian delegates to the Russian Duma declared their support for the tsar.

The course of the Great War with its appalling casualties, the chronicle of alternate advances and retreats to secure a few kilometres of mud, the tactical errors which squandered millions of lives have been fully documented and analysed elsewhere. In the Baltic, the Latvian army was mobilised in 1915 and the tsar permitted flags and insignia with Latvian emblems and inscriptions, the first time in 700 years that an imperial power had given them official recognition. Although it was bitterly said among the troops that there was little difference between serving a tsar with a beard or one with a moustache (i.e. the Kaiser), the army loyally followed the directive of the Allied Command to halt the German advance and maintain 'the Daugava line'. This the Latvian Rifles, as they came to be called, did for two years, a remarkable achievement given that they had little artillery and hardly any support from Russian troops. Their staunch resistance prompted Field Marshal von Hindenburg's observation that he would have taken Rīga long ago had it not been for 'the eight bright stars in the sky' (the eight Latvian Rifle regiments). But the German advance could not be stemmed much longer without additional military aid, and events in Russia were to preclude support for troops on the Baltic front; Livonia would soon be occupied by German forces.

The year 1917, it is widely agreed, marked one of the great fault-lines of European history: it witnessed the entry of the United

States into European affairs and saw the collapse of the Russian Empire. At the beginning of the year Russia was in turmoil with a widespread famine caused by a breakdown in the transportation system, a corrupt and incompetent government, a demoralised army and a rioting population. The tsar abdicated on 15 March, but the provisional liberal–socialist government which replaced him failed to restore internal order, still less address the low morale of the Russian troops or contribute meaningfully to the war effort. All over Russia the cry arose for 'peace, land, bread!' and, as history records, Lenin's Bolsheviks seized power in October 1917 and set in motion the process that would transform Russia into a Marxist state committed to the destruction of the political and social bases on which the sovereignty of Europe's democracies rested. Lenin abolished the elected parliament—not until 1990 would free elections once more be held in Russia—and initiated the dictatorship of the proletariat. Russia and Germany signed an armistice agreement on 15 December 1917 at Brest-Litovsk, but while Lenin's withdrawal from the war undoubtedly strengthened his position in Russia, it angered the Allies who saw it as a betrayal. This was later to be reflected in the peace negotiations, for the Allies strongly supported Czech, Slav, Balkan and Baltic nationalist aspirations, which resulted in considerable territorial losses for Soviet Russia (from 1923 the Union of Soviet Socialist Republics).

Meanwhile in Latvia the economy lay in ruins: all rolling stock, machinery and raw materials had been evacuated to Russia in 1914 or appropriated by the German invading forces. Churches, schools hospitals, railway stations, bridges and public buildings had been blown up by retreating Russians or advancing Germans; international trade had virtually ceased; over a fifth of the population had fled.[24] Germany had occupied Kurland in July 1915 and remained entrenched. The German–Balts petitioned the German chancellor to annex the Baltic provinces, and the Reichstag agreed to do so in April 1916. The position for the native Balts was grim. Although the provisional government in Russia was more liberal than the tsarist regime it had replaced, the most the Baltic peoples could expect would be 'a free Baltic within a free Russia'. The Latvians proceeded to elect a series of provisional territorial councils in March 1917 for Vidzeme (Livonia), Kurzeme (Kurland) and Latgale in March 1917.[25] These councils, along with the municipal authorities, the army and several key social and political organisations, unanimously resolved to form a united Latvian Land Council to embody the nation's political autonomy. On 5 July, however, the Russian provisional government passed a declaration granting only limited powers of self-government for Livonia and Kurland. To counteract this another council meeting was called on 30 July in Rīga, which passed resolutions declaring the nation's right to self-determination: Latvia would govern itself through an elected constitutional assembly with full legal, executive and judicial powers as a politically autonomous state within the Russian Empire.

The leaders of the July council could not have predicted the rapidity of Lenin's rise nor the equally rapid dissolution of the Russian Empire, although the fall of Rīga on 3 September and the rapid German advance into Livonia had been anticipated as strong probabilities. They were quick to respond to both. On 16 November 1917 the first Latvian National Assembly met at Valka, a town on the Latvian–Estonian border still unoccupied by the Germans. It was here that the first Diet of the Livonian Confederation had been held in the fifteenth century and now Valka became the temporary political capital of the Latvian nation.[26] Delegates met to form the Latvian Provisional National Council (LPNC) and to elect a Supreme Board to serve as its executive, chaired by V. Zamuelis with K. Skalbe as secretary.[27] Its first act was to publish a proclamation of Latvia's independence and to distribute it throughout the country. It also established an official gazette, the *Lihdums* ('The Promised Land'). On 5 January 1918 the LPNC head of foreign affairs announced to the Russian Assembly (soon to be dissolved by the Bolsheviks) that Latvia had seceded and severed all political ties with Russia. In the same month the LPNC charged J. Čakste, former representative to the Russian Duma and later to become the first President of Latvia, and Z. A. Meierovics, later Latvia's foreign minister, to obtain recognition for Latvia's sovereignty abroad.[28]

During these negotiations, however, Germany and Russia were still arranging details of the Brest-Litovsk Armistice and it was not until 3 March 1918 that a peace treaty was signed. By this agreement Russia ceded the Baltic to Germany: Kurland would be absorbed by Prussia; Livonia and Estonia would be under German control; Russia would retain only Latgale. To counteract these measures the LPNC met during 26–28 June 1918 to protest against the territorial cessions of Brest-Litovsk and called on the Allies to recognise Latvia's independence. On 11 November 1918 the Allied powers signed an armistice with Germany and on the same date the British Foreign Secretary wrote to the provisional Latvian Foreign Minister Meierovis confirming his government's recognition of Latvia's sovereignty.

> I have the honour to acknowledge with thanks your letter of the 30th ultimo in which you enclose a copy of your appeal to Great Britain and the Allies to give their protection to Latvia.
>
> I am happy to take this opportunity of repeating the assurance which I gave you on the occasion of your recent visit. His Majesty's Government have viewed with the deepest sympathy the aspirations of the Latvian people and its desire for liberation from the German yoke. They are glad to reaffirm their readiness to grant provisional recognition to the Latvian National Council as a de facto independent body until such time as the Peace Conference lays its foundations of a new era of freedom and happiness for your people. In the meantime His Majesty's Government will be glad to receive you as the informal diplomatic Representative of the Latvian Provisional Government.
>
> (Signed) A. Balfour

The LPNC, now re-named the Latvian National Assembly, met in Rīga on 17 November to elect J. Čakste President, G. Zemgalis Vice-President and K. Ulmanis Prime Minister. On 18 November the independent Republic of Latvia was proclaimed and that date remains the official National Day of Independence.

Notwithstanding the recognition of the new Baltic republics by the Allies, however, neither the German occupying troops nor the Russian were minded to relinquish their ambitions to dominate the littoral, and battles were to continue for another eighteen months. Mindful of the need to halt Bolshevik ambitions to annex the Baltic, the Allies had stipulated that German forces should remain in place until local military and police units could be set up, thus conveniently, if unintentionally, supporting Germany's plans to retain control of the Baltic in the new European order. The Red Army's fresh advance into Latvian territory was a violation both of the armistice agreement and the declaration by Lenin and Stalin that the peoples of Russia had the right to self-determination. On 3 January 1919 the Bolsheviks marched into Rīga and promptly nationalised all landed property, implemented a policy of forced labour, and set up revolutionary tribunals which began a reign of terror. The units of the Latvian armed forces which might have repelled them were still scattered north and south of the Daugava. Some existed independently, others had been absorbed into Russian or German divisions, but in any case detaching them to form a Latvian national army was at the time impractical. While the German occupying troops did indeed help to counter the invading Bolsheviks, there is no doubt that their presence also signalled Germany's long-term interests, as was shown by the interference of General von der Golz, commander-in-chief of the German armed forces in the Baltic, who played a game of intrigue by alternately supporting different representational governments in Kurzeme and Vidzeme.

The many campaigns, attacks and counter-attacks, coups and counter-coups, the complex diplomatic manoeuvres of the various international powers and the internal divisions in the newly formed Baltic governments themselves are too detailed to discuss here.[29] But briefly, a contingent of Latvian Bolsheviks headed by one Pēteris Stručka attempted to set up an alternative Latvian Soviet Socialist Republic in that part of Vidzeme still unoccupied by German forces. It lacked popular support and only lasted a few months from December 1918 to May 1919, but it forced the legitimate provisional national government, at the time headed by Kārlis Ulmanis, to flee to Liepāja. Another rival authority was established by the clergyman Andrievs Niedra, who felt that Latvia's survival depended on cooperating with Germany. Von der Golz alternately supported Ulmanis, Niedra and the local German–

Balts, playing each against the other while covertly serving Germany's ambitions to control the Baltic. Nevertheless the Ulmanis government prevailed, supported by the population as a whole, by the Western powers—who ordered the withdrawal of German forces—and by the recently re-formed Latvian National Army. However, it was not until May 1919 that Rīga was liberated from the Red Army and not until 8 July that the lawful Latvian government was able to return to the capital.

Meanwhile the Latvian government's delegates to the Paris Peace Conference, which culminated in the Treaty of Versailles on 16 June 1919, had been successful in securing *de jure* recognition for Latvia's sovereignty (Article 433).[30] However, conflict with the Red Army continued, with the latter unsuccessfully attempting to re-take Rīga in the autumn of 1919, and the eastern region of Latgale remained a battle zone. Latvian troops, later supported by divisions from the Polish army, eventually succeeded in ousting Russian forces and on 1 February 1920 an armistice was signed between the Republic of Latvia and Russia. Notwithstanding this, skirmishes continued, especially along the borderlands, until the end of June. Finally the February armistice was ratified by a peace treaty on 11 August in which Russia agreed the boundary with Latgale, relinquished all claims to Latvian territory and recognised that nation's sovereignty.[31]

The hard-won independence of Latvia was only one story among the many of eastern Europe. For us living a century after the Great War it is difficult to imagine the sheer scale of the continent-wide seismic convulsions that shook the political and economic structure of Europe, still less the appalling cost in human lives and suffering. Simply in terms of population shift the re-configuration of the European map was extraordinary. Of the 104 million people in the eastern European nations (Finland, Estonia, Latvia, Lithuania, Poland, Czechoslovakia, Austria, Hungary, Rumania, Yugoslavia, Bulgaria, Greece, Albania), eighty million had been detached from the three great empires which had hitherto dominated continental Europe. The foundations of the old order had been destroyed and the task of rebuilding, especially for the new nations, was almost inconceivably daunting. Writing in 1919 the young economist John Maynard Keynes tellingly summarised the human and economic cost of the Great War:

> We are at the dead season of our fortunes. Our power of feeling or caring beyond the immediate questions of our own material well being is temporarily eclipsed [...] We have been moved already beyond endurance, and need rest. Never in the lifetime of men now living has the universal element in the soul of man burnt so dimly.[32]

It was in these circumstances that the republics of Estonia, Latvia and Lithuania came into being.

Map 7. The Eastern Front during the Great War of 1914–1918

Map 8. The Baltic States in 1920

5

THE SHAPING OF A NATION-STATE

The Economics of Liberty

In 1914 over 2,500,000 people lived in Latvia; in 1920 that figure had fallen to 1,600,000, and although by 1925 approximately 220,000 exiles had returned, Latvia had lost nearly 30 per cent of her population. Proportionately speaking, no other country in the Great War had suffered such a loss. The countryside was devastated, the economy shattered, and the new nation was faced with crippling war debts from the prolonged struggle for freedom against both Germany and Russia after the First World War. Germany had refused any reparation on the grounds that the loss of German landed property was deprivation enough; Russia agreed compensation but only sent one token payment along with the return of monetary deposits, personal property and the state archives, which had been sent abroad for safe keeping. Latvia was deeply in debt to the Allies for services and armaments supplied during the fight for independence and owed Britain £1,303,000, the United States $5,775,000 and France 5,000,000 francs.[1] It would be hard to imagine more unfavourable circumstances attending the birth of a new state.

However, by the autumn of 1920 the boundaries of Latvia had been confirmed: Russia had relinquished all claim to Latgale; the Estonian–Latvian frontier had been agreed on 22 March (with the disputed border town of Valka partitioned); the peace treaty with Germany concluded on 15 July. Only the fine details of the frontier with Lithuania remained to be settled and that was achieved in March 1921. The new republic covered 65,791 square kilometres, a little smaller than Ireland though larger than Belgium, Denmark, Estonia, Lithuania, the Netherlands or Switzerland. The three official regions of the nation and their sizes were, and still are, Vidzeme (formerly Livonia, 35%), Latgale (24%) and Kurzeme plus Zemgale (Kurland, 41%). In the first years of independence the demographic composition was roughly 76% Latvian and 24% minority peoples, of whom about 12% were Russian, 5% Jewish, 3% German, and 4% Estonian–Lithuanian–Polish. The cultural, political and economic rights of all national minorities had been guaranteed by the Latvian National Council Proclamation of Independence of 18 November 1918, which had also decreed universal suffrage for both sexes. At the end of 1919 a general amnesty offered citizenship to those Latvians who had joined the Bolsheviks or the Germans and to the German–Balts who had supported Germany's plans to annex Latvia. Subsequent legislation on 18 December 1919 extended citizenship and civil liberties to minorities, including their right to education, either in state schools or in their own schools, the only stipulation being that the curriculum include Latvian history and language. Furthermore both types of schooling would be state-subsidised. By any standard these were liberal measures.

The task of reconstruction that faced both the provisional government and the later elected Assembly of 1 May 1920 was formidable. In 1920 Latvia was still primarily an agricultural country with nearly 80 per cent of her economy tied to the land. What industry there was had been destroyed, the factories gutted and the machinery shipped to Russia. Moreover nearly half the agricultural land was still concentrated in the large private estates, most of them German-owned. With a depopulated land, 40 per cent of which was not under cultivation, and with hundreds of thousands of starving workers, war veterans and landless peasants who lacked any means of subsistence, immediate action was urgently needed. The provisional government opened a register of the landless in January 1919 and began re-allocating land in April. Taking Denmark as its model, the government passed a Land Reform Act on 16 September 1920 which re-apportioned all agricultural land exceeding 110 hectares into farming lots sufficient to support a family. This was achieved by creating a Land Fund of nearly 3,500,000 hectares drawn from the large estates, whether state, church, municipal or privately owned. The Land Fund both registered existing farms and supervised the creation of new ones; forests, peat bogs and large inland bodies of water, however, would be state-owned to ensure conservation. Farmers who received allotments were required to buy them but were given long-term mortgages and credit to purchase the essentials for farming; they also received support from government agricultural schools and cooperative associations. As a result of the Land Act, smallholdings of 20–50 hectares became the norm, accounting for about 75 per cent of agricultural land, with larger farms of 50–110 hectares comprising about 20 per cent.

Not surprisingly these radical measures were bitterly opposed by the *Ritterschaft*, the association of German barons who for centuries had controlled the Diets of Livonia and Kurland. The *Ritterschaft* had been abolished by law on 29 June 1920 but the German landowners, arguing that the compensation for the loss of their estates was insufficient, took their case to the League of Nations. It was rejected and almost overnight Latvia became a nation of independent, self-sufficient smallholders.[2] Despite predictions by some Western economists that agriculture and grain production would fall dramatically following the break-up of the large estates and thus preclude economic recovery, in practice both cultivation and stock farming (especially dairy production) flourished. The young government had avoided famine, had ensured social stability and had laid sound foundations for restructuring the economic life of the nation.

Those foundations were strengthened by the intensive legislation carried out in the second half of 1920 and throughout 1921, which aimed to foster private enterprise not only in farming but also in commerce, industry and fishing through low-interest loans and long-term mortgages. Larger projects such as repairing the damaged rail network, road system, ports and harbour installations as well as essential public services remained state-controlled. To help finance the latter, two state monopolies on alcohol and tobacco were established and the revenues also used to fund the building of new schools and public libraries. The official national currency, the Lat, was introduced on 3 August 1922. Based on one gold franc—or 50 paper Latvian roubles—it stabilised the economy and helped to avoid the inflation and currency fluctuation that dogged many countries after the First World War. The Latvian State Bank and the Agricultural Bank opened in 1923 and the Mortgage Bank in 1924.

In addition to the immense task of creating a viable fiscal policy and of implementing its wide-ranging agricultural reforms, the new government embarked on an ambitious programme designed to stimulate international trade, taking advantage of Latvia's historical position as a conduit for shipping between western Europe and the Russian hinterland. The three major ports of Rīga, Ventspils and Liepāja with their important rail links to Russia (involving both broad and narrow gauge rails) were repaired and modernised. Special tariffs were introduced for Russian transit goods and a concession issued for a Soviet Transit Bank. Rīga also built processing plants for the Russian timber that came down the Daugava while Ventspils erected a huge grain elevator, at the time the largest in Europe, in the expectation of handling Russian grain exports. In theory these were all perfectly sensible measures, but the government could not have predicted that the Soviet Union would bypass the Baltic, shipping most of its grain and raw materials through the Black Sea ports and the remainder through Leningrad (St Petersburg), nor that it would no longer import agricultural produce and material goods from the West at all. Thus the expensive harbour installations lay idle and Latvia's rich agricultural output no longer flowed East. Notwithstanding this blow, the economic life of the nation continued to strengthen, albeit slowly, as other government initiatives such as support for industry took effect, supplementing revenue from the export of timber, flax, dairy and meat produce to Western markets.

Parallel to the economic reforms, the political structure of the new nation-state was firmly grounded in Western models of liberal democracy. After months of intensive work, the new Latvian constitution was passed by the Assembly on 15 February 1922 providing for: a unicameral parliament, the Saeima; a president to be elected for a term of three years; a prime minister and cabinet; and the separation of the legislative, executive and judicial branches of government. The constitution guaranteed freedom of speech and of the press and the right of assembly and also promised equal rights and opportunities for all citizens, as well as cultural autonomy for national minorities. It could be amended only by a two-thirds parliamentary majority. The Saeima itself consisted of 100 delegates drawn from the five electoral districts of Vidzeme, Latgale, Kurzeme, Zemgale and Rīga, to be elected by a secret and proportional ballot; the president was then elected by a simple majority of the Saeima. The first national elections were held on 28 October 1922 and the first official sitting of the Saeima was on 7 November in the same year.

However, the scrupulously fair and egalitarian voting procedure depended on an immensely complex system of calculation which after a trial period had to be simplified: the election of the first Saeima had generated no fewer than twenty-two political parties. In the effort to guarantee representation for all degrees of political opinion as well as to ethnic and religious minorities, the first Saeima had also passed a resolution in July 1923 granting the right to any group of at least five persons to register as a political party. Although in theory laudable, in practice it proved an unworkable system: at one point there were over forty political parties and the first four Saeimas (of 1922, 1925, 1928 and 1931) consisted of 22, 27, 27 and 24 parties, respectively.[3] Broadly speaking, the minority groups supported five major coalition parties which polled the following percentages of the national vote in the first Saeima:

(1) Social Democrats (six parties, socialist in character favouring industry and urban, as well as some rural, workers) 38%;

(2) Democratic Centre (nine parties, mostly professional and middle class in nature) 13%;
(3) Agrarian Bloc (seven parties, liberal though not socialist) 25%;
(4) Conservatives (seven parties, largely Christian nationalist in composition) 9%;
(5) National Minorities Coalition (ten parties) 15%.

Between the first and fourth Saeimas these percentages remained roughly the same, apart from the two strongest parties where there was a shift in power: in the 1931 election the vote for the Social Democrats fell to 28 per cent while the Agrarian Bloc moved up to 34 per cent. The largest component of the increasingly influential Agrarian Bloc was the Farmers' Union, which also produced a significant percentage of Latvia's statesmen.[4] The unwieldy internal political structure, however, combined with the international economic crisis of the 1930s, would precipitate radical reforms, as will be seen below.

Meanwhile the new nation-state had received encouraging international support. By 20 June 1921 Latvia had been recognised *de jure* by all the major European powers, on 28 July by the United States of America, and on 22 September Latvia became a member of the League of Nations. The latter has been called the single most important and imaginative outcome of the 1919 Peace Treaty of Versailles. Not only did it confirm the principles of national autonomy, but it transcended European membership: twenty-six of its original forty-two member states were non-European. It was flawed by two serious omissions however: neither the United States nor Russia had joined and this was to have grave consequences that eventually led to the League's dissolution. The United States increasingly withdrew into continental isolation while Russia, which had not been consulted in the political reconfiguration of Europe, concentrated on implementing a revolutionary communist programme profoundly anti-pathetic to Western capitalist democracy and destined to shape European and indeed Asian history for much of the twentieth century.

For the present, however, a surge of optimism flowed through the new Baltic nation-states, whose representatives met to consider mutually beneficial commercial and defence agreements designed to create a 'free Baltic sea'. The Latvian Foreign Minister Zigfrīds Meierovics proposed the unification of rail, telegraph and telephone systems, a common tariff policy and the establishment of a Baltic Court of Arbitration as well as a permanent Baltic Council to be located in Rīga. Sensible and far-sighted though the proposals were agreed to be, they foundered on a number of issues. Finland withdrew, reluctant to compromise relations with the Scandinavian nations, which were neutral, or to antagonise Russia. Poland and Lithuania also declined to join the proposed confederation or indeed to participate in any further conferences at which the other was present, locked as they were in disagreement over the fate of Vilnius which both claimed. After sustained but fruitless diplomatic negotiations, only Latvia and Estonia signed a mutual Defence Alliance in November 1923 and registered this with the League of Nations.

Such setbacks notwithstanding, the triumph of liberalism and democracy that had swept away the old European order and created political self-determination for tens of millions of people released a corresponding wave of energy and enthusiasm in the newly created nation-states. But this, as we shall see, was compromised from the outset by the fundamental economic fragility of the new Europe. The complex but powerful commercial infrastructure of pre-1914 Europe had been shattered beyond repair and, in addition to the devastation caused by the war, both national and international recoveries were hampered by severe inflation in the older states and constricting tariffs and exchange controls implemented by the new ones in their efforts to nurture their fledgling economies. Further-more Germany, the single most important industrial powerhouse on the continent, was crippled by the draconian reparation demands which delayed her recovery, while Russia was now cut off from the continental trading network by an intransigent government locked in communist ideology. Poverty and hardship were nothing new to the native inhabitants of the Baltic states of course, and it is a testament to their determination and vigour that despite the dissolution of the old European economic system they were able to survive at all. Yet the very liberal conditions which had created Latvia, Lithuania and Estonia would also begin to undermine the new republics' politics and economies in ways that could not have been predicted, while to the east the shadowy menace of Russia was to loom ever larger. Nevertheless, the decade of the 1920s in the Baltic countries was on the whole charged with a sense of energetic optimism coupled with a sober understanding that austerity was necessary for the sake of a better future.

Florescence

The two decades of freedom for Latvia from 1920 to 1940 witnessed a blossoming in music, literature, architecture, the visual arts and crafts which all flourished in despite of the country's economic hardships. The seeds of that flowering, sown during the National Awakening in the previous century, were nurtured by government initiatives and support for education and the creative arts. Jānis Rainis, widely regarded as Latvia's premier poet,[5] was appointed Minister for Education and 15 per cent of the national budget—a figure far higher than that for most European states—was allocated to increase the number of primary and secondary schools as well as vocational and technical institutes.[6] A State Music Conservatoire and an Academy of Fine Arts were founded to complement the University (established in 1919, it incorporated higher education institutes such as the Rīga Polytechnic, dating from 1862) while generous subsidies supported Rīga opera and ballet, at the time considered among the finest in Europe. The first director of the Music Conservatoire and of the Latvian Broadcasting Company was the composer Jānis Vitols,[7] who actively encouraged the study of music in schools and subsidised the traditional song festivals held throughout the country. With choirs numbering as many as 10,000 voices and audiences of 100,000, these festivals were integral to the nation's sense of itself and would be fundamental in preserving national identity later in the century when the country was annexed by the Soviet Union.

The nation's architectural legacy was protected by the new Board of Monuments which was created to locate and maintain edifices of national value. A number of the Hanseatic buildings in Rīga's Old Town owe their survival to this Board, as do the many traditional wooden buildings, castles and churches in the provinces. Rīga is also home to one of the most extensive areas of art nouveau, or Jugendstil, in Europe. Over a third of its buildings were built in this high-spirited style during the last decade of the nineteenth and the first decade of the twentieth century, a number of them designed by the well-known Russian architect Mikhail Eisenstein.[8] The art nouveau movement also stimulated the development of a distinctively Latvian architectural style which came to be known as National Romanticism. This had evolved from Jugendstil and had been modified by incorporating elements of vernacular architecture—the steep roofs, gables and beams of traditional wooden houses—along with ethnographical elements and folklore. In 1924 the Board of Monuments launched one of its most important initiatives: the creation of an extensive open-air ethnographic museum on the shores of Lake Jugla, a few kilometres north of Rīga. Under its aegis traditional buildings dating from the seventeenth to the early twentieth centuries were brought from Latvia's three regions, re-assembled, and stocked with items of historical interest. It was, and still is, one of the most extensive such museums in Europe and has been designated a UNESCO World Heritage Site.[9]

The preservation of the nation's history was fostered in other ways too, with the new Institute of Latvian History and the State Museum of Folklore as well as by the state-subsidised provincial museums, the most important of which were located in Jelgava, Cēsis, Liepāja, Rēzekne and Daugavpils. The Institute and Archive of Latvian Folklore continued the work of collecting the *dainas* and other folklore begun by Krišjānis Barons in the previous century. Painting and sculpture were stimulated by the opportunities to travel freely abroad—many artists studied in Paris (two sculptors were pupils of Rodin)—and the painter V. Purvītis became director of the Rīga Art School, later renamed the Academy of Arts.[10] These and other artistic ventures were supported by the Fund for Cultural Achievements.

In literature Jānis Rainis, who had been a leading figure in the National Awakening, influenced a new generation of poets, novelists and dramatists. They in turn were part of that era of radical experimentation and innovation in the arts which we now call Modernism. As elsewhere in Europe, modernist writers drew their inspiration from a wide variety of sources. Some, concerned to transmit a humanist strand from earlier times, grounded their works in traditional farming life, myth, folklore and landscape, while seeking new ways in which to present universal, timeless truths of human existence and psychology. Others, inspired by sources as different as the French Symbolists, Imagism and Japanese poetry, challenged the structures and conventions of the past and sought expression through fresh forms and styles. France was particularly important, for many Latvian writers had spent their years of exile in Russia where, eschewing both German and Russian cultural models, they had turned to the Romance languages, to the classics of French, Spanish and Italian literature as well as of classical antiquity, which could be found in libraries there.

Not surprisingly the 1920s also witnessed a wave of translations into Latvian, driven by the nation's hunger to feel itself part of a wider international community of culture and intellectual endeavour. The fascination for Japanese lyric poetry, for Sanskrit texts (linguistically akin to Latvian) and for the literatures of India as well as works from the English canon testified to this. These various sources in turn stimulated a correspondingly vigorous experimentation in style and form in the vernacular.[11] Parallel to these literary innovations, and sometimes informing them, ran a rich vein of satire which turned an ironic eye on party politics, corruption, and the consumerism of the *nouveaux riches*, always fertile ground for social criticism. The voices of public conscience also found ready vehicles in the vigorous proliferation of literary magazines and newspapers. By the late 1930s in Rīga alone there were forty-seven newspapers and 154 magazines in several languages—Latvian, Liv, Russian, German, Jewish, Polish. Between 1918 and 1939 the Latvian State Library published fifteen indexes of Latvian literary and scientific texts, recording that over a thousand volumes of fiction, poetry, translations and works in the sciences and social sciences were published each year.[12] In short, the 1920s were a period of dynamic celebration, of growing confidence, of reaching out, a dramatic renaissance in which art, music, architecture, literature and the sciences united to become a powerful cultural script.

Cultural flowering and economic development were grounded in the belief that the nation's identity was inextricably linked to the land itself. It would be hard to over-estimate the immense psychological boost that such a sense gave the population during the years of economic hardship. To the strong emotional bond with the land was added the exhilarating recognition that for the first time in centuries people were working for the good of their own country rather than for the profit of German–Balt landowners or a distant Russian government. Although the young state was faced with a devastated countryside and the complete destruction of its industry, there was a collective will to restore and to rebuild, a sense of national ownership which paralleled the strong growth of the nation's cultural life. This also accounted for what may be seen as a general collective trust in the fledgling government's ability to initiate, direct and control social and economic policies, transcending local criticism and dissent. Over 25 per cent of the national budget went into economic reconstruction; and as the economy stabilised and revenues began to flow steadily into government coffers, 13 per cent of the annual budget was devoted to social services such as healthcare, family allowances and a liberal superannuation scheme which offered pensions after the age of fifty-five.

Active government support enabled the steady growth of small-scale factories, particularly in timber and flax production, which together accounted for 40 per cent of exports, in metal, textiles, clothing and shoes, and chemicals.[13] As the land reforms began to take effect agricultural exports grew rapidly. For example in 1921 dairy exports totalled barely 15,000 kg; by 1925 that figure had catapulted to 7,000,000, placing Latvia only slightly behind Denmark, Sweden and Ireland; by 1930 the figure was 18,500,000 and by 1938 23,000,000. Grain production, especially wheat, increased sevenfold and sugar beet tenfold during the years of independence. By 1925 the pre-war figure for livestock had been regained and meat, especially pork products, was once more exported. Thus despite international predictions that the country would need massive foreign investment to achieve economic stability, let alone growth, Latvia had completely transformed her economy in less than a decade. Not only was she self-sufficient in the staples necessary for subsistence, but she had turned cripplingly negative import/export figures into a healthy and positive balance of payments.[14]

Shipping was slower to recover, given the failure of the expected trans-shipments between the Baltic and Russia through Latvia's ports. However, freedom of trading and shipping in the Baltic was confirmed through a series of international conventions at which representatives from the countries bordering the Baltic agreed to abolish visas and to create shipping lanes and other common policies for commerce and navigation. Following the normalisation of relations with Russia, treaties were signed by Latvia, Lithuania, Estonia and Finland to provide for arbitration in commercial and civil matters.[15] Then a number of government initiatives were introduced to lessen the country's dependence on power sources from abroad. Although Latvia was nearly self-sufficient in heating, thanks to the vast peat and timber reserves, she was vulnerable to fluctuations in electricity supplies and prices. This was meliorated by building the first hydroelectric dam across the Daugava.[16] But perhaps the most impressive achievement of the young state was that in a remarkably short period it had attained fiscal health. Not only had the Bank of Latvia succeeded in stabilising the Lat, contrary to international expectations, it had dramatically increased the country's gold reserves in the first decade and would continue to augment them in the second.[17] The national debt stood at only 1 per cent, compared to the 12 per cent average elsewhere in Europe. It was for these reasons that although the stock-market collapse of 1929 and the worldwide Depression that followed it undoubtedly affected the Latvian economy adversely, the repercussions were not as devastating as in many other countries in the developed world.

The Crisis of the 1930s

The gradual recovery of prosperity in Latvia during the post-war years was part of the wider pattern in Europe. Between 1925 and 1929 agricultural production on the continent passed pre-war figures and industry was rapidly increasing in output. The international return to the gold standard had renewed confidence in national currencies, and with the help of massive investment and loans from the United States European manufacturing and trade surged. However, this growth rested on insecure foundations, for it depended on the continuing domestic prosperity of the United States. Throughout the 1920s its booming economy, which seemed unstoppable, accounted for nearly 40 per cent of the world's coal and over half its manufactured goods. But the stock-market collapse of 1929 which shattered the US economy precipitated a worldwide financial crisis and Europe's recovery and the significant rise in living standards came to a halt. In a sense the new states of eastern Europe suffered less psychologically and—proportionately speaking—economically, for they had less to lose. Nevertheless the effects were severe and generated social unrest and a new stridency in nationalistic aspirations that undermined some of the idealistic liberal principles that had informed the Peace Treaty at Versailles. While international agreement on the principles of self-determination and nationality remained unchanged, the economic crisis exacerbated the problems in nation-states where geographical, historical, ethnic and cultural realities had cut across the new national boundaries.[18]

Across Europe the economic crisis fed the rise of powerful and opposing ideologies that promised reform and regeneration, most significantly that of Marxist communism in the Soviet Union and fascism in Germany and Italy. In the Baltic republics, as in others bordering the USSR, it was the fear of the Marxist threat that would precipitate political changes to the liberal constitutions and policies of the early years of independence and would replace them with more authoritarian regimes. However, it should be noted that the traditional ideological division of Western politics into 'left' and 'right' has little meaning in the Baltic republics, where political divisions were, and are, not based on party doctrines but rather on particular economic and social policies, themselves infused by deeply held loyalties to the nation's history, to the concept of a homeland and to a distinctive cultural heritage. Having so recently achieved independence, the indigenous populations of the three Baltic states were nationalistic in the sense of wishing to extol the flowering of their cultures in a domain that they now owned. This showed itself in the celebration of nature and the beauties of the landscape, and it was a powerful unifying force which transcended the specific criticisms of governmental policies or cynicism about the political process as a whole.

At the same time the proliferation of political groups and views each demanding formal representation in the Latvian voting system was soon recognised as unworkable in practice. Indeed, in contemporary terms most of Latvia's political parties were actually no such thing but rather small groups which coalesced around specific individuals, slogans or interests. The voting and legislative systems founded on consensus and compromise may indeed have expressed the wide diversity of political opinions in the country, but they became increasingly unstable. Governments based on coalitions could be, and were, dissolved after a vote of no-confidence in the Saeima. Moreover, general confidence in the older generation of statesmen and representatives who had fostered the economic, cultural and social development of the new state foundered in the worldwide Depression of the 1930s. The electorate were increasingly bewildered by the costly failure of government-led projects, by the lack of a unified and coherent economic strategy and by the way that political factions supported the vested interests of minority groups which appeared to operate at the expense of the nation's economic health. As a result, in all three Baltic republics constitutions were suspended and authoritarian regimes imposed.[19]

Widespread disillusion, then, was born of acute economic insecurity, and calls for constitutional reform to end parliamentary disunity and factionalism increased. The large Social Democratic Party, allied to a number of minority interests in business and industry and favouring closer ties with Russia, was opposed to such reform, as were the Conservative Nationalists who wanted stronger links with Germany.[20] In 1933 the currently dominant Agrarian Bloc, headed by the influential Farmers' Union, called for constitutional amendments, but the proposal was opposed by the Social Democrats and their allies and failed to reach the necessary three-quarters majority vote in the Saeima. This in turn sparked the constitutional crisis of 15 May 1934. Prime Minister Kārlis Ulmanis and Minister of War General Jānis Balodis, both of whom had been leading figures in the struggle for independence, dissolved the Saeima and declared a national state of emergency. They formed a National Unity government whose aim was to stabilise the economy and to reform the constitution. The *coup d'état* was endorsed by the President, Alberts Kviesis, and the Supreme Court in accordance with Article 81 of the existing constitution which permitted the cabinet to pass laws when the Saeima was not in session, though these had to be ratified retroactively. Political parties were abolished and power vested in the cabinet of ministers chaired by Ulmanis, who in 1936 also became President. Although mildly authoritarian, the new government was hardly a dictatorship: there was no political persecution, no secret police, no racial discrimination, nor did it subscribe to the tenets of fascism. Rather the new regime was seen as a necessary means of dealing with the growing internal and external threats to Latvia's economy and sovereignty. Under the aegis of Kārlis Ulmanis, who had been prime minister in previous governments and who headed the Farmers' Union, industry was re-organised, unemployment reduced, the welfare programme expanded, and increased funding for agriculture secured. After 1935 there was once again a steady rise in prosperity as the economy stabilised and foreign trade picked up, helped by a small devaluation of the Lat in 1936, and the general standard of living also began to rise.[21]

The Ulmanis government commanded great popular support and Ulmanis himself successfully steered a moderate middle course in his reforms. He had no time for extremist factions, whether leftist agitators who advocated loyalty to an international labour movement rather than to the nation-state or the unpleasantly reactionary *Pērkoņkrusts* ('Thundercross') group whose symbol proclaimed their sympathies with Nazi Germany.[22] Ulmanis simply marginalised such extremists politically and focused on hastening economic recovery and on strengthening the welfare programme. He got on well with national minorities, recognising the important contribution of the German–Balt and Jewish communities to the economy, and if his government also attracted calls of 'Latvia for the Latvians' this was perhaps inevitable in a country that had so recently emerged from centuries of oppression and was fiercely determined never again to be ruled by an ethnic minority or foreign power. Yet Latvia's history throughout had been one of tolerant coexistence with racial and religious minorities, and during the two decades of independence the general expectation was that coexistence would gradually become full integration. The powerful sense of national unity as well as the exhilarating momentum of social and cultural development were aided by a vigorous press and the new technology of radio. The economy was viable, a new civil code had been implemented in 1938, the population had recovered and reached two million,[23] the profitless divisions and disputes of the Saeima seemed a thing of the past—in short the country's health and prosperity were a cause for optimism.

It was otherwise in the area of international diplomacy and negotiation: fears were increasing over Germany's growing militarism and the looming threat of Marxist communism from Russia. All the states having a common frontier with the Soviet Union had signed the Kellogg-Briand Pact of 1929 renouncing war as an instrument of national policy. This was followed by the conclusion of a non-aggression pact between Latvia and Russia on 5 February 1932, but notwithstanding these treaties the growing international tension, coupled with the recognition of the three Baltic republics' vulnerability, undoubtedly contributed to popular support for their authoritarian regimes. In fact the deteriorating international situation would have made no difference had these states retained their parliamentary democracies. The Baltic Entente, which was implemented in the years 1934 to 1939 for the purpose of establishing common economic tariffs, cultural exchanges and mutual defence across Latvia, Lithuania and Estonia, was in any case powerless against the predatory ambitions of Germany and Russia.

When Adolf Hitler came to power as president of Germany on 19 August 1934, that country's re-armament gathered greater momentum in preparation for the conflicts to come. In the same year secret negotiations began between Germany and the USSR, which had been admitted to the League of Nations on 18 September, with the aim of demarcating their respective spheres of influence in the Baltic. Nazi propaganda, both covert and open, was disseminated in all three Baltic republics, advocating their incorporation into the Third Reich, while the USSR presented itself as their protector in the event of invasion. Soviet Russia's proposals to station troops there were vigorously rejected by the Baltic republics, which formally declared their neutral status: Latvia and Estonia in December 1938 and Lithuania in January of the new year. These protocols notwithstanding, Germany annexed Memel (Klaipēda) on 21 March 1939, while the USSR proceeded to construct new railways lines to the borders of Finland and the three Baltic republics.

Throughout the summer of 1939 the USSR sought the agreement of Britain and France to permit its occupation of Latvia, Lithuania, Estonia and Poland for defence purposes in the event of renewed German aggression. The Baltic states were not consulted in these negotiations. However, these diplomatic manoeuvrings were negated by the Treaty of Moscow, the Molotov–von Ribbentrop Pact, signed on 23 August 1939 between Germany and the USSR. Ostensibly a treaty of friendship and non-aggression, the pact actually served to formalise zones of influence in the Baltic, demarcating the northern frontier of Lithuania as the limit of German interests and sanctioning the occupation of Latvia, Estonia and Finland by Russia.[24] As history records, Germany annexed Austria on 12–14 March 1938, absorbed Czechoslovakia in March 1939 and then invaded Poland on 1 September 1939. On 3 September 1939, honouring their agreement to support the latter against invasion by a foreign power, Britain and France declared war on Germany.

In the Baltic the immediate response to Germany's aggression had been to reiterate the policy of neutrality but the declarations were in vain. Germany and the USSR had already agreed to partition eastern Europe between them, though this did not make them firm allies as the course of World War Two would reveal. However, for the moment Stalin's strategy was to entrench himself firmly in the Baltic. This he achieved by using the pretext that an incident involving an interned Polish submarine was a threat to Soviet security and then announcing that Baltic ports were giving aid to hostile U-boats. On 28 September 1939 Estonia was forced to sign a treaty leasing all her islands to Russia for ten years to use as military, naval and air force bases and permitting the deployment of 25,000 Soviet troops on her territory. Faced with the implications of the infamous Molotov–von Ribbentrop Pact, the example of Estonia's compromised sovereignty, with sixteen divisions of the Red Army massed on her borders, and in the absence of support from Britain and France, Latvia also signed a Pact of Mutual Assistance with Russia on 5 October 1939; Lithuania followed suit on 10 October. The Soviet Union agreed to respect Latvia's sovereignty but nevertheless took control of the Gulf of Rīga, occupying the strategically important ports of Ventspils and Liepāja as well as several airfields. Shortly thereafter 30,000 Soviet troops marched in. Soviet agents also arrived and began drawing up lists of 'anti-Soviet' persons and planning the mass deportation of the local population, to be replaced by Russians. Thus, despite assurances from Moscow that the independence and sovereign rights of Latvia and Estonia would be honoured, these countries were now effectively under Soviet rule. The implications of this incursion had been foreseen by Hitler, who stepped up his repatriation of German–Balts, the *Volkdeutscher*. By the beginning of 1940 nearly 50,000 German-speaking residents had left Latvia and the remainder had departed by May, ending the presence of an elite sector that for nearly 700 years had dominated the area. Meanwhile the USSR had been expelled from the League of Nations on 14 December 1939 for invading Finland, which was forced to cede its Karelian territories and the city of Viipuri to Russia and to sign a peace treaty on 12 March 1940. Stalin had succeeded in his ambition to occupy the Baltic.

6

WORLD WAR II AND ITS AFTERMATH

The First Soviet Invasion

The rapprochement between Germany and Russia and the capitulation of Finland brought home to the Latvian government and people that any possibility of surviving the war as a neutral state was fast disappearing. Accordingly, the Ulmanis government took a decision on 17 May 1940 to provide for the country's political continuity in the event of invasion. This took the form of delegating the state's authority to two ambassadors, Kārlis Zariņš in London and Alfreds Bilmanis in Washington DC. The two ambassadors were empowered to appoint diplomatic and consular agents as well as representatives to international conferences. Although these measures did not establish a government-in-exile, they did ensure that the voice of free Latvia would continue to be heard internationally. With some foresight Latvia's state gold reserves were also transferred, the bulk to the United States and the rest to Britain and Switzerland. The precautions were well-founded for on 14 June 1940 Joseph Stalin accused first Lithuania and then Latvia and Estonia of having failed to honour their mutual assistance pacts with the USSR and for conspiring against Soviet Russia. He presented Lithuania with an ultimatum: to accept additional Red Army troops, which would be added to the existing Soviet garrisons, and to agree to the election of a new government 'friendly' to the

Soviet Union. On 15 June the Lithuanian government accepted the terms and its president fled. In the absence of Western aid—and with several divisions of the Red Army on their borders—Estonia and Latvia had no choice but to accept the demands Stalin issued on 16 June. It is telling that the Soviets did not wait for an official reply but on 17 June ordered 200,000 Soviet troops to enter Latvia, supported by tanks and air force. In all, an estimated 800,000 Russian soldiers were stationed in the three Baltic republics.

Kārlis Ulmanis dissolved his cabinet and on 18 June was summoned by Andrei Vishinsky, the notorious public prosecutor who had presided over many of the Stalinist purges of the 1930s. Ulmanis was informed that a new cabinet and prime minister would be appointed with Soviet 'assistance'. The latter was Professor August Kirchenšteins, who formed a puppet government on 20 June that included a few figures from the hitherto banned Latvian Communist Party, itself composed of scarcely 150 members. That party and the Communist Youth Organisation emerged from their suppressed underground activities to liaise with the Soviet security forces (the notorious NKVD) and, with the support of the Red Army, began their work of propaganda to convince the Latvian population that it had been living under a reign of terror from which the Soviets had liberated them. Freedom of the press was abolished and both newspapers and radio were devoted to disseminating Soviet propaganda.

On 5 July it was announced that 'free elections' would be held on 14 and 15 July and that all political candidates had five days in which to present their programmes along with proof that these had been circulated to the electorate. However, no election material could be printed without the approval of the Minister of Information, a Soviet appointee, and in any case many of Latvia's Party leaders, parliamentarians and local officials had been arrested, deported or executed. The five electoral districts were given a single list of Soviet-approved candidates and voting was mandatory upon penalty of losing one's employment. The election results—98 per cent in favour of the Communist candidates—were announced in the foreign press twenty-four hours before the vote counting had been completed. Similar farcical 'free' elections were held in Lithuania and Estonia. These were followed by staged demonstrations in which the local populations called for the establishment of a Soviet Latvia. These 'spontaneous' calls were accompanied by a flood of nearly identical telegrams sent to the new government at its first meeting on 21 July also urging Latvia's incorporation into the USSR. On the same day Kārlis Ulmanis was arrested and deported to Russia and on 31 July General Balodis also disappeared. These two great founders of the Latvian nation-state were never heard of again.

The officials of the new government were a mixture of a few self-serving local collaborators, some members of the existing Latvian Communist Party and a number of administrators with Latvian surnames who had left Latvia during the war for independence to make their careers in Soviet Russia. They were also survivors of the Stalinist purges of 1936 and 1938 and so completely obedient to the Kremlin's directives. At the first sitting of the new government on 21 July all of Latvia's institutions and sources of wealth were nationalised. Capitalism and private enterprise were abolished and, although agricultural collectivisation was not implemented, farmers were restricted to owning a meagre 10 hectares of land. By the end of September 1940 every aspect of commercial, industrial and agricultural activity as well as transport had been nationalised. The banking system was destroyed as worthless Soviet paper roubles flooded into the country with an official exchange rate of 1 rouble per Lat, resulting in massive loss to Latvia's collective wealth. Rampant inflation followed and by January 1941 the cost of living had risen tenfold while salaries had merely doubled. Small retailers were still permitted to operate, but their shops and goods were systematically looted by the Red Army. Warehouses, granaries, hospitals, pharmacies were stripped; industrial and agricultural machinery and raw materials were shipped east for the Soviet war effort.

Meanwhile on 30 July an official delegation had departed for Moscow to present the will of the liberated Latvian people to the Supreme Soviet Council and on 5 August 1940 Latvia was formally declared a Soviet Socialist Republic and became a member of the USSR.[1] The illegality of these proceedings was condemned by the international community, led by the United States and Britain, and the legations of the pre-war republics remained in place. Only Nazi Germany accepted the Soviet annexation of the Baltic states. But although the *de facto* takeover was not recognised *de jure*, the reality was that Latvia was forced to accept a Soviet-designed constitution on 24 August which made her politically, economically and socially completely subservient to the USSR without any hope of secession. Soviet law now held sway throughout the country, the Latvian attorney general was controlled by his Soviet counterpart in Moscow, and laws were held to be retroactive to 1920, ignoring the two decades of independence. Special tribunals and courts were set up from whose decisions there was no escape or appeal. Political parties of course had been abolished to be replaced by a single Communist Party which would enforce the 'dictatorship of the proletariat'. In effect there was a two-tiered power system: the Communist Party ruled in Latvia, Lithuania and Estonia but was itself subservient to the Communist Party of the USSR and its secretary, Joseph Stalin.

The systematic indoctrination and terrorisation of the population proceeded throughout 1940. All educational institutions from primary school to university were placed under new management and forced to run courses on Marxist–Leninism. Censorship regulated the press and radio, the official language once more became Russian, and even street names were replaced with Soviet ones. The Latvian military (numbering about 20,000) was denuded of arms and equipment and either disbanded or incorporated into the Red Army. Over a thousand of its officers were imprisoned, deported or executed. The Home Guard, the *Aizsargi*, was dissolved. By the end of 1940 only a small number of 'reliable' officers, that is those who had thrown in their lot with the new regime, remained. Russian troops everywhere openly patrolled the streets of what was now designated the Baltic Military District with Rīga as its headquarters. Rīga was also the centre for the activities of the infamous secret police which began its programme of night-time arrests and mass deportations to central Russia and Siberia, targeting officials of Latvia's legitimate government, the professional classes, teachers and the clergy. In one night alone (13–14 June) over 34,000 men, women and children were herded into cattle trucks and sent to Siberia in what must have been inconceivably appalling conditions. Most perished in the severe winter that followed.[2] Throughout Latvia churches were declared state property and many were transformed into cinemas, army clubs, even bowling alleys; services could only be held on payment of an exorbitant fee, while the public rental for church property was ten times higher than for the equivalent house space. Religious instruction was banned in schools and the university's theology faculty shut down. Publication of religious works, Bibles, hymnals, even calendars was prohibited. Faced with the rapidity and ruthless efficiency of the

9. Railway wagon, typical of those used to deport many thousands to Siberia on 14 June 1941 (reproduced by kind permission of the Museum of the Occupation of Latvia)

Soviet takeover and its terrorist methods, the population could only watch in silence and incredulity as their hard-won economy was shattered, their lands once more sequestered, and they themselves reduced to virtual slavery.

At this juncture the course of the Second World War changed dramatically for on 22 June 1941 Hitler turned on his erstwhile ally Russia. Having invaded and secured Belgium, the Netherlands, Luxembourg and France, and with Italy having allied itself with Germany, Hitler felt strong enough to challenge Russia's territorial gains. There was more to this than military tactics however, for Hitler also nursed a deep and abiding personal hatred for Bolshevism and for what he regarded as the racially inferior Slav peoples. In his view it was the destiny of Germany to impose Teutonic civilisation on the Slavic east whose role in the new scheme of things would be to provide *Lebensraum* (living-space) and raw materials for the Reich. The attack on Russia, code-named Barbarossa, was carried out by three million soldiers from the *Wehrmacht* across a 2,000-mile front. The German northern army heading for Leningrad (formerly St Petersburg) swept into Lithuania, reached Rīga on 1 and 2 July, and Estonia on 7 July. As in the First World War, the Baltic countries again found themselves a front-line battleground.

Despite initial gains, Hitler's invasion of Russia was to prove unsuccessful and his armies were in retreat from Moscow by Christmas, but they remained in the Baltic. Here they had been greeted as liberators from the Soviet terror and helped by large numbers of local civilians who formed impromptu guerrilla units to harry the Soviet troops. The Red Army retreated in disarray, along with the Stalinist government officials, Communist Party members, security forces and police who had been imposed on the Baltic states, as well as by a large Jewish contingent which had originally fled to the Baltic to escape German-occupied Poland. Freed of the hated Soviet presence, local organisations in all three republics began the task of re-creating their pre-war administrative structures on the assumption that their independence would be restored. They were quickly disabused of any such notion. The German High Command speedily put in its own institutions, laws and officials to replace the Soviet ones. The Baltic peoples would find that they had merely exchanged one kind of dictatorship for another.

Nazi Occupation and the Second Soviet Invasion

When German troops arrived in Rīga on 1 July 1941 they were greeted with cheers and with flowers as liberators in the confident expectation that the republic would be restored. All over Latvia the national flag was raised, the national anthem and Latvian songs were broadcast over the radio, and in villages, towns and cities the hated symbols of Soviet Russia were publicly torn down and burned. The partisans who had fled to the forests emerged to help set up skeletal administration units.[3] But they were perceived as a potential threat by the German authorities who promptly issued a proclamation prohibiting Latvian military and home guard uniforms and ordering the immediate surrender of all firearms. The partisans were then formed into police battalions under German command; subsequently many were sent out of Latvia to serve on the eastern front, from Finland to the Black Sea. On 28 July a dismayed populace listened to the announcement that Latvia was now part of a new German province, the *Ostland* (East Land) composed of the three Baltic states and White Russia. There was no doubt as to the Reich's colonisation and Germanisation plans for the Ostland, as an early secret memorandum, dated 2 April 1941, confirms:

> In the case of these areas the question arises whether they should be allotted the special task of becoming a German settlement area in the future, the most suitable racial elements to be assimilated. […] The necessary removal of considerable sections of the intelligentsia—particularly in Latvia—to the Russian nucleus area would have to be organised. The settlement of a German rural population in considerable numbers would have to be started […] after the undesirable elements have been eliminated […] in the course of one or two generations, this area can be joined up with the German nucleus area as a new germanized country.[4]

The newly appointed *Reichskommisar für das Ostland* was Heinrich Lohse, who immediately issued a proclamation which, far from restoring property rights to the Latvian population, stated that henceforth rent and tax must be paid to the German government. In an astonishing piece of legal legerdemain it was argued that given the frontier settlement agreement with Russia of 11 January 1941 in which Germany recognised Russia's annexation of the Baltic states, and given that private property did not exist in these countries at the outbreak of the German–Soviet conflict on 22 June 1941, it followed that Germany's conquest of these regions in a time of war meant that the inhabitants could claim no legal ownership of property or land. Furthermore it was argued that these regions had been liberated at the cost of German blood so that the Reich was entitled to compensation in the form of all property held in the former Soviet territories.[5] A German state-owned company, the *Landbewirtschaftungsgesellschaft Ostland*, was set up on 16 June 1942 to administer landed property; other state companies followed to manage industry and business ventures. The *Notenbank Ostland* issued new currency for the occupied territories in the form of German marks; although these were nominally equivalent in value to the Reichsmark, they could be used only in the Ostland.

Undoubtedly the policy of the Reich was to secure the Baltic and its resources for the war effort until such time as these countries could be fully Germanised. That process was to be hastened by the Gestapo: illegal arrests, torture and execution without trial, deportation and mass execution of tens of thousands of Latvians commenced. Next the German SS set up concentration camps outside Rīga with the aim of exterminating the Jewish population. Not only Latvian Jews but many thousands transported from Germany, Austria, Czechoslovakia and the Netherlands were incarcerated. During the years of independence the Jewish population in Rīga had numbered about 43,000 (roughly 10 per cent) and had been highly respected for its commercial and cultural contributions to the new state; indeed over a thousand members of the Jewish community had seen active military service in the struggle for Latvia's independence in 1919–20. The Second World War changed all that, for reasons which must be viewed dispassionately if we are to understand the motivation behind the deplorable role of some Latvians in the Nazi atrocities that were to follow. When the course of the Second World War made it evident that the only alternatives for Latvia were domination by Soviet Russia or by Nazi Germany, most of the Jewish population had greeted the invading Soviet army with relief and a number had served in the regime's political and administrative apparatus. But this had the effect of alienating their fellow citizens who came to identify the entire Jewish community, rather than particular individuals, with Soviet oppression and the brutality which had included the deportation of 30,000 Latvians and the execution of another 1,500 in the first year of occupation. This helps to explain, though it cannot condone, what happened in Rīga after the Nazi arrival.

Although many Jews had fled the Nazi advance, those who had remained in Rīga were now trapped. Local Latvians, remembering their suffering under the Soviets and their supporters, now turned on the Jewish community as a whole and some even collaborated with the Germans in what happened next. Shortly after their arrival the Nazis murdered over 2,700 Jews in nearby Bikernieki Forest and imprisoned an estimated 30,000 in the Rīga ghetto, which was surrounded by a high wire fence and patrolled by Latvian auxiliaries, among them the Arājs Kommando who became a byword for brutality. On the night of 30 November—1 December it is believed that 24,000 Jewish people were taken from the ghetto to nearby Rumbula Forest and massacred. Concentration camps such as Salaspils (18 kilometres south-east of Rīga) received the rest as well as the influx from abroad; within a few months half the Jews sent to Rīga had been killed. Of the estimated 15,000 incarcerated in Salaspils, only 192 survived. It is believed that 100,000 men, women and children of many nationalities were put to death in the camps during the three years of Nazi occupation. Today a line from the Latvian writer Eižens Vēveris, who was himself a prisoner in Salaspils, is engraved above the entrance: *'Aiz šiem vārtiem vaid zeme'* ('Beyond these gates the earth groans').[6]

The perpetrators of these atrocities, like the 'Butcher of Rīga', were subsequently identified and condemned at the post-war Nuremberg War Crimes Trials,[7] but it is only just to point out that in the general wave of anti-Semitism not all Latvians were colla-borators or bystanders. Some, like the Lutheran archbishop of Rīga Grinbergs, who was arrested for his protests and incarcerated in Germany,[8] hid and succoured their Jewish fellow citizens at great risk to themselves and their families.[9]

In the autumn of 1942 Latvia's local authorities once more appealed to the Germans to restore Latvia's international status as an independent republic. This was summarily dismissed, as was the proposal to create a Latvian army of 100,000 for the defence of the realm. However, Hitler did agree to the formation of a volunteer Latvian legion to be called the *Waffen SS Legion Lettlands* and mobilisation commenced in February 1943 to register both commissioned and non-commissioned officers; this was followed by a labour conscription on 11 May. Of the 50,000 men who were mobilised, 25,000 were sent to serve as auxiliary units in the German army, 10,000 to act as labour units, and only 15,000 to form the legion itself which was deployed along the eastern front. The plight of these units was unenviable: they were under the command of a hated occupation power while another equally hated force stood at Latvia's border poised to invade. Many young Latvians fled into the forests to avoid conscription and organised their own independent guerrilla groups. Later they became known as the 'Forest Brothers' (see below) and would continue to harass the Soviet military for many years to come.[10]

Although the legion was commanded by German officers, it was deeply committed to defending Latvian territory and it pressed for the same recognition that the Latvian Rifle regiments of the First World War had received. In this respect the legion had some success for orders were once more given in Latvian, the national anthem was played at roll call, and Latvia's colours and insignia were permitted on the uniforms. It was for this reason that after the war Latvian troops were not regarded as members of the *Wehrmacht* but as distinctively Latvian and therefore not subject to arrest but only to discharge.

Germany's defeat on 2 February 1943 at Stalingrad marked the beginning of her long retreat; by the spring of 1944 the front was at Estonia's border and in August battle raged in Vidzeme between the Latvian legion and the invading Russian army which had swept across Latgale earlier in the summer. Vilnius fell to the Russians on 13 July, Tallinn on 29 September and Rīga on 13 October 1944. However, a few days earlier on 9 October Latvian military units had crossed the Daugava into Kurzeme to mount a final defence. Though vastly outnumbered and ill-equipped, these units held out against Russian attacks throughout the winter of 1944–5. Meanwhile urgent diplomatic entreaties to Germany had some result: on 20 February 1945 the German government finally agreed to the formation of a Latvian National Council. This may have been prompted by rumours of the outcome of the historic meeting at the Crimean resort of Yalta on 4–10 February when the 'Big Three'—Roosevelt, Churchill and Stalin—had met to consider the reconfiguration of Europe after Germany's defeat, which was now imminent. The USSR's *de facto* takeover of the eastern European states it had occupied before Hitler's declaration of hostilities against it was tacitly accepted by the United States and Britain, who were unwilling to antagonise Stalin. However, neither the fate of the Baltic republics nor their rights under the Atlantic Charter of 1941 were ever discussed. This would consign them in the decades to come to a kind of limbo, suspended outside the domain of international law. On the one hand their incorporation into the USSR could not be accepted *de jure*, on the other they were no longer sovereign states and so could not be represented at conferences or given a seat in the United Nations. For all the eastern European countries, Yalta would remain a bitter memory of a shameful betrayal by the Allies.

In any case the hastily assembled Latvian National Council which had rallied in Kurzeme could do little for a land in turmoil that was also witnessing the juggernaut advance of the hated Red Army. On 7 May, a day before the official announcement of Germany's capitulation to the Allies, the council issued a proclamation announcing the creation of a provisional Latvian government. This measure was doomed, for in the meantime the Latvian legion itself had been disbanded. Its commander had praised the bravery of his men but, recognising the impossibility of stemming the Red Army's onslaught and that capture by the Soviets would be tantamount to a death sentence for his troops, he ordered his units to surrender to the British, Americans or French. In the light of the rapid Soviet advance and with all hope of military protection gone, the members of the provisional government as well as other surviving officials of the republic fled overseas.

The Russian army's re-entry was to mark the resumption of the large-scale deportation of the Latvian people, especially from Kurzeme which had been inundated by refugees who had fled Latgale and Vidzeme to escape the Bolshevik advance. In desperation Latvia's overseas representatives repeatedly appealed to the Western powers to intervene on their behalf, to halt the Russian invasion and return the Soviet Union to its 1939 frontier, to restore Latvia's independence. It was a hopeless effort. Kurzeme surrendered on 9 May and the Red Army immediately reinstated Soviet law and policy. From 12 May 1945 it began to implement a truly draconian conscription which marshalled all men between the ages of sixteen and sixty-five and all women between eighteen and forty-five into military units and labour brigades. In June 50,000 Latvian farmers and their families were deported to the USSR to be replaced by an equivalent number of Russians. And Latvia disappeared into the grey nullity of Soviet rule.

Exile

On 9 October 1944, a few days before the Soviet army entered Rīga, one of the last refugee ships to leave the still unoccupied port of Liepāja set sail for Germany, the crossing to Sweden being deemed too hazardous. The vessel carried the author's parents and, unbeknownst to them, another family whose nine-year-old daughter would return nearly half a century later to become the first woman President of a free Latvia; it would also be under her energetic leadership that Latvia would become a member of the European Union. But few of the tens of thousands who joined the mass exodus by ship that autumn to swell the numbers who had preceded them—an estimated 300,000—would ever return, and the consequences of this were profound. Latvia had already lost a very high percentage of her professional classes who had been killed or imprisoned or who had fled the Soviet terror of 1940–1. Those who had remained now crowded the quays to escape another wave of executions and deportations. It was a pattern repeated all over the Baltic. Indeed, as the Canadian–Latvian historian Modris Eksteins has cogently observed, the reality of 1945 for eastern Europe was to be the 'displacement, not only of a few million refugees [...] but of an entire civilisation and its intellectual foundations'.[11]

The cataclysm of the Second World War in which fourteen million Europeans perished, with another estimated twenty–twenty-five million deaths in the USSR, was followed by the logistical nightmare of re-locating tens of millions of displaced persons and refugees.[12] It has been called—and surely was—the greatest social problem the West has ever faced. Rootless, starving and traumatised, millions of human beings lay in the camps, took to the roads or scavenged in the streets of ruined cities and towns, scrabbling for survival. The collapse of civilised societies meant that all too often the bare essentials for existence could only be found by robbing, cheating or looting. With catastrophe on so great a scale and faced with such overwhelming masses of brutalised human beings, the Allied powers were presented with a near-impossible task. This may go some way to explaining the attitude of their commanders who all too often lost sight of the humanity of the people they were dealing with, collectively calling them 'human rubble', 'the scum of Europe', 'locusts', and 'disease carriers' to be quarantined behind barbed wire.[13] Initially the Allies had divided these uprooted peoples into two groups: 'displaced persons' (DPs) were the survivors of the concentration, slave labour and re-location camps, and it was assumed that they would be returned to their homelands; the term 'refugee' was at first applied to Germans who had fled the Soviet advance or had been expelled from their homes in eastern Europe. In practice it was a distinction without a difference and caused considerable confusion, especially for those DPs who could not return to their Soviet-occupied homelands—their plight would more properly put them in the category of refugees in today's terminology. Neither term, however, could even begin to encompass the horrific scale of the human tragedy in the immediate post-war years.

> Collaborators, resistance fighters, SS soldiers, Jews, peasants, professors, prostitutes, children, paupers, bankers, criminals, clergymen. Every nationality, age, social class, type. They were all present amidst the devastation. They headed in every direction. Frightened, dirty, bewildered. Carrying, pushing, stumbling, hobbling, pleading.[14]

The DP and refugee camps set up by the Western Allies with the aid of the United Nations Organization Relief and Rehabilitation Administration (UNRRA) had to house, clothe and feed this mass of wretched humanity. Every building or complex of any size was pressed into service—former prison camps, army barracks, warehouses, schools, churches, barns, private residences. Conditions were often basic in the extreme, with only a couple of toilets and washing facilities for several hundred people; not surprisingly disease was rife. Although the feared epidemics of typhus, cholera and other deadly diseases were kept at bay, others such as whooping cough, tuberculosis, diphtheria and scarlet fever ravaged the malnourished population. Food was barely sufficient to support existence and without the illegal black market many would have perished. Indeed, as the novelist Heinrich Böll was to write of Germany then: 'Anyone who did not freeze to death in a destroyed city could only have stolen his wood or coal and anyone who did not starve to death must have acquired his food, or had someone else acquire it in some illegal fashion.'[15]

Notwithstanding the grim conditions and as relief measures began to be implemented, efforts were made to raise morale in the camps. With the help of the UNRRA schools and cultural activities were established, including choirs, orchestras and dance companies. The Latvian ballet corps, which had escaped abroad intact, reformed itself in Lübeck. In December 1945 a Baltic university—later renamed the Baltic Studies Centre—was created in Hamburg and two years later it enrolled 1,200 students with 200 faculties teaching

10. Refugee carts and cattle passing the Freedom Monument in Rīga, 1944 (reproduced by kind permission of the Museum of the Occupation of Latvia)

300 courses. This was supported by a library which had grown to 10,000 volumes by 1948. As bodily strength and mental health slowly returned to the exiles, sports once more became popular, despite the lack of equipment. These efforts went some way to meliorating the sense of living in a political and social limbo, but they could not erase the pervasive fear that dominated every waking moment in the camps: the fear of where the inmates would be sent next. Those who could find the money risked everything to escape the German DP camps for neutral countries such as Sweden. Those who could not were haunted by rumours. Would the pre-1939 national boundaries be honoured or would the Western powers bow to the Soviet Union's insistence that the territories it had occupied during the war should be regarded as the USSR's rightful domain and sphere of influence. But to be returned to USSR-controlled territory was tantamount to a death sentence, for the Soviet Union had decreed that the citizens of any country it had occupied in 1940—the Baltic States, Poland, Ukraine among them—were *de facto* Soviet citizens. This in turn meant that those

who had fled their homelands were by definition either enemy collaborators or defectors who had betrayed the Communist cause, with all that that implied.

The repatriation of nationals had been part of the Yalta agreement and in June 1945 Germany was partitioned into four sectors to be administered by the USA, Britain, France and the USSR. The fate of those who found themselves in the Russian sector was now sealed.[16] Between 1945 and 1947 the Allies forcibly repatriated over two million DPs from the east European states and thus condemned them to death, to imprisonment or to the forced labour camps of the infamous Gulag Archipelago. Another three million were returned to their homelands from the Soviet-controlled sector to face a similar fate. However, as the ideological division between the Western democracies and the Soviet Union escalated and as news of the horrors inflicted on the returned refugees began to reach the West, British and American policy was modified. In 1947 it was agreed that those DPs who had lived in countries outside the USSR in 1939 would not be returned but sent to countries prepared to accept them—Sweden, the United Kingdom, Canada, Australia and Argentina being the most open. Other democracies were less welcoming, such as the United States whose pre-war isolationist policy strictly limited the number of immigrants from any one country.[17] In 1948, however, the more liberal Displaced Persons Act was passed which allowed 10,000 refugees a month from Europe to enter the country, though the processing was painfully slow, for the United States was wary of admitting anyone with the slightest connection to Communism or Nazi-ism.[18]

The plight of the dispossessed and deracinated peoples of the three Baltic states was particularly acute. Yet their cultures did survive, for if the mass executions and deportations had decimated the ranks of the educated and the intelligentsia, the survivors nonetheless preserved their languages and traditions in their new homelands. In the immediate post-war years of 1945–50 over a thousand books were published by Latvian exiles in Sweden, Denmark and Germany. Despite dispersal and exile, the core of the nation's heritage remained intact, the form and pattern of its distinctive life re-created to be transmitted to the next generation. This was as true of the Latvians who had remained in their occupied country as for those who had escaped abroad. Both were exiles, but for both the preservation of heritage was far more than a mere lament for a lost past; rather, it was driven by a powerful and instinctive belief in the validity of their culture's right to self-preservation, without which the life of any individual must be impoverished. As in previous centuries—and irrespective of the degree of political enfranchisement—the Latvian people resisted amalgamation into alien uniformity.

The reality for the peoples of Latvia, Lithuania and Estonia in the final months of 1944 and the first half of 1945 was the return to power of the hated Communist Party. That return was met not only with justifiable fear and suspicion but also with active resistance. In Latvia an estimated 10,000 soldiers and civilians fled to the forests to continue a guerrilla war against the Soviets.[19] These 'Forest Brothers' were well-armed with equipment from their former army units, which they augmented through raids on local Soviet military bases. The Forest Brothers commanded immense support and were supplied by the rural communities in secret. From their forest retreats they were able to harass the Soviet authorities and to evade or defeat the Red Army units sent out to destroy them. In the aftermath of the Second World War, and as tensions between the West and the USSR grew into the 'Cold War', the Baltic nations continued to nurse the hope that the international power struggle might yet result in the restoration of their liberty. As the years passed that hope gradually faded, but it was not until the early 1960s that the last of the partisans left the forest.

The reinstated Communist Party in Latvia, headed by Jānis Kalnbērziņš,[20] presided over a devastated landscape and a ruined industrial system, and faced an acute shortage of personnel with which to begin its rule. Although some Baltic-born Communists who had resided in the USSR were sent out by Moscow, the shortfall had to be made up by recruiting Russians who had no knowledge of the local culture, still less of its language. This largely Russian-staffed administration, viewed with unremitting hostility, could not even communicate with the very people it was supposed to rule. The lack of qualified staff was exacerbated by restricting higher-level posts to Party members, but that membership itself was so hedged with restrictions that applications were minimal: no one whose relatives had been deported or had emigrated to the West, or who had collaborated with the German occupation during 1941–4, or who had been associated with any 'anti-Soviet' organisation or activity during the years of independence, was eligible.[21] The result was an administration staffed by the few locals who could meet the requirements plus a large influx of mediocre Party members from Russia. Similar restrictions permeated every sector of employment and generated a system of truly Orwellian 'double-think'. Thus, in order to get a job one had to be vetted to ensure there had been no anti-Soviet activities in the past (still less the present), obtain a Party card, demonstrate a competence in Russian, and in public profess undying loyalty to the Party while in private fiercely sustaining one's personal beliefs in, and hope for, a free Latvia.

Latvia had lost nearly a fifth of her population. Industrial output had dropped by half and agricultural land lay waste; it was urgent to revitalise both. But under Soviet doctrine the labour force was not employed according to its qualifications and skills but on the criterion of loyalty to Party and state. In agriculture, too, there were grave difficulties; given that agricultural output was still based on the private ownership of small farms, immediate collectivisation would clearly spell ruin. As a temporary measure, the Soviet-led government permitted the existence of these smallholdings but requisitioned 20 per cent of each farm's produce for the state. In the meantime government propaganda on the benefits of collec-tivised farming would slowly convince the population to give up its lands voluntarily. That there could be any recovery at all under such conditions was extraordinary, but it was surely driven by the nation's history of stoic endurance, its love for the land and its collective memory. The population had enjoyed two decades of independence and would transmit that memory to its children; it had then endured a war in which it had suffered successive occupations by ideologically opposed powers; it now found itself ruled by a totalitarian regime. Its strategy for survival would be the same that had served it in the past: to cultivate a double morality. Hatred of the occupying power and resistance to its ideology had to be concealed beneath a veneer of compliance in order to survive, but the nation's language, culture and values would be hidden and nurtured in secret. It was a kind of exile, a passive inner emigration, but it would be powerful enough to withstand the decades of privation, purges, propaganda and the systematic rewriting of history that followed, as the next chapter will show.

Map 9. The Baltic States in 1945

- - - - - 1938 borders	▨ Additions to Lithuania 1939–40
· · · · · June 1940 Lithuanian border	▨ Loses for Estonia and Latvia 1945
- · - · - Post-1945 borders	

7

LATVIA, SSR

Sovietisation

The period of economic reconstruction from the end of the Second World War to Stalin's death in 1953 was as much geared to altering the nation's collective psychology as it was to restructuring its industry and agriculture on Communist principles. Faced with a hostile population, the Party leadership and its administrators implemented a draconian programme of censorship and police surveillance. All books, newspapers and journals published before 1945 were scrutinised and any publication which expressed positive views on Latvia's independence or Western democratic values in general was removed and destroyed; some items survived in specialist collections, but access was limited to a small number of stringently vetted researchers.[1] Literary, historical and political works from the past were only permitted if they could be shown to have anticipated Marxist–Leninist doctrine, lauded Russia and Russian culture, praised the 1917 Revolution and the Bolsheviks, or were critical of Latvia's years as a nation-state. Contemporary authors were restricted to approved topics that justified Communism, depicted socialist realist scenes, or celebrated the 1917 Revolution and its aftermath. It became mandatory to praise Marx, Lenin and Stalin and for all artists to produce work that demonstrated the ideological values of Marxism.

Such censorship was overseen by the new Academy of Sciences in Rīga, modelled on its counterpart in the Soviet Union, which prepared long lists of banned titles and shorter ones of approved texts. Under the auspices of the Institute of Communist Party History, Latvia's history was completely re-written to conform with Marxist–Leninist doctrine. Thus her past was redrawn as a period when the population had been enslaved by bourgeois capitalism from which the Latvian people had been delivered by the USSR. This was deemed to be a telling example of the process of historical inevitability that had witnessed the glorious international socialist revolution and the establishment of the dictatorship of the proletariat among all enlightened peoples. It was this version of history that was now taught at every level in schools and institutes of higher education. University faculties such as theology and philosophy were closed and the language of instruction, as well as of administration, was Russian. All current teaching and research had to be based on Marxist–Leninist principles. The Sovietisation of the system included the re-certification of school teachers in 1950 and nearly a thousand were denied the right to teach at all. Schoolchildren of both sexes were obliged to undergo military training and to participate in all official parades.

To this indoctrination and propaganda was added something even more damaging. Notwithstanding the revolutionary achievements of the present prosperous era, as official sources declared, it was clear that society would be riddled with survivors from the earlier, unenlightened capitalist phase of history. This segment of the population would not have been conditioned to accept Communist beliefs and so by definition was prone to obstructionist and deviant ways of thought and behaviour. In short, it was a threat to society and it therefore followed that such persons must be identified and removed. Latvia had already lost at least half of her professional and intellectual elite through executions, deportations or emigration. Those who remained were now forced to comply with Party doctrine as a matter of survival. Secret police surveillance permeated every aspect of daily life; people disappeared and were never seen again. This 'normalisation of terror', as it has been called, was hardly less pervasive and pernicious than that depicted in Orwell's classic novel *1984*. It also created a system of informers and denouncers that would grow insidiously as the shortages in food, housing and basic consumer goods became ever more acute, undermining the moral fibre of the nation.

Under directives from Moscow, Latvia's material output and that of the other Baltic states was to be redirected to fuel Stalin's ambitious plans to make the USSR a great industrial power. The Five-Year Plans of 1946–51 and 1951–5 also ensured that the Baltic economies would be subservient to, and inextricably entwined with, that of the Soviet Union. The plans concentrated on developing and subsidising heavy industry at the expense of agriculture and local consumer industries. This achieved an impressively rapid growth in the USSR's industrial output but at the cost of starving agriculture and light industry of essential investment, resulting in chronic shortages and privation and catastrophic environmental damage. Other measures proved equally disastrous for the native Latvians. Moscow's official policy was to dilute the indigenous working population by importing more compliant Russian workers. Here it was the farming community that would suffer most. In 1945 there were about 280,000 agricultural smallholders in Latvia— the '10-hectare' restrictions of 1940–1 having been reinstated—but most had refused to surrender their lands to establish the recommended communal *kolkhozes*, despite extensive propaganda and the punitive taxes imposed on private farms.[2] Impatient of the delay, Moscow directed the local administration to remove any farmers who persistently avoided collectivisation and justified this by designating them obstructive, anti-social elements, as *kulaks* (broadly speaking any prosperous farmer who was able to employ others).[3] Accordingly, in March 1949 44,000 Latvian farmers were rounded up, deported to Siberia and replaced by Slavic immigrants.[4]

By the end of 1951 over 98 per cent of Latvia's farms had been merged into the officially approved collectives, a shattering blow psychologically as well as economically. Agricultural production declined steeply: grain production dropped to half pre-war levels and by 1956 to barely a third, while the acreage of land under cultivation fell to half what it had been in the days of the republic. Demoralised by the collectivisation process, many farmers left to seek employment in the towns. Those who remained were permitted small garden plots for each family, but by definition a 'family' meant all the generations living together or even near to each other. The number of hens, pigs and cattle each family was allowed to keep was also strictly limited. Nevertheless, although these garden plots represented only 5 per cent of the total land under cultivation, they produced 66 per cent of all the vegetables raised, 50 per cent of the meat and milk and 70 per cent of the eggs. This ensured survival for those on the land, but it could not alleviate the acute shortages of the most basic foodstuffs for the towns and cities. For senior Party members and government officials—the *nomenklatura*—such privation of course was non-existent; the rest of the population managed as best it could through the Black Market or by 'knowing someone'.

The misery of enduring shortages in food and consumer goods was compounded by the lack of housing. The properties of those who had fled or been deported to Siberia had been taken over by Russian administrators, demobilised soldiers and the influx of new settlers. It is estimated that at least half a million Slavic immigrants flocked into Latvia, exacerbating the problem of already inadequate housing and supplies. This influx also left deep scars on the national psyche of the population as it saw itself reduced to a subservient class in its own homeland. By 1952 the proportion of Latvians had sunk to a mere 54 per cent, while in Rīga they comprised only a little over a third of the citizenry. Starved of the essentials for normal life, with its economic wealth siphoned off to service Moscow, subjected to a barrage of relentless propaganda which it knew to be false, and with its very history rewritten, it is little wonder that the nation was overwhelmed by a sense of bitterness and despair.

The death of Stalin on 5 March 1953 and the ensuing power struggles in the Kremlin with the emergence of Nikita Khruschev as First Secretary of the Communist Party at first had little impact on life in the Baltic republics. However, at the Tenth Party Congress in 1956 Khruschev vigorously denounced Stalin as having deviated from the true path of Lenin and for having succumbed to 'the cult of personality', thus distancing himself and the Party from the atrocities of the Stalinist period which had claimed tens of millions of lives throughout the USSR. What followed was an easing of the extreme repression in Russia and its satellite republics and a tacit return to Lenin's teaching to respect the integrity of the nations that formed the Union. The years from 1957 to the mid-1960s have been called 'the thaw' and saw the publication of many works criticising the Stalinist era, of which Alexander Solzhenitsyn's *One Day in the Life of Ivan Denisovich* (1957) is perhaps the most famous. A wave of new works emerged in the Baltic written by young authors who had known little apart from the war and Soviet rule but whose vision of their nation had been nurtured by the older generation who remembered the years of independence. The celebrated Estonian novelist Jan Kross published a book of poems in 1958 which chronicled an exile's life in the coal mines of Siberia; the Latvian author Ojārs Vācietis wrote a novel about the deportations of 1949 and in 1958 openly published a poem protesting against the 1956 invasion of Hungary; and another novel (1963) by the Lithuanian Mykolas Slockis depicted events in the Second World War and the patriotic activities of the Forest Brothers.

Censorship remained and many works failed to secure the necessary approval for publication, but artists nevertheless found increasingly inventive ways to evade the censor's office. For example, if a work had appeared in translation in a Moscow book or periodical first, its approval locally could hardly be withheld. Then there were covert and coded ways of bypassing censorship through the use of complex allusions, symbols and metaphors: a poem describing the natural beauty of a Soviet Socialist Republic could just as easily express a love for one's homeland; a novel ostensibly focusing on an approved socialist–realist theme could be subversive according to how it was read. Western classics were quietly translated and published and even some pre-1940 Latvian authors re-appeared in the bookshops. Such measures demonstrated considerable courage, for expulsion from the Writers' Union could mean a life-time ban on the publication of a writer's work. Nonetheless resistance to the Soviet regime and to Sovietisation continued to grow steadily in both open and hidden ways, nor was it confined to the towns and cities. For example, a collective farm near Bauska (south of Rīga) had been named *Uzvara*, which means 'victory'. To the Soviet authorities it designated the victory of Communism but to the locals it articulated the hope for an eventual victory over their oppressors.[5]

The thaw also set in motion the reprieve of many of the men, women and children who had been sent to the Gulag. About 30,000 were released on 1 July 1960 with the right to return and live in Latvia.[6] Politically, too, the period of the thaw gave those Latvians working in the system greater opportunity to manipulate it from within, as well as to voice their discontent with Russification, the chronic shortages and the flood of Russian immigrants. However, the Latvian Communist Party which by now numbered over 78,000 incorporated a wide spectrum of opinion. Hard-liners loyal to Moscow, such as Arvīds Pelše of the Latvian Central Committee, rigidly adhered to Comintern doctrine, while those like Eduards Berclavs, First Secretary of the Rīga Central Committee, pressed for moderate reform. Under the guise of improving Latvia's contribution to the USSR economy, Berclavs attempted to increase Latvian control over local industry so as to shift emphasis away from heavy industry, which depended on the Soviet Union for its raw materials and imported workforce, to more traditional light industries which used native resources. With mounting popular support, he also argued for increasing the proportion of Latvians in senior positions, halting the settlement of Russian immigrants in Rīga, increasing housing for native Latvians and fostering Latvian culture. His attempt failed, for the Russians appealed to the Kremlin and denounced the incipient 'bourgeois nationalism' of Berclavs and his supporters. Khruschev was forced to come to Rīga in 1959 to intervene. Jānis Kalnbērziņš and Eduards Berclavs were dismissed from office and in the ensuing purges of 1959–60 some 2,000 Latvian Party members were expelled and the thoroughly russified Arvīds Pelše was confirmed in post.[7]

Pelše remained until 1966 and although he was able to contain the discontent and the calls for reform and liberalisation, his attempts and those of his successor Augusts Voss to crush Latvia's heritage were unsuccessful. Despite censorship, repression, propaganda and the indoctrination of young Latvians through *Komsomol* (the Communist youth organisation), the nation's culture and language survived. It did so partly through the covert efforts of many native Communist officials, who often justified their collaboration with the Soviets by maintaining that outward compliance enabled them to work in Latvia's interests, and partly through underground publications and other activities. After Pelše's term of office ended, resistance to Moscow was fuelled afresh by the events of 1968 when Alexander Dubček's experimental 'socialism with a human face' was crushed. Even committed Communists were shocked by the brutality of the Soviet invasion of Czechoslovakia and the suppression of the 'Prague Spring' and many, especially the younger members, felt that the Soviet Union had forfeited any claim to their loyalty. Dissent grew and underground activities in all three Baltic states strengthened. In public Latvian culture may have been marginalised and denigrated, but in private it was fostered. Thus, although the churches were closed or turned into secular cinemas, bowling alleys or Red Army clubs, and street names replaced with Soviet ones, literature and the arts and crafts still kept alive the values of a civilisation which the older generations embodied and secretly passed on to those who had known little but Soviet rule. Music was especially vital for it was a reminder of the nineteenth-century National Awakening and the original establishment of the National Song Festivals. Under Soviet rule such festivals were virtually the only opportunity for legal gatherings and the Baltic states took full advantage. Although it was mandatory to concentrate on Soviet patriotic songs, singing in the vernacular continued to affirm each nation's consciousness of itself; communities and choirs transmitted the heritage of the *dainas* and folksongs, ensuring that the memory of the people's origins in antiquity and their centuries-old customs were preserved.

As Latvia slowly recovered from the Second World War and adapted to Soviet rule, a measure of material prosperity returned, helped by the nation's tradition of hard work. There was high demand throughout the USSR for the consumer goods produced in the Baltic states and although shortages of nearly everything were still common, Latvia, Lithuania and Estonia soon achieved the highest standard of living in the USSR, though that fell far short of Western norms. Shipbuilding in Rīga and Liepāja was resumed and helped the economic recovery, even if the large fishing fleets were almost entirely Russian-manned for fear that Latvian crews would defect. The white sands of Jūrmala, the resort outside Rīga, became a popular holiday destination for Russians. It was a different picture in agriculture, however, where the farming community had been utterly demoralised by the collectivisation process; many had emigrated to the towns and indeed by 1980 70 per cent of Latvians lived in urban areas as compared to 30 per cent before 1940. Notwithstanding the slight easing of political restrictions during the thaw and the improvement in the economy, life in general continued to be grim. Gradually the pleasant wooden vernacular architecture of the provincial towns and the fine buildings of the major cities fell into disrepair, public facilities decayed for want of basic investment and maintenance, dirt and squalor (generally blamed on the Russian population) defaced the previously immaculate streets and buildings, and everywhere the ugly concrete high-rises built in Soviet brutalist style blighted the urban landscape. As the Latvians saw their countryside increasingly polluted by heavy industry and their communities physically degraded, it is little wonder that alcoholism and the suicide rate rose to become among the highest in Europe.

Between East and West: the Cold War

When Churchill spoke of an 'iron curtain' descending to divide Europe in 1946, few could have foreseen that it would remain in place for over four decades. Despite the profound ideological differences between the Western democracies and the USSR, there had been a measure of agreement on the need to prevent a resurgence of Germany's power and to hasten the decolonisation of European empires across the globe. But as the rifts in policy deepened, it became increasingly clear that every possible non-military strategy must be employed to contain Russia's power and expansionist ambitions. Accordingly, the post-war American Marshall Plan of 1947 was designed not only to aid Europe's recovery and economic reconstruction but to give economic help and financial support to key countries like Greece and Turkey which bordered the USSR. The Soviet Union refused to participate and in 1949 set up its own association COMECON (Council for Mutual Economic Assistance) in order to coordinate and control the Communist economies of eastern Europe. It countered the creation of the new international defence alliance NATO (North Atlantic Treaty Organisation) of 1949 with a similar alliance of its satellites known as the Warsaw Pact (1955).[8] Throughout the 1950s and 1960s the aim of these two groups of states was to use every means possible short of outright war to increase their security. Propaganda, subversion, surveillance, support for guerrilla activities, even outright bribery of governments of neutral or uncommitted states were normal policy. As one eminent historian has aptly summarised: 'The Cold War was a blight which left little of the world untouched, and became a seeping sewer of crime, corruption and suffering for more than thirty years. But it was also the source of a protection for western Europe behind which it could grow a new future.'[9]

Such a protection and such a future were of course denied to the Baltic states whose economies continued to subsidise the Soviet Union's industrial expansion, the growing arms race and, from the 1960s onwards, the ambitious space exploration programme. Food and consumer goods remained in short supply and here, as elsewhere in the USSR, protests at the curtailment of civil liberties and the poor material conditions of existence grew ever louder. In 1964 Khruschev was removed from office by a group of internal Communist officials supported by the army; after some political jostling he was succeeded by Leonid Brezhnev (1906–82) who remained in post until his death. Brezhnev's period of office saw a dramatic increase in Soviet military might—expenditure for the military rose to 50 per cent of GNP—which undoubtedly stimulated the

USSR's industrial profile, but because of his neglect of the wider economy his time in office became known as the 'Era of Stagnation'. It was also to precipitate the crises of the 1970s which in turn would lead to the eventual dissolution of the USSR.

Despite routine propaganda promoting the economic success of the various Five-Year Plans, the stark reality was that statistics were more often than not falsified and socio-economic growth sluggish at best or non-existent. And despite sporadic attempts at political liberalisation and the devolution of some authority from Moscow to the individual Soviet Socialist republics, international tensions ensured that the military and internal security services operated as if it were wartime. Although the production of consumer goods had risen slightly and unemployment figures were low—most jobs were guaranteed for life—it became increasingly difficult to maintain the fiction that the standard of living throughout the USSR was equivalent to or better than that in the West. It was equally apparent that nominally independent east European countries like Hungary, Czechoslovakia and Poland were considerably more affluent than the Soviet Union itself and that both were inferior to the Western economies. Most societies in the USSR still operated through the Black Market and a non-currency exchange system of bartering goods and services. Chronic shortages, an incompetent distribution system, ineffective quality controls, an increasingly disillusioned workforce that knew the imposed quotas were impossible to achieve and that the widely proclaimed successes were a fiction, all contributed to economic stagnation.

The Baltic states were better off than most of the interior republics of the Soviet Union and were even referred to as 'our West', the term itself unconsciously ironic and a telling admission of the Communist economy's failures. Their shortages could be meliorated by covert bartering, by some smuggling of goods at the ports and, more importantly, by acquiring hard currency sent by relatives abroad which could be used to buy consumer items normally unavailable to those who only had Soviet roubles. But discontent grew, fed by the inferior quality of USSR-produced items, the glaring disparity between the privileges enjoyed by Soviet officials and the citizenry at large, and above all by the policy of Russification. By 1980 only one in five Russians living in Latvia had any command of the native tongue. There was a pervasive fear that the indigenous language would be lost, for the chronic shortages also meant that most couples delayed having children and when they did limited the number to two. Healthcare was poor, infant mortality rose, and in the absence of reliable birth control methods abortion became routine, with predictable consequences for the health of women. As unrest grew, graffiti slogans calling for the expulsion of the Russians appeared more frequently, as did food riots. Meanwhile Soviet attempts to block radio transmissions from the West had only limited success and gradually international news seeped into the Baltic borderlands and contributed to the rising tide of dissatisfaction.

Other non-aggressive, coded forms of protest increased: flowers in the national colours (the Latvian flag is maroon–white–maroon) appeared on the graves of earlier patriots and the statesmen of the Independence years; the same colours decorated clothing, food items, and the arts and crafts produced for visitors and tourists whose numbers increased during the 1970s as international travel restrictions eased. The underground press flourished, producing newsletters, poems, books and plays which were circulated in typescript. All this inevitably came at a price. People still disappeared or were condemned to long periods of exile, some for the most trivial offences: one youth who had broken a lightbulb in a train was sentenced to ten years' hard labour in Siberia.[10] The Latvian poet Vizma Belševica (1931–2005) was banned from publishing after writing a poem in which she obliquely compared the invasion of the Red Army to that of the Teutonic Knights.[11] Her work has remained highly influential in Latvia.

The émigré populations abroad continued their protest against the Soviet annexation of the Baltic states and were remarkably successful in keeping the plight of their nations alive in their host countries through lobbying and through their legations and consulates. Contrary to Soviet expectation, they had not become assimilated into the communities that had received them but had preserved their languages, customs and traditions so that a new generation grew up with a consciousness of its Baltic heritage. Given that a high proportion of those exiles were professional people, they were able to produce books and newspapers in their vernaculars as well as in English and other international languages. And, crucially, they corresponded with friends and relatives in their homelands, sending letters, parcels and literature. Although these were censored, they were also a valuable source of information about life in the West and a powerful psychological reminder that Latvia, Lithuania and Estonia had not been forgotten.

During the Brezhnev years Moscow slowly relaxed its control over domestic cultural affairs in its republics and in the 1970s, as the principles of *détente* began to infiltrate the Cold War mentality of the USSR, a series of cultural exchanges were established between the Soviet states and the West. Although these were designed to demonstrate the benefits of life in the USSR and to woo back the younger generation of exiles, inevitably they also revealed the glaring disparities between the Communist and capitalist systems in the general quality of life, material wealth and degree of individual liberty. Even the most loyal Communists travelling abroad were shocked to find that the rouble was not recognised as an international currency and by the liberal atmosphere and political freedom that were taken for granted. Travel to the USSR on the other hand was strictly controlled by the state agency Intourist and visitors were monitored by KGB agents who routinely interrogated any locals who had spoken to Western tourists. Hotel bedrooms and public areas alike were 'bugged' as a matter of course. Nonetheless the iron curtain was becoming porous in a way undreamt of a generation ago.

This relaxation in cultural affairs was paralleled by a shift in the political composition of some states in the USSR: by 1980 the majority of Communist Party members and holders of government offices in Lithuania and Estonia were no longer Russian. In Latvia native administrators were still in a minority and were still dominated by those Russified Latvians who had returned in 1944; both they and their successors would vigorously oppose the growing independence movement. Nonetheless, if senior positions in Latvia remained under Russian control during the 1970s—for example, the post of second secretary of the Party was always reserved for a Russian—in practice it became increasingly possible to circumvent Moscow's directives. Local policies could be and often were shaped by native Party members, many of whom discreetly supported nationalist activities. These could take a number of different forms but one of the most popular and effective was to protest against environmental damage. Thus on 14 September 1973 the Latvian parliament was able to create the Gauja National Park, at a stroke preserving the heartland of Latvia's heritage while protecting one of the most beautiful wilderness areas in Europe from the degradation of collective farming and industrial pollution.[12]

Not all such efforts were successful of course and the 1970s were also known as 'the death years' for Latvia's national tree when thousands of oaks were felled in the name of Soviet collectivisation. But local conservationists and authorities alike were able to resist the wholesale destruction, saving many ancient oak stands and replanting others. Their efforts were inspired by a group of dedicated professional women led by the poet Imants Ziedonis. For over two decades they rescued oak trees, restoring the stone circles and ditches that had protected them, as well as sacred boulders, springs, castle ruins and pre-historic mounds to preserve Latvia's cultural landscape and ensure that its historical resonances were not lost to future generations. The 'Green Sun' symbol they carved and left behind at these sites can still be seen today. Ziedonis became an iconic symbol for rebellion not only in Latvia but throughout the Soviet Union and strongly influenced the younger generation of poets. He was particularly adept at creating a poetry of political protest by using time-honoured images from the *dainas* and references to folklore that both celebrated the natural world and obliquely criticised the occupation of his native land.

> I rooted the linden in–
> Ah, Lord, I planted her in the midst of the yard!–
> And the linden sprang to the air.
> Ah, Lord, Lāčplēsis sprang from the linden,
> And the nine fair sons of Koknēsis.

They rooted the linden out–
Ah, Lord, they rooted the linden out of my land.
Uprooted the linden tree–
And set her down–
Ah, Lord, down beyond the sea.[13]

Other forms of protest were more overt, such as the frequent riots that attended popular rock concerts during the 1970s when nationalist slogans were chanted, the passive refusal to understand when addressed in Russian, cheering non-Russian sports teams, boycotting Communist-approved books.[14] Agitation and appeals continued to grow despite arrests and prison sentences. In 1974 a group of Latvian Communists headed by Eduards Berclavs signed a protest against Russification and others followed. On 23 August 1979, the 40th anniversary of the Molotov–von Ribbentrop Pact, a petition with signatories from the three Baltic countries was sent to the United Nations protesting against their illegal annexation. It was succeeded by others in December 1979 and January 1980. And despite the teaching of Marxist–Leninist historical doctrine that economic growth and the re-allocation of labour resources would result in the abolition of national identities to produce the 'Soviet individual', the reality was in fact the reverse. The percentage of the population who remembered the years of independence might be declining, to be replaced by those who had been indoctrinated by a Soviet version of history, but this failed to stem the rising tide of nationalism, and resentment against the Soviet socialist regime grew ever stronger. Ironically it would be the Soviet-created Supreme Councils for each republic that would hasten the fragmentation of the Union. The function of these parliaments with their native majorities had been largely symbolic, primarily to rubber-stamp Moscow's directives, but as nationalist aspirations grew they would become a powerful legal weapon to use against the USSR.

Brezhnev's term of office also witnessed the signing of the Helsinki Accord, which would later become a manifesto for dissent and calls to liberalise the USSR. At the time the Conference on Security and Co-operation in Europe, held in Helsinki Finland during the summer of 1975 and attended by 35 European states plus the USA and Canada, was announced throughout the Soviet Union as a triumph for Brezhnev and Soviet diplomacy. While the Accord was designed to improve relations between the Communist bloc and the West, and did indeed reduce Cold War tensions, it was not a binding treaty. Its articles were also open to very different interpretations. On the one hand the ten points—which included respect for the inviolability of national frontiers and for territorial integrity as well as non-intervention in a state's internal affairs— were hailed by the Soviets as a confirmation of their post-war gains in eastern Europe, on the other the NATO nations reaffirmed their non-recognition of the forced incorporation of the Baltic states into the USSR. The wording of the final act of the Accord was fluid, simply stating that the frontiers of Europe should remain stable but could be changed by peaceful means. The Helsinki Accord also included among its principles respect for human rights and fundamental freedoms including those of thought, conscience, religion or belief, and this would later inform protests throughout the USSR.

Brezhnev died in 1982 to be succeeded for two years by Juri Andropov, head of the KGB, who was followed for only one year by Konstantin Chernenko, who died in 1985. Both were elderly, embodied the ethos of the old regime, and were incapable of countering the swelling opposition to Party control in eastern Europe, signalled most dramatically by the growth of the Solidarity movement in Poland. In 1980 workmen in the Gdansk shipyards had formed a non-Communist trade union (*Solidarmošč*) in the wake of the election in 1978 to the throne of St Peter of a Polish Pope. Jean-Paul II was an outspoken critic of Communism and his support for his native land gave hope to tens of millions of all faiths still living in Communist countries.[15] The Solidarity movement spread in spite of efforts to suppress it. Bewildered by the mounting crises and discontent throughout the Soviet empire, in 1985 the Party elected Mikhail Gorbachev to lead it. Gorbachev's credentials were impeccable: he was one of the younger generation of Party politicians (b. 1931) who had risen through the ranks on merit; he was able, energetic, a committed Communist yet open to new ways of thinking; in short, he offered a way for the Party to evolve and to counter the growing crises. Within two years he had persuaded many of the older generation of Party bureaucrats to accept honourable retirement and replaced them with a younger cadre of supporters who were sympathetic to change. At the twenty-seventh Party Congress of 1986 he announced the new policies of *glasnost* (openness), *perestroika* (reconstruction) and *demokratizaatsia* (democratisation), encouraged vigorous debate about ways of stimulating the economy and addressing the growing rebellion in the USSR republics and, most significantly, initiated a new era of dialogue with the West. Under his leadership, Moscow slowly began to relinquish a measure of internal control to its constituent states. That overall authority still rested with the Party and Moscow, so it was not questioned, nor its agents of enforcement—the KGB, police and army—but the very possibility of open discussion in which it could be admitted that the Party had been wrong in its economic policies and that reform was needed resonated throughout the USSR.

In the Baltic states Party leadership became increasingly divided: traditionalists who were trained to follow Moscow's directives without question were still in power but unsure how to proceed in the growing climate of liberalisation. Young Party members and emerging nationalists alike embraced the new degree of freedom and pressed for further reform, while others simply waited to see which way the proverbial political wind would blow. Latvia was still in the grip of the local KGB head Boris Pugo, who was the Party First Secretary and would remain so until 1988.[16] An ethnic Latvian, he had ruthlessly suppressed nationalist dissent but now faced a dilemma: he wished to maintain strict control but given the new instructions from Moscow he was compelled to soften his authoritarian rule and to begin replacing the older generation of hard-liners with younger members committed to reform who would be appointed on merit rather than through Party patronage. During his final years in office, opposition to Party dictates had swelled to immense proportions. In 1986 a massive protest was mounted against another hydroelectric dam on the Daugava river, a project which had been approved by Moscow but which would entail ecological disaster, devastating a large swathe of the river valley. The Daugava symbolised the nation's deepest cultural roots and embodied its history: it was 'the river of our destiny, the river of our souls' as an old Latvian saying puts it. To the fear of ecological damage was added local anger at the prospect of yet another influx of Russian workers. The storm of protest could not be ignored and in November 1987 Moscow cancelled the project, a victory that would have been inconceivable only a few years earlier. It was also proof that Moscow itself agreed in principle that the protection of a country's environment was a matter for its own government and not for the Soviet Union, a striking departure from previous policy.[17]

Gorbachev's *glasnost* and *perestroika* resulted in the slackening of central control and undoubtedly offered greater freedom to voice nationalist aspirations. However, those very policies also presented the Supreme Soviet with a dilemma: *glasnost* meant acknowledging the errors of the past but, as Anatole Lieven has lucidly summarised, 'Since the entire communist claim to legitimacy and to positive achievements was based on lies, this honesty would sooner or later bring down the whole system.'[18] For the native Balts a popular way of discrediting the Soviet past was to counter the official celebration of key Soviet events such as the 1917 Revolution with rallies commemorating the nation's own anniversaries. On 14 June 1987 the Helsinki-86 group, founded by a number of dissident Latvians the previous year, mounted a demonstration at the Freedom Monument in Rīga to remember those whom Stalin had deported in 1941. In the past such a gathering would have been dispersed and its leaders imprisoned, but both KGB and police were now in a quandary: they could scarcely deny protesters the right to demonstrate against Stalin when official policy from Moscow itself had recently re-confirmed that denunciations of the old dictator should be encouraged. Moreover the protesters now invoked the principles of the Helsinki Accord, to which the Soviet Union and the members of the Warsaw Pact had been signatories, arguing that their rallies could not be illegal.

Lacking support from Moscow and so unable to use violence against these nationalist demonstrations, the KGB, police and local Party administrators resorted to harassment, detained activist leaders, and withheld the permits necessary for holding public gatherings, but completely failed to stem the mounting tide of popular protest. In all three Baltic states the numbers of demonstrators swelled to hundreds of thousands. On 23 August 1987 the Helsinki-86 group organised a mass meeting to protest against the signing of the Molotov–von Ribbentrop Pact and the Soviet annexation of the Baltic states, and on 18 November Latvian Independence Day was publicly celebrated for the first time since 1940. Another mass rally on 25 March 1988 at the Freedom Monument commemorated the victims of the Soviet 'terror' and on 14 June the forbidden Latvian flag was carried openly through the streets of the capital. When at the great Baltika Song Festival of June 1988 the national flags of all three Baltic republics were triumphantly raised together it became clear that the era of Soviet hegemony must be nearing its end.

The Singing Revolution

On 23 August 1989, the fiftieth anniversary of the signing of the Molotov–von Ribbentrop Pact, two million Baltic men, women and children formed a human chain reaching from Tallinn through Rīga to Vilnius, a distance of over 600 kilometres, to sing their way to freedom. It was one of the greatest and most moving demonstrations of modern times and its emotional impact on the international audience as film footage from hovering helicopters was transmitted to the West was dramatic. For half a century the Soviet Union had denied the existence of the secret protocols between Germany and Russia over the latter's annexation of the Baltic states, but after the 'Baltic Way' demonstration Gorbachev appointed his lieutenant Alexander Yakovlev to investigate. Although the original documents had vanished, a single microfilm copy had survived in British hands. It was examined by the Federal Government of Germany which on 1 September 1989 declared that the protocols were genuine but

11. Crowd demonstration on the banks of the Daugava on 18 November 1989 (reproduced by kind permission of the Museum of the Occupation of Latvia)

179

invalid. On 29 December the Congress of Soviets passed a similar declaration and formally denounced the protocols as illegal from the moment of their signing. This public acknowledgement of the illegitimacy of Soviet rule in the Baltic opened the way for the governments of Latvia, Lithuania and Estonia to regain control of their countries.

* * *

The 'Baltic Way' or the 'Baltic Chain' was only the most dramatic visual embodiment of the pro-independence movements which had been growing in force and numbers since the previous year. Public debate had been encouraged by Moscow as a way of emerging from the stagnation of the Brezhnev era and this had resulted in renewed discussions in the Soviet Baltic republics over their status within the USSR. The summer of 1988 saw the formation of Baltic pro-independence parties: *Sajūdis* in Lithuania, the Latvian National Independence Movement and in Estonia the National Independence Party. All three declared that any compromise on sovereignty was morally and legally unacceptable and called for independence and the restoration of their national languages as the official means of communication. At the other end of the political spectrum were the parties formed by Communist hard-liners, most of them Russian and other non-ethnic immigrants, who were afraid of being deported and who pressed for a return to the old, rigorous *status quo* of Party rule.[19] Between these opposites were the moderate Popular Front Parties of the three republics. These consisted for the most part of Communist liberals who advocated reform and enhanced autonomy for their states within the framework of the existing USSR. The Popular Fronts attracted the largest membership and thus were in a good position to moderate between the other two factions; they vigorously took advantage of the new policy of openness to organise debates about the political structures, economies and futures of their nations.[20]

A striking example of the revelations that were made public under *glasnost* had come about at the Latvian Writers' Union meeting on 1–2 June 1988: a senior Communist Party member who had been active in Rīga in 1940 declared that in fact there had been no popular revolution or support for the Soviet invasion, contrary to what was affirmed in the official history books. Similarly the previously Communist-controlled institutes and university faculties of history now acknowledged the appalling extent of the executions and deportations of 1940. Another important result of *glasnost* came in August when Gorbachev ordered the release of many Baltic political prisoners and sent Alexander Yakovlev to meet the Baltic heads of government with a firm promise that the persecution of dissenters and nationalists would cease forthwith. Later, speaking on a BBC programme, Yakovlev recalled:

> I had to admit to them that we had an empire, that there really was a centre which dictated to the republics. I had to agree with them. Anything else would have been blasphemy. So I supported them, and I still think I was right.[21]

It is no wonder that faced with Moscow's changing policies and the growing local calls for autonomy, hard-line Communist administrators and the *nomenklatura* rapidly lost their sense of purpose.

Although the official government structures and offices as set out under the Soviet constitutions of the three Baltic states remained, 1988 saw the fragmentation of the Soviet system. The increasingly rapid departure of members from the Party was paralleled by the equally rapid growth of new, alternative political parties, especially the Popular Fronts. Encouraged by internal confusion over the powers of the police, security forces and the army, plans for restructuring the Baltic governments grew apace. Estonia was the first to declare sovereignty on 16 November 1988, followed by Lithuania on 11 May 1989, and both later formally announced their withdrawals from the Communist Party.[22] Latvia was in a more delicate position, hampered because nearly half her population was non-native (in 1989 Latvians formed only 52.5 per cent of the population) and Party membership and administration were still Russian-dominated.[23] But on 31 May 1989 the Latvian Popular Front Party issued a proclamation calling for complete independence and on 28 July, immediately following the Supreme Soviet's declaration in Moscow that it had delegated management of their economies to the Baltic republics, the Latvian Supreme Council also passed a decree declaring sovereignty.

Given the uncertainty over Moscow's reaction and—for the Balts—the worrying lack of immediate support from the international community, such calls for sovereignty fell short of pressing for full independence in the sense of a complete separation from the USSR. Large sectors of the population still hoped for some kind of accommodation within a reformed Soviet system, but nationalist calls for independence became an irresistible force after Moscow's admission in December 1989 that the 1940 annexation of the Baltic republics had been illegal. To this was added the news from Moscow that at the next sitting of the Supreme Soviet a new 'Law on Secession' would be passed, imposing a ten-year moratorium on any republic choosing to leave the USSR. In order to bypass this forthcoming regulation, Lithuania declared full independence at the first sitting of its newly elected parliament in March 1990 and began to form its own national army, helped by large numbers of deserters from the Soviet forces. Gorbachev ordered the Lithuanian parliament to rescind its decree and when it refused imposed an oil blockade which, however, was lifted after diplomatic negotiations.[24]

The Latvian and Estonian Supreme Councils acted with more caution, but eventually enough Russians joined the Popular Front Parties which then forged alliances with the more militant Independence Parties to secure the two-thirds majority of seats necessary for their Supreme Councils to declare independence.[25] On 4 May 1990 the Latvian Council officially denounced the Soviet annexation of 1940 as null and void, declaring the country independent; Estonia followed a fortnight later. The new Latvian government was headed by Anatolijs Gorbanovs, an astute and able man who had effectively led the country since 1988.[26] He was a popular figure, effective in reassuring the local Russian population and able to liaise with Dainis Īvāns and Ivars Godmanis of the Popular Front Party (*Latvijas Tautas Fronte*) and Andrejs Krastiņš, leader of the radical National Independence Party (*Latvijas Nacionālās Neatkarības Kustība* or *LNNK*). With the agreement of both parties the independence proclamation was followed by an appeal to the United Nations and the international community.

> We appeal to you not to leave the Baltic States at the mercy of the totalitarian superpower, the USSR, which has never abandoned any territory which it has occupied. We urge you to exert economic and diplomatic pressure on Moscow, so that it starts immediate negotiations with the Government of Lithuania. We urge you to support Latvia and Estonia in the same way. In 1938, 1939, 1940, and 1945 the small nations of Europe were left to their fate. We believe and hope that support for Gorbachev by the governments of the democratic states does not mean the betrayal of the Baltic States in 1990. We believe that broad and unequivocal support for the Baltic States does not undermine the security of any other state.[27]

To the dismay of the Baltic nations international recognition was slow to come, and although negotiations with Moscow continued they were dominated by fears of a Soviet backlash and anxiety that support from the West would fail. There was good cause for such fears, for on 15 May Soviet loyalists had organised mass demonstrations outside the Latvian and Estonian parliament buildings and later in the month Soviet officials loyal to Moscow attempted to form an alternative government in Estonia. The Western democracies did employ every diplomatic means possible to put pressure on Gorbachev to show restraint and their efforts undoubtedly helped to moderate, though they did not stop, subsequent Soviet military intervention. In September 1990 a series of bombs exploded in Soviet military sites in Latvia, almost certainly the work of hard-line Communist agents, the *provokatsia*, while OMON (the special police) defected from the Latvian Ministry of the Interior to re-affirm its allegiance to Moscow. A few weeks later the Soviet High Command announced that it intended to begin a programme of forced conscription. In December National Salvation Committees were formed in all three Baltic states under the auspices of Soviet Union officials. Although their identities remain unknown, it is likely that the two most powerful and committed Communists to hale from the Baltic—Boris Pugo and Alfrēds Rubiks—were actively involved in conducting these and other counter-independence campaigns.

Soviet army units were mobilised to enforce conscription on 2 January 1991. In Rīga protesters were confronted by paratroopers who also sought to occupy the press headquarters but were repelled by civilians armed only with a few hunting rifles. On 11 January more paratrooper units attacked the Press Centre in Vilnius and on the night of 13 January they attempted to storm a number of major government installations. They were confronted by hundreds of citizens who erected barricades and formed a human shield around key buildings and the television and radio stations, blocking the advance of Soviet tanks and armoured carriers. Few had any expectation of surviving the Soviet advance.[28] It was a demonstration of extraordinary courage and a dramatic statement of national solidarity. On 20 January Soviet tanks, supported by OMON, also rolled into Rīga to take the Ministry of the Interior. The Latvian film director Juris Podnieks recorded the events and his footage was shown on Western television networks only a few hours later. As a shocked international community watched, machine-gun fire was heard and the cameraman Andris Slāpiņš fell, the camera tilting at a crazy angle to the street as his dying words were recorded: 'Pick up the camera—and *film...*'[29]

The succeeding months witnessed many scenes of stoic endurance against police harassment, especially by the border guards who were routinely subjected to Soviet brutality in an attempt to provoke incidents that could be used as an excuse to deploy Soviet troops. Essentially, however, the position was one of watchfulness and stalemate while discussions with Moscow continued. But the Soviet Union itself was in the process of disintegrating, with nine of its constituent states having either declared independence or asserted a degree of sovereignty, including the powerful Russian Federation. The economic crisis continued and there was a real threat of civil war as Gorbachev, caught between the conflicting demands of the reformist and reactionary factions of the Soviet Union, tried to accommodate both. On 19 August a *coup d'état* by Communist hard-liners attempted to remove him from power and on 21 August armed vehicles under OMON rolled into Rīga again, heading for the Cathedral Square and the parliament building. Batons and tear gas failed to disperse the unarmed populace who came to the defence of their legal government. The Soviet attack halted and troops withdrew when news came that the *coup* in Moscow had failed, primarily because Boris Yeltsin, the popular and charismatic President of the Russian Federation, had rallied the nation to support Gorbachev. After the conflicts of August 1991 the Communist Party was officially banned in all three Baltic states and its properties seized. Most politicians and administrators who had been members announced themselves as apolitical figures henceforth, committed to the nationalist cause and the republics' independence, though a number of intransigent hard-liners were arrested. In the days that followed, the Baltic states received international diplomatic recognition and on 6 September 1991 the Soviet State Council officially recognised their independence. A few days later Latvia, Lithuania and Estonia were admitted as members of the United Nations.

Map 10 Latvia today

8

IN A FREE STATE

Transition

If independence and international recognition had been achieved on a wave of optimism, the nation now faced formidable political, economic and social difficulties. True, the threat of fresh incursions from the East was fast receding as the USSR itself disintegrated,[1] but the process of disentangling the new republic from the Soviet infrastructure and of forging productive links with the international community was dauntingly complex. Indeed, after half a century under Soviet dominion the problems facing the country were far more acute than they had been in the early years of the first independence period.

The most pressing task was to restructure the government itself, though a simple return to the 1922 constitution was unlikely to meet all the needs of a late twentieth-century republic intending to integrate itself into the wider European network. Of equal urgency was economic reform for a system still inextricably linked to the old Soviet one: the currency remained the Russian (formerly Soviet) rouble; Communist Party assets could be confiscated but had to be re-allocated according to transparently fair and legal principles; the fact of a large Russian military presence in the country and its withdrawal had to be addressed;[2] the entire Soviet welfare system with its centralised budget had to be transferred and new sources of revenue and distribution established. Then there was the sensitive question of citizenship. Almost half the population was non-Latvian, but to offer citizenship to all current residents without restriction (as Lithuania, with her small percentage of non-indigenous peoples, had done) seemed to many in Latvia and Estonia a betrayal of their nations' hard-won sovereignty. Citizenship was automatically granted to all residents and their descendants from the period of the first republic and Gorbanovs declared that it would be available to anyone who applied for it, but debate over the qualifying criteria was prolonged and heated: what level of language competence should be required; and could former Communist Party hard-liners and the privileged *nomenklatura* apply, or for that matter members of the Soviet secret services, the infamous KGB, and senior Soviet army officers. It was often pointed out that under international law occupying forces were not entitled to voting rights.

Although it was acknowledged that many high-ranking and experienced Russian Party officials had placed their services at the disposal of the new republic and were essential for its functioning during the transition period, the very fact of their presence caused understandable resentment. Many felt that their government should be staffed by those who had suffered during the five decades of occupation. In the first elections the Russian population were largely disenfranchised but the Citizenship Law, passed on 25 November 1993, regularised the criteria for citizenship in accordance with the norms of the European community. These granted unconditional citizenship to all children born in Latvia, as well as to applicants who had five years' residence and a basic conversational competence in the language.[3] A further law on the status and rights of non-citizens was passed on 12 April 1995 which entitled them to permanent residential status, internationally recognised travel documents, exemption from military service, and the right to maintain their national languages and traditions.

The political restructuring of the country was perhaps the most straightforward task, for the old constitution could be used to give authority to the transitional government while revisions were drafted. Accordingly, the 1990 elections for the Latvian Supreme Council were held under a combination of the old Soviet procedures and the provisions of the 1922 constitution. Although this transitional system itself was criticised as technically not legal, the provisional government was legitimate in the sense of having been fairly elected and recognised as temporary. Moreover the leaders chosen—Ivārs Godmanis, Anatolijs Gorbanovs and Dainis Īvans— commanded strong support across all the ethnic groups and were able to effect the most pressing legislative reforms, to implement the revision of the constitution, to negotiate with the international community and the USSR, and address ways of dealing with the growing economic turmoil. It is a testament to their energies and intelligence that they achieved as much as they did.

The revised constitution restored the system of a unicameral parliament, the Saeima, consisting of 100 members elected by proportional representation for a term of four years. This body also had the power to elect a president as Head of State,[4] who was tacitly deemed to stand above party politics. Unlike the confron- tational political systems of the United States and the United Kingdom (dominated by two or three political parties respectively), that in Latvia was modelled on European democracies founded on the principles of consensus and of governing by coalition. Each Cabinet of Ministers would be formed from several parties and would pass legislation by a simple majority. As in the first independence era, it was anticipated that such a process would ensure a democratic plurality of views in parliament even if this meant that no single party would be in control. Such a multi-party approach (see Chapter 5) permits a wide range of political views but its disadvantage is that coalitions can be fragile political entities, prone to dissolve when one or more political parties withdraws. Thus in the first election the largest party was the moderate Latvia's Way which gained 32 per cent of the seats, though even with its coalition partners it secured only forty-eight votes out of the Saeima's 100. Nonetheless the transitional government of 1990–3 achieved a legal and non-violent transfer of power and implemented the new legislative, executive and judicial systems.

That success was darkened by other factors, however, as the fledgling state struggled to re-enter the community of Western nations and to regain 'normality', as opposed to the perceived 'deformation' of the Soviet period. Central to that struggle was the urgent need to stabilise and manage its economy. Like Estonia and Lithuania, Latvia had signed agreements with the European Free Trade Association (EFTA) and like them sought to re-introduce its distinctive national currency. The Lat was restored in March 1993 as the official currency and after an initial period of high inflation remained comparatively stable, in dramatic contrast to the hyper-inflation of the Russian rouble.[5] But the West was slow to invest in the Baltic and could offer only limited—and often conflicting—economic advice in a situation that was unprecedented in modern experience. While everyone recognised the paramount need to manage a rapid transition to Western capitalism, it was an almost impossibly daunting task given that the entire commercial system had been centralised in the USSR. In the short term this meant a dramatic fall in living standards as incomes and pensions declined in value, prices rose, and the threat of inflation loomed. It is estimated that half the population lived at or below the official poverty level during these transition years and not surprisingly criticism of the government grew. Unemployment levels rose sharply as former state-owned companies were dissolved; those who remained in public-funded positions such as the civil service, healthcare and education suffered drastic reductions in their salaries. The tax system was in turmoil with government regulations in flux or non-existent and the nation's GDP dropped by a third.

The scramble to privatise state-owned companies, enterprises and facilities was also insufficiently regulated, the government fearing to impose strict controls lest it hold back the country's entry into Western markets. Purchase prices for companies and real estate were ludicrously below actual values. New companies of doubtful provenance appeared with capital funding from unknown sources, some almost certainly through the illegal appropriation of former Party funds. They were formed and dissolved with no purpose but to make a quick profit. This in turn gave rise to a *nouveau riche* class whose conspicuous consumption caused great resentment across all sectors of the population. Equally damaging was the impoverishment of the nation's intellectual and professional life: funding for research was virtually non-existent and academic publication went into hibernation. The articulate professional classes were prominent in voicing their dismay at the crass economics of the *nouveau riche*—still today popularly referred to as the 'Russian mafia'—as their own salaries were slashed. But after half a century of intellectual stagnation there were no resources, financial or human, to begin the task of raising the quality of the nation's teachers and especially of those in its higher education institutions whose degree programmes fell far short of European standards.

The expectation that there would be a flood of aid from returning émigrés was also doomed to disappointment. The substantial Latvian communities in the United States, the United Kingdom, Australia, Sweden and Germany had lobbied vigorously during the decades of Communist occupation, but few were prepared to leave the countries which had given them sanctuary and an affluent standard of living. Their children, having left Latvia at a very young age or been born abroad, were now fully integrated into the host societies and comfortably employed. However, some support for the new republic was forthcoming from both the business and academic expatriate communities: the latter set up educational scholarships and fellowships and sometimes were able to arrange sabbatical leave to their parents' homeland. It was expatriates who created the important Occupation Museum in Rīga, for example, and others returned to help in business and to serve in the government—in the parliamentary elections of June 1993 it was émigrés from Germany, the United States and Australia who were elected to the key ministerial posts of Justice, Finance and Welfare.

In that same election the moderate Latvia's Way party gained a healthy percentage of votes and formed a coalition with the Agrarian Union, the third most popular party, while the Saeima elected Guntis Ulmanis (grand-nephew of Kārlis Ulmanis of the first republic) president. As expected, the composition of this parliament also included a wide spectrum of different political and economic views, with parties such as the National Harmony and Equal Rights particularly committed to integrating Russian residents into the republic. It is greatly to the credit of this—and successive—governments that they were able to avoid punitive legislation to redress historical wrongs and instead channelled reforms in accordance with European and internationally accepted norms. Thus when legislation was passed to re-affirm the primacy of Latvian language and culture, corresponding protection was given to minority languages and peoples. Much more difficult was the task of formulating legislation that would stimulate entry into the free market economies of Europe while protecting vulnerable commercial areas. If vigorous debates and disagreements over economic policies dominated the elections of 1995 and 1998, it is only fair to acknowledge that both governments were successful in maintaining the nation's equilibrium through negotiation and compromise.[6]

However, none of the immediate post-independence governments succeeded in passing sufficiently powerful tax laws and import–export regulations to stem the rampant financial manipulations of unscrupulous entrepreneurs. The government, legitimate business concerns and the population at large failed to recognise the dangers of notorious 'pyramid' schemes in which consortia, businesses and banks offer very high interest rates to depositors but then crash because the original investors, having made their profit, withdraw. This resulted in the banking crisis of 1995–6 when several major banks collapsed and the Bank of Latvia had to intervene. Government legislation was rapidly passed to prevent a recurrence of such practice but, as so often in the early years of independence, action came too late. Retraining the civil service and key personnel in other government sectors was also damagingly slow. Many officials were still enmeshed in Soviet-era protocols and had little idea how to carry out new directives and reforms. The lack of firm sanctions from the government meant that corruption flourished among customs officials and the police, and few sectors of society could claim to have had clean hands. Even some politicians and academics were seen openly awarding themselves bursaries, fellowships and other emoluments. Yet throughout the economic turbulence and social hardship the idea of forging a Scandinavian-style welfare state remained the universally accepted, if distant, goal and slowly the country began to make modest gains. The GDP rose steadily after 1995 along with the general standard of living and both were far ahead of the Russian Federation. Not surprisingly the numbers of Russians returning to their homeland therefore declined dramatically, also encouraged to remain by the liberal citizenship laws.[7]

The state's political, social and economic growth and ties with the West grew stronger with its membership and active participation in several key international organisations. While diplomatic relations were maintained with the former Communist states and with the powerful Russian Federation, neither Latvia, Lithuania nor Estonia accepted Russia's invitation to join the Commonwealth of Independent States in 1992, electing rather to become members of the Council of Baltic States created in the same year. Soon the newly formed European Community (later to become the European Union) included the Baltic states in its international aid programme and provided both funding and expertise to facilitate their entry into the free market economy. In 1995 all three Baltic republics became associate members of the EU. The most important consideration for these newly restored states however remained defence. In 1991 all three joined the Conference on Security and Cooperation in Europe (CSCE) which had been set up in 1975 to address matters of security, human rights, common environmental and economic factors; in 1995 this body was renamed the Organisation on Security and Cooperation in Europe (OSCE). Subsequently OSCE was instrumental in helping the Baltic governments draft legislation that ensured the rights of minority cultures within their states in accordance with international norms.

Perhaps the most ardently sought after goal in the eyes of the Baltic republics was admission to the North Atlantic Treaty Organisation (NATO). On one level nothing could seem more appropriate than to join this defence alliance, but in the early 1990s NATO was still a potent symbol of the international military alliance that had opposed the USSR during the Cold War and now it was faced with the problem of how to admit former Communist states without antagonising the Russian Federation, which was bound to see such a move as a security threat to itself. In addition, NATO was founded on the premise that its member states would contribute to its mutual defence policy, but the Baltic republics had no armed forces to speak of and Russian troops were still stationed on their territories. Granted that the Baltic states wished to leave the Russian sphere of influence, an alternative proposal advocated a course less inflammatory to Russia's sensibilities: to designate the eastern Baltic a neutral, nuclear-free zone, but this met with understandable scepticism. Finally in 1998 the United States proposed a Charter of Partnership in which the Baltic republics should be granted membership of the EU, OSCE, the World Trade Organisation and NATO. The process of integrating them however was to prove lengthy and complex, involving patient and delicate negotiations, not least because the Baltic populations themselves were bewildered by the seemingly endless process of evaluation and guidance from external bodies on the requirements for entry; at times this must have seemed perilously close to undermining their newly-won sovereignty. But through a scrupulous and transparent process of modifying existing laws and passing new ones, the necessary international protocols and guarantees were eventually adopted by all three republics.

The transition to membership of an international, Western community of nations brought with it other difficulties, especially in the acute shortage of qualified personnel not only for Latvia's business sectors but crucially for the new Ministry of Foreign Affairs. Under the Soviet occupation Moscow had handled international relations, but now neither an understanding of the former USSR's protocols nor a knowledge of Russian was of the slightest use. English was the accepted international language but there was a catastrophic lack of speakers. In the general reorientation towards the West it was often untrained teachers who were recruited to staff these new posts while basic language skills could be acquired by the civil service, but this was an unsatisfactory ad hoc arrangement at best and had the additional and undesirable effect of reducing the number of qualified teachers in the system, with predictable consequences for educational standards.

Local staff had to be found to man the new commercial enterprises and services which had attracted international funding, especially from Sweden, Denmark and Germany. This entailed far more than learning new languages, however: three generations had to be retrained to adopt completely different codes of behaviour and values. The Soviet system of ensuring jobs for life irrespective of the quality of the work was now defunct; personnel had to be reschooled to understand that employment was not an unquestioned right but depended on performance. The dour and lackadaisical Soviet-style service (familiar to anyone who visited the USSR during the Intourist days) was no longer acceptable. This process of re-education was facilitated by short courses as well as summer schools run by foreign companies now eager to invest in the Baltic, and many of the nation's young people were sponsored to travel abroad to learn new skills. But though such measures hastened the process of modernisation and Westernisation it is also true that significant numbers of the older generation were unable to adapt or to grasp the need for transparency after the decades of secrecy and lack of accountability.[8]

Nonetheless by the late 1990s Latvia was firmly set on her new course. Parliamentary democracy had been successfully re-established and fair elections held; the economic downturn had been reversed; the country was now a member of several key international organisations; the last Russian troops had departed; the reminders of the decades of humiliating occupation had been expunged—Cyrillic street names and signs changed back to the Latin alphabet and their pre-1940 designations, the statues of Lenin and other Soviet figures removed, and most non-Latvians in public service were at least attempting to communicate in the state language. The restoration of cultural wholeness could continue with confidence. Above all, the election of 1998 was to give Latvia a new president who would be eminently suited to represent her in the outside world.

Integration

The appointment of Vaira Vīķe-Freiberga marked a turning point in Latvia's international profile. Formerly a professor at the University of Montreal and a Fellow of the Royal Society of Canada, she possessed internationally respectable credentials as well as experience at senior management level and she was untainted by any dealings with the 'Russian mafia'. Moreover she was fluent in English, French, German and Spanish in addition to her native Latvian. Impatient with inefficiency, unfulfilled promises and corruption, Russians and Latvians alike enthusiastically embraced her appointment as president in 1999 and her re-election in 2003.[9] Her high standing in Latvia was soon followed by equal popularity in the eyes of the international press and media for whom she rapidly became 'news'. Articulate and urbane, she was a commanding presence at the negotiating table and more than a match for interviewers. As she once pointed out, governing an eastern European country was not unlike chairing a university faculty of independently-minded academics—and both were like trying to herd cats—but there is no doubt that under her aegis Latvia moved far more rapidly towards full membership in the EU and NATO than would otherwise have been the case.

The drive to join the EU was fuelled by far more than the obvious economic benefits that membership would bring. Equally powerful was the country's sense of itself as part of the liberal democratic tradition of Europe from which it had been temporarily divided during the decades of the Cold War. This perception however had the unintended side effect of widening the gap between ethnic Latvians and the large Russian-speaking minority and threatened to delay Latvia's admission to the multi-ethnic and multi-national membership of the EU. President Freiberga was particularly active in addressing ways of hastening the process of naturalisation and the integration of minority peoples through state-funded initiatives such as the National Programme for Latvian Language Training and the Social Integration Programme. By the early years of the new millennium the European Council acknowledged that these and other liberal measures had been effective and towards the end of 2002 Latvia, like Lithuania and Estonia, had met the criteria for entry to the EU. On 13 December of that year the European Council agreed it would offer all three Baltic republics a Treaty of Accession on 16 August 2003, subject to each holding a national referendum on entry,[10] and Latvia, Lithuania and Estonia joined the EU on 1 May 2004. As President Freiberga observed, this put 'a full stop to the sequels of the Second World War' and ended the fragmentation of Europe.[11] Since their entry the three Baltic governments have continued efforts to integrate their ethnic minorities more fully and, indeed, in 2004 President Freiberga announced the creation of a post at ministerial level in Latvia specifically for this purpose.[12]

Entry into NATO was deemed as important as membership of the EU and this too was contingent on Latvia successfully resolving internal ethnic tensions, any remaining external territorial disputes, and on demonstrating its ability to contribute to the alliance's military strength.[13] Not surprisingly the process was delayed by strong opposition from the Russian Federation. Although the 1998 Baltic Charter of Partnership, pioneered by the USA, had specified admission to NATO in principle, achieving this in practice was a long and delicate process. The Russian President Vladimir Putin repeatedly voiced his opposition, though his objections were gradually modified by Russia's desire for more constructive ties with the Western democracies. In the end the Baltic states were formally invited to join the alliance at the 2002 NATO summit in Prague, the Protocols of Accord were signed on 26 March 2003, and the three republics became full members on 29 March 2004.

These successes were paralleled by the rapidly growing economies of the Baltic which enhanced their credibility as viable nation-states. By 1998 most of Latvia's foreign trade had shifted to the EU while exports to the Russian Federation had declined to about 17.5 per cent and imports to 13.5 per cent. A large proportion of the latter was due to energy resources: Latvia remained dependent on Russia for natural gas and for most of its oil needs though the country also had, and has, large renewable energy sources of its own, mainly from the three hydroelectric dams on the Daugava which provide 70 per cent of its electricity, the remaining 30 per cent derived from fossil fuels. The strong economic growth with its shift to Western markets along with the country's increasing importance as a trans-shipment centre for goods and raw materials through the ports of Rīga, Liepāja and Ventspils meant that it was able to weather the Russian financial crisis of August 1998 better than expected.[14]

One of the fastest growing areas of the economy was, and still is, the service sector. The Scandinavian countries and Germany invested substantially in new hotels, restaurants and department stores and were active in training staff to run these commercial ventures. Within a few years over half the country's GDP was generated by this rapidly expanding area. As transit services at the ports grew and tourism and light industry flourished, the GDP growth rate between 1998 and 2006 shot up to become one of the highest in Europe.[15] Economic reforms, low labour costs and a highly skilled workforce attracted foreign investment and the economic boom earned Latvia, along with Lithuania and Estonia, the soubriquet of the 'Baltic Tiger' economies. In 2006, for example, Latvia's economy grew by 11 per cent and by 2007 the Baltic states had the highest growth rate and lowest unemployment figures in Europe. In the years immediately following admission to the EU it is estimated that between 80,000 and 100,000 Latvians with higher education qualifications went abroad in search of better-paid jobs, migrating principally to Sweden, the UK and Ireland where salaries for manual labour were higher than their professional salaries in Latvia. In the short term this meant a severe shortage of skilled personnel in many areas, but after a few years this trend slowed to a trickle and in some cases has been reversed.

The global financial crisis of 2008 stopped this burgeoning growth and the Baltic states were among the hardest hit in Europe. Latvia's GDP dropped by more than 20 per cent (at one pointing falling as low as 26 per cent) and by mid-2009 the three Baltic republics were experiencing one of the deepest recessions anywhere on the globe. It is greatly to the credit and hard work of their peoples, who stoically endured the necessary austerity measures, that the severe fiscal contraction of 2008–9 was as short-lived as it was. Economic recovery was rapid and by 2010 Latvia again had a steady growth rate of 5.5 per cent accompanied by low inflation and low unemployment. The global recession however has also meant the curtailment of investment in vital areas such as health and education. In 2009 there were only fifty-nine hospitals in the country (down from ninety-four in 2007 and 121 in 2006) and healthcare remains the second lowest in the EU.[16] Resources for education have been equally hard hit, many schools have been closed and standards in higher education in particular, lag behind the rest of Europe. But under the auspices of the EU and other overseas funding agencies many talented young people have won scholarships for study abroad and have returned to work in their homeland. As their numbers strengthen, so too will the professional and intellectual foundations of the country. It is encouraging that overall the United Nations Human Development Index of 2011 ranked Latvia forty-third out of 187 countries and designated the country's quality of life and achievement 'high', along with the other nations of Europe (as distinct from the lower ranking given to the Balkans, Ukraine and the Russian Federation, for example).

Today Latvia's economy continues to flourish with Rīga as an increasingly important international financial and commercial centre. Unemployment is down to 7 per cent and the index for inflation in 2011 was only 1.3 per cent, though that rose to 3.4 per cent in 2012. The Lat was one of the highest-valued currencies in the world with a strong international credit rating of 'stable' and 'positive', and Latvia entered the euro-zone on 1 January 2014.[17] Although Latvia's GDP is still only about 65 per cent of the EU average, that in itself is an extraordinary figure given that in 1999 its GDP per capita was only 25 per cent of the EU average. The government debt is low, about 36 per cent of GDP, the central bank has comfortable reserves and a number of the leading private banks are owned by very solid Scandinavian giants.

The State of the Nation

In less than two decades Latvia achieved the remarkable feat of effecting a transition from the closed economy and political stagnation of a Soviet state to a Western free market economy and a stable political system as the elections of 1998, 2002, 2006 and 2010 have confirmed. The multi-party coalition style of government has proved successful and if initial enthusiasm for political leaders is often followed by disillusionment this too is a familiar enough pattern in most Western democracies. The widely predicted flare-up of ethnic tensions has come to nothing and the country has shown itself mature enough to integrate its minority peoples in accordance with modern democratic principles. Today the country's population is estimated at just under 2,220,000, of whom about 62 per cent are Latvian and 27 per cent Russian.[18] In February 2012 a constitutional referendum was held to consider whether or not Russian should become a second official language: the proposal was rejected by three-quarters of the voters (out of a 71 per cent overall turn-out). Although over 290,000 Russians are still not citizens, this will alter as new generations born on Latvian soil become integrated naturally into the life of the nation. English is the most popular international language, especially for tourism and commerce, and many people also speak German and Swedish.

The visitor to Latvia today will be struck by the dynamic and optimistic atmosphere and the modern facilities but will also notice the social and economic disparities that still exist, particularly in urban areas where the dismal legacy of Soviet slums remains, a painful contrast to the affluent and renovated areas. Nonetheless such eyesores from the Communist era are gradually disappearing. Rīga is once again a thriving hub of commercial activity with a cosmopolitan population and it became the Cultural Capital of Europe in 2014 for which it also adopted as its unifying symbol amber, the shining sun-stone, which has danced in and out of the nation's consciousness and history since pre-historic times. In the same year Latvia entered the euro-zone and the country will also assume the presidency of the Council of Europe in 2015. The ports of Liepāja and Ventspils have regained their importance as centres of trade and trans-shipment and the smaller towns and agricultural communities in Kurzeme and Vidzeme a measure of their traditional prosperity. Latgale remains the poorest region for historical reasons, but this 'Land of Blue Lakes', open meadows and vast forests is also becoming an increasingly popular tourist destination.

Latvia's coastline is some 500 kilometres long with fine, white beaches largely untouched by commercial resorts but dotted by charming, traditional fishing hamlets; inland her unspoilt wetlands, lakes and woodlands are rich in wildlife and attract tens of thousands of visitors from abroad each year. Indeed one of Latvia's greatest assets is the number and variety of her pristine eco-systems, protected in the many national parks[19] and nature reserves. With one of the lowest population densities in Europe—only thirty-seven people per square kilometre—it is no wonder that rare bird species and wildlife flourish in natural habitats. In 2012 the country was awarded the highest international rating for environmental performance.[20] This emphasis on preserving the natural habitat should come as no surprise for, as this chronicle has shown, the landscape was and continues to be an unusually powerful integrating factor in the nation's identity and sense of itself. Long before recorded history this most ancient of surviving Indo-European languages articulated the reality of a landscape in which humanity and nature are harmoniously intertwined and that legacy remains undiminished today.

The Latvian people's national consciousness and identity also continue to be affirmed in the contemporary world through the powerful renaissance of its cultural heritage since independence. The Five-Year Song Festivals grow in stature and popularity while internationally renowned musicians represent the nation abroad: the conductors Mariss Jansons and Andris Nelsons, the great violinist Gidon Kremer, the many talented singers and choirs, the composer Pēteris Vasks, the lucidity, beauty and simplicity of whose music has won him wide acclaim. Space forbids giving more than a token nod to the other arts, but many architects and artists have also achieved international renown: the 'architectural sculptures' of Ojārs Feldsbergs are found as far away as Japan. Other luminaries have included the painter Mark Rothko (1903–70) who was born and lived in Daugavpils before emigrating to the United States. His family have agreed to donate a dozen paintings to the new Rothko gallery in his home city.

Karāļi nak un karāļi iet... ('Rulers come and rulers go') runs the old Latvian proverb, but the land and its people remain. The story of Latvia chronicles the phenomenon of a national consciousness which enabled communities deprived of freedom for nearly 800 years to survive with their language and culture intact, surely one of the most extraordinary sagas in Europe's history. Today we live in an age of globalisation which poses a different kind of challenge to the Baltic states, threatening 'the disenchantment of the world' that so often follows the growth of materialism, as Max Weber warned. Yet the future of a Latvia whose economy is now firmly integrated into the EU and whose membership of NATO and the UN guarantees international support suggests otherwise, for the nation is free as never before to celebrate its language and distinctive heritage and to nurture the homeland that gave rise to both. It has been said that the age of romantic nationalism has ended, that the future lies with the great superpowers which control our ever more tightly-knit global economy. This may well be, yet history has shown that empires which seemed eternal to those who lived in them have vanished, and that it is the creative diversity and vigour of national cultures and languages that have survived. It may be argued with equal cogency that the future health of the world and its peoples, no less than the health of the biosphere, depends precisely on maintaining that diversity.

POSTSCRIPT

A PERSONAL NOTE

My father, who was born in 1907 and died in exile in 1997, encapsulated over his lifetime the dramatic changes in Latvia's fortunes during the twentieth century. Born into a nation which was a province of Russia, he later saw his family massacred by an invading troop of Bolsheviks; as a youth he grew up in the days of the First Republic; as a young man he took a law degree at the University in Rīga and subsequently represented his country as a diplomat, serving in Paris, London and Berlin. When the Soviets invaded again in 1944 he fled Latvia with my mother, only to be interned in a German camp, where I was born. Had it not been for my father's linguistic skills as an interpreter, which earned us a few extra rations, we would never have survived. In 1950 he was appointed to the Latvian Legation in Washington DC where he helped keep alive the plight of his occupied country in the eyes of the West. He lived to see independence and to enjoy the reports of my first visit to his old university and his homeland. Like others of their generation who fled, his life and that of my mother no less than the lives of those who remained in Latvia are a testament to the resilience of a brave people and an undaunted nation.

The experience of a first-generation immigrant child growing up in a household which spoke Latvian, German and English showed me that the sense of belonging to an exiled people was essentially an emotional and cultural phenomenon rather than a political one. It was the language, the songs, myths and folklore that sank into my consciousness and those of my peers and that made us feel distinctively Latvian even while we sought to embrace the way of life of our adopted countries. It was also this sense of living simultaneously in two radically different worlds that gave us insight into the emotional—and sometimes conflicting—demands entailed in the concepts of 'homeland' and 'nation'.

Much has been written about the emergence of the Baltic states since the 'Singing Revolution'. But although contemporary historians have scrupulously addressed the facts of their economies, political systems and demographic compositions, few have engaged with the most fascinating and fundamental question of all: what determines the psychology of these nations' identities and what generated and preserved their sense of self? All too often theoretical discourses are about 'power elites' and ignore the simple truth that 'nationalism has to be understood by aligning it, not with self-consciously held political ideologies, but with the large cultural systems that preceded it, out of which—as well as against which—it came into being'.[1] For Latvians, Lithuanians and Estonians, those cultural systems are inextricably entwined with their ancient languages and the world views these embody. Wittgenstein's famous dictum that 'the limits of my language are the limits of my world' may be paraphrased with some justice as 'the history of my language is the history of my world'. The Enlightenment philosopher Johann Gottfried Herder was right when he declared that the oral literature and songs of the Livonians *were* their history and heritage.

Different sovereignties, languages, religions have flowed over the Latvian landscape and its inhabitants, but their passing has always left the core of the language and culture intact. This suggests that there is something intrinsic to that people's sense of itself as a nation which is not dependent on dynastic or religious particulars; it is founded in the Latvian language which affirms that the life of humanity is rooted in the very nature of things, and that in turn informs and gives meaning to the mundane facts of existence—to life and death—and to the historical circumstances of conquest, servitude and suffering.[2] It was because of this innate linguistic affirmation of a shared worldview that the vicissitudes of politics, economics and social history have failed to undermine the national identity of the Latvians. This is not to diminish the importance of the powerful historical forces that have shaped the fate of this people nor to ignore the impact of such phenomena as the growth of literacy, industry, commerce and technology. Rather, the aim of this study has been to redress a balance that appears to have been lost between such undeniable historical developments and the powerful emotional bond that knits together a community of individuals who regard themselves as a nation. It is my hope that the preceding pages have given the reader a clearer insight into that deepest stratum of Latvia's identity.

NOTES

PREFACE

1. Hugh Seton-Watson, *Nations and States* (Boulder, CO: Westview Press, 1977) p. 5.
2. Ibid., p. 1.

1. ORIGINS

1. For lucid and informative discussions of this complex issue see the Bibliography entries for Barry Cunliffe, Marija Gimbutas, J. P. Mallory and Colin Renfrew.
2. At Zvejnieki ('the fisher-folk') where over three hundred burials, which provide evidence of continuous human habitation from the seventh to the third millennium BC, have been identified and partially excavated. More remain to be discovered, making this the single largest Stone Age burial find in northern Europe.
3. From the fifth millennium BC successive waves of these mysterious Eur-Asian steppe people had flowed across the continent, changing the ethnic and linguistic configuration of Europe, and by the last quarter of the third millennium BC almost the whole continent had been transformed economically and socially by the population shifts and mergers that had come about as the result of the Kurgan migrations. Their last great out-reach into east-central Europe in the third millennium BC, however, initiated the beginning of a more stable era which would see the gradual formation of individual Bronze Age cultural units.
4. In Ghassul, Palestine, an amber bead (bearing the distinctive chemical signature of Baltic *succinite*) was found at a site known to have been inhabited between 4600 and 3600 BC. See *Amber in Archaeology*, eds. C. W. Beck and J. Bouzek (1993); *Amber in Archaeology*, eds. C. W. Beck, I. B. Loze, J. M. Todd (2003); J. Todd, 'Baltic Amber in the Ancient Near East', *Journal of Baltic Studies*, xvi.3 (Fall, 1985).
5. For maps of the ancient amber trade routes see J. M. Navarro, 'Prehistoric Routes between Northern Europe and Italy defined by the Amber Trade', *The Geographic Journal*, LXVI, 6 (1925); and Marija Gimbutas, *The Balts* (New York: Praeger, 1964) p. 58. See also *Amber in Archaeology* (eds. C. W. Beck et al.).

6. For example, when Heinrich Schliemann excavated Mycenae, Tiryns and the levels of Troy, he found tens of thousands of Baltic amber beads.
7. See J. P. Mallory, *In Search of the Indo-Europeans: Language, Archaeology and Myth* (New York: Thames & Hudson), ch. 3 and Gimbutas, *The Balts*, ch. 1.
8. A distant echo of that name and of the vanished pastoral life of the Neuri is still preserved in the Latvian term 'Juri' or 'Jurģi', which refers to the old annual custom of moving a household, its horses and cattle to summer pastures.
9. For an account of this remarkable journey see Barry Cunliffe, *The Extraordinary Voyage of Pytheas the Greek* (Penguin: 2001).
10. Pliny the Elder, *Natural History: A selection*, trans. John F. Healy (Penguin, 2001), book 6, ch. 11.
11. *Austravia* is cognate with Baltic 'austrums' (which means 'east'), while 'abalus' is the Indo-European for 'apple' (in Latvian 'abols').
12. Tactitus, *De Germania*, trans. J. B. Rives (Oxford: Clarendon Press, 1999), Ch. 71. Pomponius Mela had identified 'Scadinavia' in AD 43 and a little later Pliny the Elder refers to 'Scatinavia'.
13. It is also worth noting that 'gals'/'galas' means 'end' in the Baltic languages. The eastern region of Latvia is still called Latgale, i.e. where the land of the Lats ends.
14. Pliny, *Natural History*, book 6. The expedition probably set out after the Great Fire of AD 64, following which Nero built a new Circus and staged games of spectacular extravagance.
15. See Arnolds Spekke, *The Baltic Sea in Ancient Maps* (Stockholm: M. Goppers: 1961), pp. 9–11; J. R. Bacon, *The Voyage of the Argonauts* (Methuen, 1925); and Mara Kalnins, *The Ancient Amber Routes: Travels from Rīga to Byzantium* (Rīga: Petergailis Press, 2012), ch. 5.
16. See J. R. Bacon, *The Voyage of the Argonauts*, p. 113.
17. Gimbutas, *The Balts*, p. 109.
18. However, many of the eastern Balts who remained became Slavonicised and their descendants make up a large percentage of the population of present-day Belarus.
19. Jordanus, *De Rebus geticis*, ch. 23.
20. *Anskar: The Apostle of the North 801–865*, trans. from the *Vita Anskarii* by Charles H. Robinson (Mitchell Press, 2011) ch. xxx, pp. 97–100.
21. The domain of the Semigallians (who lived in what is today southern Latvia and northern Lithuania) is also named in Scandinavian chronicles, which record an attack by Danish Vikings in 870.
22. *Saxo Grammaticus: The History of the Danes*, trans. by Peter Fisher, ed. Hilda Ellis Davidson, p. 43. See also the account of an assault on King Dorno of Kurland (pp. 40–1).
23. *Egils Saga*, trans. and ed. by Christine Fell (Toronto: University of Toronto Press), section 53, p. 79. See also section 46, pp. 65–8, for the account of Egil's raid on the Kur household.
24. F. Balodis, *Det Äldsta Lettland*, cited in Bilmanis, *A History of Latvia* (New Jersey: Princeton University Press, 1951), p. 36.

25. A small Baltic tribe known as the Tālavians were gradually assimilated into the larger Latgallian group. It was also in the mid-tenth century that the generic name for the Old Prussians was mentioned by the Arabic traveller Ibrahim-ibn-Jacub, who affirmed that the Baltic 'Brus' people spoke a distinctive language and were courageous fighters against the Viking 'Rus'.

26. The Old Prussians were slowly assimilated into the German lands (see ch. 2). The Russian chronicles (Laurentius and Hypatius) of the eleventh and twelfth centuries record warfare between the Russian dukes and the Baltic Galindians (first mentioned by Ptolemy in the second century AD—see Map 3—as inhabiting south-eastern Prussia). The later Slav accounts locate a branch of this tribe in the area south-west of Moscow and are important in confirming that a Baltic people successfully resisted eastern Slav expansion for several centuries. The Galindians were also listed among the ten Prussian tribes in 1326 by Duisberg, annalist of the Teütonic Order, but then pass out of history.

27. The types of graves and burial rites signalling a differential into distinctive tribal units remained fairly stable from the first centuries AD until the early medieval period. Each tribe possessed its own customs, whether of cremation, burial in barrows, urns, pits or flat graves, in communal or isolated cemeteries. See Gimbutas, *The Balts*, for what is still the best summary of such archaeological evidence.

2. A CONQUERED PEOPLE

1. *Two Voyagers at the court of King Alfred* [Ohthere and Wulfstan], trans. by Fell, ed. Lund (Williams Sessions Limited, 1984), pp. 23–5.

2. The custom of preserving the dead and leaving them unburied was common throughout ancient Indo-European cultures, as were methods of embalming and preserving the bodies.

3. Adam of Bremen, *History of the Archbishops of Hamburg-Bremen*, trans. by F. J. Tschan (Cambridge University Press, 1992), p. 199.

4. Ibid., p. 197.

5. The persecution of, and atrocities against, the Baltic Prussians after the Teutonic Knights had conquered them in the thirteenth century are amply documented. Old Prussian as a language disappeared in the seventeenth century and 'Prussia' became an independent German monarchy in 1701.

6. All translations of the *dainas* (from *Latviešu Tautas Dziesmas*, eds Svābe, Straubergs and Hauzenberga-Šturma) are by the author.

7. W. Mannhardt, 'Letto-prussische Gotterlehre', *Lettisch-Literarische Gesellschaft*, vol. 21 (Rīga, 1936), p. 17. Cited in Gimbutas, *The Balts*, p. 192.

8. Hundreds of these huge mounds still dominate the level expanses of the Eur-Asian steppe.

9. Even today one of the metaphors for dying in modern Latvian is to take the journey *aizsaulē*, ('beyond the sun').

10. Traditionally the *veļi* hover around the homestead and watch over the inhabitants. However, they can also be malicious if not propitiated; they are subject to *Veļu māte*.

11. *Lāčplēsis* is the national hero of the Latvians, symbolising their unity and their struggles over the centuries against invaders. According to one version of the legend he was overcome by the Black Knight (perhaps a folk memory of the Teutonic Order) and drowned in the river Daugava but will rise again to restore the Castle of Light, emblem of independence. The myth, which has clear parallels with other legendary heroes, such as King Arthur, was important in fuelling the struggle for independence in the nineteenth and twentieth centuries.

12. The Latvian parliament is still called the *Saeime*, while *pagasts* refers to a parish.

13. See the entry for the year 1209 in *The Chronicle of Henry of Livonia*, trans. by J. A. Brundage (Madison, WI: University of Wisconsin Press, 1961), p. 92.

14. By Henry the Lion on the site of an old Slavonic town, Lübeck became the hub of the commercial and economic alliance of towns and guilds that formed the Hansa (see ch. 3).

15. Lifland—or Livland—appears on a Scandinavian rune-stone dating from the mid-eleventh century. The area had been known as the Liv kingdom of Iduma, cited in the Norse sagas, and it later became part of Vidzeme (the middle land), today the northernmost of Latvia's regions.

16. Ernemordus departed for Rome in 1169 to obtain papal blessing, but then disappears from history.

17. 'The treacherous Livonians [...] poured the waters of the Dvina [Daugava] river over themselves saying: "We now remove the water of baptism and Christianity itself with the water of the river."' Brundage, *The Chronicle of Henry of Livonia*, p. 34.

18. Ibid., pp. 38–9.

19. Ibid., p. 37.

20. See Spekke, *The Baltic Sea in Ancient Maps* (Stockholm: M. Goppers, 1961), p. 17.

21. In 1186 Pope Celestine III had also expressed the interest of the Holy See by granting 'the remission of all sins to all those who would take the cross and go to restore' the newly founded church of Meinhard. Similarly in 1198 Albert had secured the blessing of the papacy which 'in enjoining the Livonian pilgrimage for the plenary remission of sins, made it equal with that to Jerusalem'. Brundage, *The Chronicle of Henry of Livonia*, pp. 29–30; p. 36.

22. As a matter of policy the Knights built castles next to or over the stronghold of a conquered native chieftain, lord or king. The Master of the Order was responsible for the administration of the district on behalf of the Rīga bishopric.

23. This right was later confirmed by the Lateran Council of 1215 which had introduced the measure to counteract the tendency of secular princes to nominate bishops.

24. Reval was re-named 'Daani-linn', that is 'fortress of the Danes', hence 'Tallinn'.

25. Henry of Livonia was Latvian, possibly one of those sons taken hostage at the

beginning of Albert's rule and sent to Bremen or Rome to be educated. His good Latin earned him a position as Albert's secretary and he was given considerable responsibility: e.g. he was sent to give religious instruction to the sons of King Tālivaldis in 1214. He made several trips to Rome, assisted Bishop William of Modena, and prepared the *Chronicle* which, though it supports church policy and the invasion of the Baltic, also shows sympathy for his fellow Balts.

26. Originally founded in 1190 as a charitable institution, akin to the Templars and Hospitallers, the *Fratres Hospitalis Sanctae Maria Teutonicorum per Jerusalem* were re-formed in 1198 as a military order of crusading knights. Its membership was exclusively German.

27. It is likely that King Lamikis perished defending his realm, for there is no record of his having reached Rome for the agreed coronation ceremony in 1232.

28. The site of this historic battle is still unconfirmed: suggestions include Vecsaule, (Old Saule) not far from the castle and town of Bauska in Zemgale, Latvia, and Šiauliai, a little further south in northern Lithuania.

29. The Teutonic Order was strictly hierarchical and consisted of three classes: the knights, who were of noble birth, the clerics and professionals (such as lawyers, physicians, architects), and the lay brothers (soldiers, workers and artisans). In addition the Grand Master could call on auxiliary military forces from the minor nobility who owed feudal allegiance to the Order.

30. In one version of the Lāčplēsis legend the hero is killed by the 'Black Knight'; in another they kill each other and both fall into the river Daugava.

31. In 1242 the Russian Prince Alexander Nevsky liberated Pskov; he captured sixty mounted knights who were crossing frozen Lake Peipus, but later signed a peace treaty with the Livonian Order.

32. However, Gediminas and his son Algirdas also halted the advance of the Tatars. Lithuania and Poland were joined in 1386, creating a vast Commonwealth which stretched from the Baltic to the Black Sea.

33. In the eighteenth century Herder was to write: 'Humanity shudders at the thought of the blood shed in the savage wars, in which the Old Prussians were wiped off the face of the earth and the Kurs and Latvians reduced to slavery.' *Ideen zur Philosophie der Geschichte der Menschheit*, XVI, 2 (1784–91), cited in Spekke, *History of Latvia: An Outline* (Stockholm: M.Goppers, 1957), p. 152. See also the grim account by the Königsberg chronicler of the Order, Peter von Duisberg, in the same volume by Spekke.

34. Despite its emotional language, ch. 6 in Bilmanis, *A History of Latvia* (New Jersey: Princeton University Press, 1951) is still the most lucid summary of the complex and lengthy process by which this happened.

3. THE POLITICS OF SURVIVAL

1. Several German and Scandinavian municipalities, though none of the Hanseatic towns, have a stag on their coat-of-arms. The *daina* may refer to one of the great

German merchant houses or guilds which traded in the Hansa. The old unit of measurement cited—*sieks* (about 12 kg)—has no precise English equivalent.

2. Although the word Hansa does not appear in written documents before 1267, the alliance of cities had begun much earlier.

3. The Hanseatic League was formally established in 1356 and regular assemblies, or *diets*, were held in Lübeck. Its membership ranged from 70 to 150 towns, and although its influence declined after the fifteenth century it remained an economic power until the end of the seventeenth century.

4. All Hansa ships flew the red and white pennant of the League; those trading from Livonia also flew the black flag and white cross of the Teutonic Order.

5. Although the Order did not come to the aid of the Hansa in the war with the Danes (1362–70) it lent its prestige to, and supported the Hansa in, negotiations with foreign powers. After defeating the Danes in 1370 the Hansa in effect controlled Baltic trade until the mid-fifteenth century (see below).

6. In theory one could serve an eight-year apprenticeship with an accredited Hansa merchant and be sponsored for entry into one of the guilds, but the high fees required would have made this all but impossible for a native, even were the patronage forthcoming and the required birth to German parents waived.

7. A strategy that was later adopted by the peasantry; those who were unable to migrate to towns could sometimes flee to a neighbouring fief where they would have the status of new settlers. In practice, however, this often meant simply falling into debt to a new lord.

8. The Hanseatic League would have been reluctant to antagonise the Teutonic Order and may have sensed an advantage in bypassing Rīga to trade directly with the rich northern Slav cities of Pskov and Novgorod.

9. Many knights had left the Order, while the qualifications for admission were becoming stricter: at one stage a candidate had to prove that he had twelve noble ancestors.

10. Pope John commanded the Master to respect the treaty and, when he failed to comply, excommunicated the Order and all its vassals in 1325.

11. In 1386 the Duchy of Lithuania and the Kingdom of Poland were united by a marriage between Gediminas' grandson Jogaila and the Crown Princess of Poland Jadwiga, establishing a dynasty which was to rule for over two centuries. The two nations were further integrated in 1569 as a Commonwealth, but although Lithuania preserved a separate administrative system, her territories were gradually diminished—ceded to powerful neighbouring states—and her culture progressively eroded by her dominant partner. The nobility came to speak only Polish and Latin, while Lithuanian merchants, artisans and peasants were disenfranchised and lost the right to own land.

12. In the first two centuries of union, the two nations were ruled sometimes jointly and sometimes separately by a King of Poland and a Grand Duke of Lithuania. After the Statutes of 1569 the two lands would be ruled by one king under a two-tiered system (see note 11 above).

13. For example, in 1424 the *Diet* established a category hitherto unknown in Livonia—the bonded serf—whereby a farmer who defaulted on his tithes or fell into debt to his lord would become a serf for ten years without wages. Furthermore, legal measures were introduced to track down and return farmers who had fled their lord's estate. The native farmers of course had no representation on the *Diet*.

14. A small residual portion of the Teutonic Order remained and was administered from Germany, but had no influence in Livonia and little in Prussia. It continued until 1809 when Napoleon disbanded it. In 1840 it was resurrected, with the Archbishop of Austria as its Grand Master, on the grounds that the founder of the Austrian Empire, Rudolf of Hapsburg, had been a Teutonic Knight in the thirteenth century. Today the archives of the Teutonic Order are in Vienna.

15. Only two copies of this magnificent work, which measures over 4 feet in height and is nearly 6 feet long, have survived. Magnus (1490–1557) also wrote a *History of the Northern Peoples* (*Historia de Gentibus Septemtrionalibus*, published in Rome in 1555), the first major scholarly account of the countries of northern Europe.

16. As in many other cultures, the snake was revered as the sacred intermediary between humanity and the gods.

17. Magnus's accompanying commentary, the *Opera Breve*, is equally ironic: '*A*. the country of Livonia, which is under the rule of the German Order of the Blessed Virgin. *B. Terra Curetum* [Kurland] on the coast of which there are repeated shipwrecks and scant comfort is given to the victims.' It is a far cry indeed from Adam of Bremen's praise for the humane Prussians and Kurs who came to the aid of mariners in the eleventh century.

18. Around 988 Prince Vladimir had agreed to accept Christianity for himself and his people and had chosen the Eastern Orthodox Church (Constantinople) over the Roman Catholic (Rome).

19. The Tsar besieged Vilnius (Wilno), the capital of Lithuania, in 1564–5 and though he failed to take the city, the very fact of the incursion so far into the country's heartland sank deep into Lithuania's collective consciousness.

20. Notwithstanding the need to defend Livonia from Russian attacks, the Livonian *Diet* had passed an astonishingly short-sighted decree in 1507 which forbade its native militia to bear swords, allowing them only pitchforks and farm implements. The landowning aristocracy preferred to hire mercenaries, but they were to prove ineffective and the lack of a strong militia undoubtedly hastened the partition of Livonia.

21. As a free imperial city, Rīga would remain independent for another twenty years.

22. The tenacity of the German landowners in retaining their holdings was to prove quite remarkable: at the beginning of the twentieth century over half of Latvia was still in their hands.

23. Magnus was half-brother to the Danish king, who at the time owed fealty to Muscovy.

24. The Lord's Prayer had been translated into Latvian by Simon Grunau c.1530 and printed in Münster's *Cosmographia* of 1550; the Catholic Catechism of 1585

and Martin Luther's Catechism of 1586 had also been printed abroad. Notwithstanding general religious tolerance there were also bitter disputes, such as the Calendar Riot of 1584–6 when Rīgan Lutherans refused to accept the new Gregorian calendar (which a papal bull had introduced two years earlier in western Europe to replace the Julian calendar), deeming it a Catholic counter-reformation plot of the Jesuits.

25. An additional levy which required every fifteen farmsteads to pay for one soldier.

26. Their position now did not differ significantly from that of the Polish and Lithuanian peasantry who were considered mere property, forbidden to leave their lords' estates or to own land in their own right.

27. The sparring for dominance over the Baltic Sea between Denmark and Sweden ended in 1645 when Denmark retired from Estonia, ceded Gotland to Sweden, and acknowledged the right of passage through her straits to Swedish shipping as well as to the ships of her dominions.

28. Eventually the Peace of Andrussovo (1667) fixed the Dniepr river as the boundary between Russian and Polish Ukraine.

29. Z. Ligers, *Histoire des villes de Lettonie* (Paris, 1946), pp. 130, 147, cited in Bilmanis, *A History of Lativa* (New Jersey: Princeton University Press, 1951), p. 169.

30. Ibid.

31. In *Scriptores rerum livonicarum* (Leipzig and Rīga, 1853), vol. II, p. 202.

32. Ibid., p. 603.

33. Although it is an exceptional statistic, by the end of the seventeenth century three-quarters of the farmers in the district of Piebalga had emancipated themselves from taxation.

34. This Latvian folksong is widely regarded as the unofficial national hymn.

35. The other major port of Liepāja (mortgaged to Prussia) and the town and district of Piltene (leased to Denmark) were subsequently integrated into the Duchy.

36. Duke Kettler's concessions included the formal recognition of land titles not by documents but by a sworn affidavit. Notwithstanding these and other measures, relations between the duke and his nobles continued to be strained.

37. Farmers in the autonomous Piltene district were also better off, able to own property, inherit land, and to expect assistance in times of hardship.

38. The *Diet* was convened by the duke every two years and had the power to approve taxes and to negotiate between the nobles and the duke. Also, in the duke's absence a new ducal council and court would assume administrative and judicial authority. Membership was from the nobility of course—peasants, burghers and clergy had no representation, though the traditional self-government of the towns through their city councils was respected.

39. For example, Courland's navy numbered forty-four warships and sixty large merchant vessels; by comparison Denmark had a fleet of twenty and Sweden thirty in the same period.

40. Cited in Spekke, *History of Latvia: An Outline* (Stockholm: M. Goppers, 1957), p. 260.
41. Ibid., p. 258.
42. Glück was pastor at Marienburg (Alūksne) in Livonia and an exceptional linguist: in addition to German, Latin and Latvian, he spoke fluent Estonian and Russian. His beautiful translation of the Old and New Testaments was achieved single-handedly in only eight years, a remarkable feat. After Marienburg fell to Russian troops, Peter the Great, recognising Glück's exceptional abilities, took him to Moscow where he established and ran a school for the sons of Russian nobles until his death in 1705. By an extraordinary quirk of fate, Glück's foster-daughter was to become Catherine I of Russia.
43. Henceforth 'Livonia' would denote only the province of Vidzeme ('the middle-land') north of the Daugava, a little over a third of modern Latvia.
44. The most magnificent of these was Rundāle palace; another was the grand ducal palace at Mitau (Jelgava). Today both are national monuments and open to the public.
45. H. Vitols, *La mer baltique et les états baltes*, p. 204, cited in Bilmanis, *A History*, p. 212.
46. In October of that same year Poland ceased to exist, partitioned among Russia, Austria and Prussia.

4. UNDER RUSSIAN RULE

1. Cited in John Hampden Jackson, *Estonia* (London, Allen & Unwin, 1948), p. 72.
2. Not until 1830 would the trade and merchant guilds again be open to all citizens and nationalities and farmers entitled to leave their lands to engage in commerce or undertake professional work in the towns.
3. He offered the deposed Louis XVIII (brother of the executed Louis XVI) refuge in Mitau, the capital of the old Duchy of Courland.
4. Merkel (1769–1850) had published his pamphlet in Leipzig (see below).
5. Manor lords also had the power to issue or deny passports for internal travel, all decisions made by the local courts had to be ratified by them, and public expenses such as schools and relief for the poor were a charge on the community, the *pagasts*, and not the manor.
6. Von Völkersahm set up a Farmers' Mortgage Bank which charged 4 per cent interest; the Bank of the Landed Nobles offered loans at 6 per cent. By 1901 a third of the lands in Kurland and Livonia had been redeemed by peasant farmers who thus became independent smallholders.
7. Anyone visiting Latvia today will still see living examples of that festival, once celebrated throughout pre-Christian Europe to ensure the growth of crops and a good harvest.
8. Herder, *Sämmtliche Werke* (Berlin: Weidmann, 1877), ix, 532. Herder (1744–1803) served as a Lutheran pastor in Rīga. A native of Königsberg, he would have been

keenly aware that the ancient Old Prussian language had become extinct in the previous century.

9. Herder's ideas became immensely influential in Germany, especially among the younger generation of Romantic poets and writers like Goethe, whom he met in 1770. After the French Revolution Herder also went on to found a new school of political thought, which was particularly important in debating the concepts of nationalism and liberty.

10. See Simon Schama, *Landscape and Memory* (HarperCollins, 1995).

11. *Die Letten, vorzüglich in Livland, am Ende des philosophischen Jarhunderts* was translated into French by the Abbé Sieyes and reached a wide audience across Europe.

12. At what point the Kurs, Letts and Livs began to call themselves Latvians is debatable. Herder still differentiated between these regional peoples in 1765, but it is likely the conflation would have occurred at the beginning of the nineteenth century with the rise in national consciousness. The name derives from the Baltic *Lat* (German *Lett*).

13. This first comprehensive collection drew together the work of earlier collections by Bergmann (1807–8), Buttner (1844) and Sproģis (1857–60).

14. Valdemārs (1825–91) is widely regarded as the father of the Latvian navy. It was largely due to his efforts that on the eve of the First World War Latvia's maritime fleet numbered 333 (274 sailing ships, 59 steamers).

15. It was at this festival that the Latvian national anthem *Dievs svēti Latviju* ('God Bless Latvia') was first sung, with both words and music by Kārlis Baumanis.

16. Cited in Spekke, *History of Latvia* (Stockholm: M.Goppers, 1957), p. 301.

17. Not surprisingly the enrolment of Latvian and Estonian students fell from 1158 in 1890 to 389 in 1900. See Bilmanis, *A History of Latvia* (New Jersey: Princeton University Press, 1951), p. 248.

18. See ch. 2, n.11. Pumpurs' (1841–1902) rich and colourful work, clearly influenced by Homer's *Iliad*, attempted to fuse the archaic traditions and myths of folklore and the *dainas* into an epic poem (a genre foreign to the ancient Baltic people). Auseklis ('the morning star') was the *nom de plume* of Krogzemju Mikus (1850–79) who greatly admired Schiller and the German Romantic poets.

19. The names of the other regions were also standardised in accordance with Latvian usage and spelling: Kurzeme (for Kurland/Courland), Zemgale, Latgale.

20. Blaumanis (1863–1908) wrote poetry, short stories and plays as well as novels.

21. The United States ambassador in Odessa to his colleague in St Petersburg. Cited in Patricia Herlihy, *Odessa* (Harvard, 1986), p. 297. In Rīga a demonstration held in sympathy resulted in forty killed and 240 wounded.

22. Cited in Benedict Anderson, *Imagined Communities* (Verso, 1983; rev. edn 2006), p. 88.

23. Ibid., as cogently argued by Anderson.

24. Roughly half a million, mostly farmers from Kurzeme who fled north of the Daugava. Latvian refugee committees, which coordinated communications, fund-

ing and self-help groups to assist with housing, employment and in setting up Latvian-language schools, were first established in Moscow and St Petersburg; eventually there were some 260 across Russian-held territory.

25. Given that Kurland was in German hands, it was the Kurlander exiles in Estonia who elected a council-in-exile for that region.

26. Subsequently the LPNC was relocated to Petrograd for security.

27. Participants across the political and professional spectrum included delegates to the former Duma; the Provisional Councils of Vidzeme, Kurzeme, Latgale; the Latvian Soldiers' Organisation; the leaders of various political groups as well as of committees on war refugees, cooperative associations, trade unions; members of the press, the professions, and prominent writers.

28. Meanwhile the Latvian Social Democrats left in German-occupied Rīga also sent a petition to the German High Command asking for recognition of a politically neutral, independent Latvia in accordance with the decisions reached by the council of 30 July 1917. Not surprisingly the petition was rejected.

29. See Bilmanis, *A History*, pp. 300–31 and Spekke, *History of Lativa*, pp. 348–56. See also Jackson on Germany's post-war intentions towards the Baltic, citing the *Memoirs* of Von der Golz in *Estonia*, p. 14.

30. The formal ratification of the Treaty of Versailles took place on 10 January 1920. The final treaty between Latvia and Germany was not signed until 15 July 1920.

31. The Bolshevik government recognised Estonia by the Treaty of Tartu on 2 February 1920 and Lithuania by the Treaty of Moscow on 12 July 1920.

32. John Maynard Keynes, *The Economic Consequences of the Peace* (Harcourt, Brace and Howe, 1919), p. 278.

5. THE SHAPING OF A NATION-STATE

1. In contemporary terms roughly £78,000,000, $347,700,000 and €45,450,000.

2. Whereas in 1905 there had been about 83,000 independent farms (with 48 per cent of the land held in the 1,338 German estates until 1918), after the 1919 Act smallholdings numbered about 150,000 and the 1935 agricultural census listed 275,698 of them.

3. For a complete list of the parties and their programmes see Bilmanis, *A History of Latvia* (New Jersey: Princeton University Press, 1951), pp. 312–14.

4. For example, Jānis Čakste, Kārlis Ulmanis, Zigfrīds Meierovics, Jānis Goldmanis and General Balodis (who had been the leading military figure in the 1918–20 struggle for independence) as well as thirteen of the eighteen prime ministers in the new state.

5. Jānis Rainis (1865–1929), poet, dramatist, essayist, short story writer and translator. His best known work is the play *Joseph and his Brothers* which has been translated into a score of languages. He is buried in the Rīga cemetery which bears his name, next to his wife Aspazija (1868–1945), also a gifted poet.

6. In 1920 there were 864 elementary and 36 secondary schools; by 1934 that figure

had risen to 2,057 and 96, respectively. Nearly 30 per cent of elementary and 14 per cent of secondary schools belonged to ethnic minorities, mostly German, Russian and Jewish, and these received the same state funding as Latvian schools.

7. Jānis Vitols (1863–1948) had taught music in the St Petersburg Conservatoire.

8. Mikhail Eisenstein (1867–1921), whose buildings at 10b Elizabetes iela, 2a and 4 Alberta iela and 4 Strelnieku iela can still be seen today. His son Sergei, born in Rīga, was the famous film-maker who directed the iconic *Battleship Potemkin* (1925).

9. The Open-Air Ethnographic Museum opened in 1932 under the directorship of P. Kundziņš and was enlarged in 1941 and 1985. There are now over a hundred traditional buildings which accommodate some 114,000 domestic, farm and craft artefacts of considerable historical value. Today the museum also hosts fairs and music festivals, while during the summer the buildings are occupied by artisans wearing traditional costumes from Vidzeme, Kurzeme, Zemgale and Latgale.

10. V. Purvītis (1872–1945) was a classical painter of Latvian landscapes. In the nineteenth century Latvia's best-known artists had been K. Huhn (1831–77) and J. Feders (1838–1909), both of whom were members and professors of the St Petersburg Academy of Art. Perhaps the finest Latvian portrait-painter was Jānis Rozentāls (1866–1916), who also studied in St Petersburg and whose house at 12 Alberta iela, Rīga, is now a museum.

11. For an historical overview see Andrups and Kalve, *Latvian Literature*, pp. 140–92; and Bilmanis, *Latvia as an Independent State*, pp. 143–50.

12. The state also adopted the Berne Convention Law (10 May 1937) on copyright.

13. From a few score factories in 1918, by 1937 there were over 5000, employing more than 92,000 workers.

14. For tables and statistics showing the growth of the economy, see Bilmanis, *Latvia as an Independent State* (Read Books, 2007), pp. 227–53, 263–302, 314–21. The government's official publication, the *Economist* (brought out in English as well as Latvian), transmitted details of the country's economy, finance, shipping, commerce and agriculture.

15. The most important of these were held in Barcelona (20 April 1921), Berne (23 October 1924) and Geneva (31 January 1928).

16. Built with Swedish assistance at Kegums in 1936 and completed in 1940.

17. Reserve funds of gold and foreign currency in the Bank of Latvia between 1923 and 1938 rose from 31.8 to 91.7 million Lats. See A. Švabe, *Latvija 30 gados, 1918–1948*, cited in Spekke, *History of Latvia* (Stockholm: M. Goppers, 1957), p. 368.

18. For example, a third of Poland's population did not speak Polish; a third of Czechoslovakia consisted of Poles, Russians, Germans, Magyars and Ruthenians; over a million Hungarians found themselves part of an enlarged Romania.

19. Estonia under President Päts had suspended the constitution on 12 March 1934;

NOTES pp. [137–149]

Lithuania had done so as early as December 1926. Estonia's constitutional reforms were implemented in 1938 but Latvia's were pre-empted by the Soviet invasion of 1940.

20. The largest foreign investor was Germany, followed by the UK and Sweden.

21. Latvia's standard of living was rated a modest sixteenth in Europe, i.e. above Portugal and Yugoslavia and only just below Greece and Czechoslovakia. The national income, which had dropped from 926 million Lats in 1927 to 754 million in 1932, passed the 2 billion mark in 1938 and by 1940 had exceeded 9 billion.

22. This Indo-European emblem was adopted in reversed form as the Nazi swastika. Nazi propaganda was disseminated throughout the Baltic from 1934 onwards, though Latvia banned the virulently pro-Nazi *Baltischer Brüderschaft* in 1934.

23. A fifth of whom lived in Rīga. In 1914 Rīga's population had been over 500,000 but dropped to less than 250,000 during World War One; by 1939 it had recovered and stood at 400,000.

24. On 27 September the two great powers modified their treaty, relegating Lithuania to the Soviets; the Treaty of Brest-Litovsk signed the next day divided up Poland between them.

6. WORLD WAR II AND ITS AFTERMATH

1. Estonia had been incorporated on 3 August and Lithuania would follow on 6 August.

2. See, *History of Latvia* (Stockholm: M. Goppers, 1957), ch. xviii for a detailed account of the Soviet terror in this period.

3. Indeed in Lithuania the partisans proclaimed independence and formed a new government, but this was dissolved by the Germans on 1 August 1941.

4. From the US State Department archives headed *Nazi Conspiracy and Aggression*, vol. 8, p. 677. The full text is given in Spekke, *History of Latvia*, pp. 398–9.

5. For the full text see Bilmanis, *A History of Latvia* (New Jersey: Princeton University Press, 1951), p. 404.

6. After the war, memorials were set up to commemorate the dead at Rumbula (1962), Salaspils (1967), Bikernieki Forest (2001) and Mežaparks (2005).

7. The history of the Holocaust has been amply documented elsewhere, though there is still some debate about the identity of the 'Butcher of Rīga'. It is likely that this was Herberts Cukurs, the Latvian aviator and SS member of the Arāj Kommando. He was cited, though not formally charged, at the Nuremberg Trials. Another figure who has been so called was the Austrian Eduard Roschmann, commandant of the Rīga ghetto from January 1943. Another candidate for the title was Rudolf Lange. See Andrejs Ezergailis, *The Holocaust in Latvia* (Rīga: The Historical Institute of Latvia, 1996); Max Kaufman, *The Destruction of the Jews of Latvia* (Konstanz: Hartung-Gorre, 2010); Bernard Press, *The Murder of the Jews in Latvia* (Illinois: Northwestern University Press, 2000); Gertrude Schneider, *The Unfinished Road: Jewish Survivors of Latvia Look Back* (Westport, CT: Praeger, 1991) and *Journey into Terror: The Story of Latvia's Ghetto* (Westport, CT: Praeger, 2001).

8. He survived to be released by the Americans after the war.

9. Among them Jānis Vindulis and the brothers Fritz and Jānis Rozentals. The heroism of Jan and Johana Lipke was formally recognised in 1966 by Yad Vashem, of the World Centre for Holocaust Research, as one of the 'Righteous Among Nations'. Roberts and Johanna Sedul were similarly honoured in 1981 as were others.

10. They were joined by a number of survivors from the main political parties of the legitimate pre-war government who set up a Latvian Central Council which became a focal point for the Resistance.

11. Eksteins, *Walking Since Daybreak* (Macmillan, 2000), p. 44.

12. Estimates range from thirty million to forty-three million.

13. See Michael R. Marrus, *The Unwanted: European Refugees in the Twentieth Century* (Oxford University Press, 1985), pp. 311–13.

14. Eksteins, *Walking Since Daybreak*, p. 220.

15. *Missing Persons and Other Essays*, trans. Leila Venrewitz, p. 26. Cited in Eksteins, *Walking Since Daybreak*, p. 169.

16. At the time the author and her parents were in Erfurt, which would be in the Soviet sector. However my father, whose legal training and command of several languages had earned him a position as translator for the United States military authorities, was advised by an official to leave before the partition agreement was formally announced. He in turn passed the word to the other Latvian refugees in the city and somehow persuaded the military to let them go. The next day a lorryload of Latvians escaped to a DP camp near Hanover, controlled by the Allies.

17. The annual quota for Latvia was 236, at which rate it would have taken over 200 years to process the refugee applications.

18. The *New York Herald Tribune* for 30 August 1948 scathingly noted that as 'matters now stand, it is easier for a former Nazi to enter the United States than one of the Nazis' innocent victims'.

19. A similar number operated in Estonia, while in Lithuania it is estimated that 40,000 partisans continued the Resistance. During the war about 140,000 Latvians had fought with German troops and about 65,000 with Red Army units.

20. Kalnbērziņš (1893–1986) had been the Latvian Communist Party leader in 1940–1; while residing in the USSR during the years of Latvia's independence he had avoided the Stalinist purges of 1936 and 1938.

21. In 1945 there were about 11,000 Communist Party members in Latvia; by the mid-1950s there were 35,000, but only a third of those were Latvians.

7. LATVIA, SSR

1. According to *1940–1991: Museum of the Occupation of Latvia* (p. 116), twelve million titles in Latvian, Russian, German, English and other languages were on the forbidden or restricted lists.

2. For example, by 1948 the taxes imposed on private farms had risen from 40 per cent to a staggering 75 per cent.

3. *Kulak* (the Russian for 'fist' as in 'tight-fisted') designated the class of richer peasants. When they stood in the way of Stalin's plans for agricultural collectivisation he decreed their liquidation as a class. It is estimated that between five and ten million USSR peasants were deported in 1929 to Siberia, northern Russia and the Urals.

4. The figures for Estonia and Lithuania were similar, about 40,000 each.

5. In Rīga there was a famous visual example of opposition. A gifted Latvian craftsman had been denied entry to a guild in an earlier century because he was not German. In retaliation he cast two enormous black cats in metal and positioned them with backsides and rudely upraised tails facing the Guild Hall. The guild hastily admitted him whereupon the cats were decorously turned around. During the Soviet occupation one was repositioned, flaunting its defiant posterior at the Soviet police and administration which had taken over the Guild Hall. To the joy of the locals, the Soviets never caught on. After Independence the cat was swivelled round again and can be seen today atop a spire opposite the Guild Hall, which now houses the Philharmonic Orchestra.

6. There are no reliable figures for the numbers who remained. For an almost unbearably moving pictorial record of life in those camps and the ways the inmates found to survive and preserve their human dignity see *1940–1991: Museum of the Occupation of Latvia* (Rīga: 2002).

7. Berclavs (1914–2004) survived to become leader of the National Independence Party and is honoured today for his efforts to slow the Russification of his homeland (see below).

8. Of the Western nations only Spain, Sweden and Switzerland did not join NATO. The members of the Warsaw Pact were Albania, Bulgaria, Czechoslovakia, East Germany, Hungary, Poland, Romania and Russia.

9. Roberts, *The Penguin History of Europe* (Penguin, 1997), p. 589.

10. His story is told in *Is it Easy to be Young?* (1986) by the Latvian film director Juris Podnieks (1950–92) who won the Prix d'Italia in 1989.

11. These lines from her poem *Marginal Notes of Henricus de Lettis to the Livonian Chronicle* epitomise the protests of the 1970s and after:

> Let me burn. Grant me a funeral pyre!
> Life was long but life's awakening—short.
> The highest of my father's sacred honours–
> Climb up the towering flame to heaven
> And cry out the injustice of
> Fiery iron that slaughtered my nation.

> [Translation by the author]

12. The Gauja river valley was, and is, unique. Formed some 12,000 years ago after the last Ice Age, it is a precious record of geological time and natural ecological

development, a miniature world with its own microclimate and a variety of pristine habitats—forest, lush meadows and uplands as well as extensive wetlands which support a vast bird population. It is also a historical entity, an important visual record of human habitation from the Mesolithic, Neolithic and Bronze Ages.

13. From 'Tree', *Flowers of Ice*, pp. 15–16 [translation by the author]. Ziedonis (b. 1933), poet, essayist and prose writer, later became chairman of the Writers' Union Board and of the Latvian Culture Foundation.

14. For example, in 1978 a three-volume history of Rīga was published: the first, *Feudal Rīga*, sold out in hours; the second, *Rīga 1867–1917*, did moderately well; but *Rīga in the Period of Socialism* simply remained on the shelves. See Plakāns, *A Concise History of the Baltic States* (Cambridge: Cambridge University Press, 2011), p. 379.

15. Karol Jozef Wojtyla (1920–2005). In 1993 he visited the Basilica of St Mary, an important Catholic shrine in the town of Aglona in Latgale. Historically Latgale had been closely associated with Catholic Poland and Lithuania.

16. Pugo would be appointed Soviet Interior Minister in the autumn of 1990 by Gorbachev but later joined the attempted coup against him in August 1991 (see below).

17. Similar ecologically-driven protests stimulated rebellion elsewhere in the Baltic. Estonia protested against state plans to open a highly toxic and polluting phosphate mine in the north-east of the country, the source of over half the country's rivers. Moscow bowed to pressure and cancelled the project in October 1987. In Lithuania resistance to Moscow's plans to develop more chemical factories became an important factor in the foundation of the independence party *Sajūdis* in June 1988.

18. Lieven, *The Baltic Revolution* (New Haven, CT: Yale University Press, 1990), p. 220.

19. These were the Unity Party in Lithuania, the Internationalist Front in Estonia, and the Internationalist Front in Latvia.

20. In Estonia the Popular Front held its first meeting on 1–2 October, in Latvia on 10 October and in Lithuania on 22–3 October.

21. Quoted in Lieven, *The Baltic Revolution*, p. 223.

22. Lithuania on 19–20 December of that year and Estonia in March 1990.

23. As late as April 1990 Alfrēds Rubiks, a committed Communist, was elected First Secretary.

24. On 25 June the Lithuanian Supreme Council agreed to a compromise: it would only begin implementing the procedures leading to independence and would postpone independence itself. Oil supplies were duly resumed but Gorbachev was fast losing patience with negotiations as subsequent events would show.

25. Gorbachev had offered Latvia full internal autonomy within the USSR, reserving only defence and international relations, but this had been rejected outright.

26. Born in 1942 he chaired the Latvian Praesidium from 1988 to 1990 and so was

effectively Head of State in the first year of Latvian's independence. At the fifth Saeima election in 1993 Guntis Ulmanis was elected President. (The years of the Soviet Supreme Councils were not recognised in the official list of parliaments. The last legitimately elected Saeima had been the fourth.) Gorbanovs was parliamentary Speaker from 1989 to 1995 and remained a member of parliament until 2002.

27. Full text given at http://www.letton.ch.
28. Fourteen died in Vilnius that night, either shot to death or crushed by Soviet tanks.
29. Slāpiņš (1949–91) was also Podnieks' cameraman for the hauntingly beautiful tribute to Latvia, *Homeland*. Another member of the camera team, Gvido Zvaigzne, also died later of gunshot wounds, as did four other civilians. Juris Podnieks survived until 23 June 1992 when his body was found in Lake Zvirgzda in Kurzeme, apparently the victim of a 'diving accident'. No one believed this. The last Soviet troops in Latvia did not withdraw until 1994.

8. IN A FREE STATE

1. On 25 December 1991 Gorbachev resigned as President of the USSR and announced its dissolution, whereupon the Russian Federation under Boris Yeltsin took over the assets of the Communist Party and the former USSR.
2. The last Soviet units did not leave the country until 1994. See Mole, *The Baltic States: from Soviet Union to European Union* (Routledge, 2012) pp. 120–8.
3. The law came into force on 22 July 1994.
4. Originally set at three years, the term of office was changed to four years in 1997.
5. IMF concerns about the lack of monetary resources had been partly assuaged in 1992–3 when the Bank of England returned £90 million of gold reserves it had held since 1940; this was followed by similar moves from the Banque de France and the Swiss Bank for International Settlements. The rate of conversion was one new Lat to 200 Latvian/Russian roubles.
6. For example, in 1995 disillusioned voters tended to move either towards the more radical Democratic Party or to the protectionist People's Movement Party; in 1998 however the vote shifted back to the centre, once again supporting the moderate Latvia's Way and the centrist People's Party.
7. In the second half of the 1990s they accounted for about 30 per cent of the population.
8. Plakans points out that the number of skilled persons leaving employment rose from 8,600 in 1991 to 22,500 in 1992, 75,800 in 1993 and 95,500 in 1994. See Plakans, *A Concise History of the Baltic States* (Cambridge: Cambridge University Press, 2011), p. 434.
9. Born in 1937, she left Latvia with her parents in October 1944, after which the family lived in several countries before settling in Canada. During her term of office as president she gained a reputation for defusing difficult situations.

Confronted by a group of Russians who challenged the law on the state language she replied with wit and conviction that if *they* agreed to learn Latvian *she* would learn Russian.

10. In Latvia the vote was 67.5 per cent in favour out of a national turnout of 72.5 per cent.

11. As announced on the BBC News on 21 September 2003 (see http://news.bbc.co.uk/1/hi/world/europe/3126100.stm).

12. In addition to the substantial Russian population in Rīga there are large enclaves in eastern Latgale, while in the industrial city of Daugavpils, not far from the Russian border, the majority of the population are Russian-speakers. The voting franchise has also been extended to the 290,660 non-citizens (about 14 per cent of the country's population), enabling them to vote in local city and council elections though not in those at national level.

13. For a useful table setting out the size of each nation's military contribution to NATO and the percentage of GDP assigned to the defence budget, see Mole, *The Baltic States from the Soviet Union to the European Union*, p. 163.

14. Roughly half the capacity of these ports is taken up by crude oil and oil products.

15. Trans-shipment, tourism and services account for about 72 per cent; timber and timber products, agricultural produce, machinery and electric goods account for about 24 per cent.

16. Often medical services and medication have to be paid for privately, leading to charges of corruption. The suicide rate is the seventh highest in the world and life expectancy is only 72.5 years.

17. In July 2013 the European Parliament and the European Central Bank confirmed that Latvia had fulfilled all the convergence criteria required for entry to the euro-zone. The conversion rate was set at 0.702804.

18. In 2012 the demographic spread was approximately: 62.1 per cent Latvian, 26.9 per cent Russian, 3.3 per cent Belarusian, 2.2 per cent Ukrainian, 2.2 per cent Polish, 1.2 per cent Lithuanian, 2.1 per cent Other. Although there are only about 400–500 native Liv speakers of Finno-Ugric origin left, the country takes great pride in preserving the remnant of this ancient Baltic people and vigorously supports its cultural activities. Latvia also has small Roma and Jewish populations. Latvians are in a minority in Rīga, which remains a vibrantly international city, and Russian-speaking peoples constitute a large majority in Daugavpils, the important industrial city in eastern Latgale.

19. The country has three National Parks, four State Reserves, twenty-two Nature Parks, 211 Nature Reserves, six protected landscape areas and one Biosphere Reserve. The area of the country is 64,589 square kilometres, 5 per cent of which are wetland. There are over 2,000 lakes and over 40 per cent of the country is still wooded.

20. The Index on Eco-Achievement placed Latvia first and second in the two main categories out of 132 nations reviewed.

POSTSCRIPT: A PERSONAL NOTE

1. Benedict Anderson, *Imagined Communities* (Verso, 1983; rev. edn 2006), p. 12.
2. Ibid., p. 36.

SELECTED BIBLIOGRAPHY

[Place of publication London unless otherwise stated]

Aasland, Aadne (ed.), *Latvia: The Impact of the Transformation* [*The NORBALT Living Conditions Project*] (Norway: Fafo, 1996).

Albi, A., *EU Enlargement and the Constitutions of Central and Eastern Europe* (Cambridge: Cambridge University Press, 2005).

Anderson, Benedict, *Imagined Communities* (Verso, 1983; rev. edn 2006).

Armstrong, J. A., *Nations Before Nationalism* (Chapel Hill: University of North Carolina Press, 1982).

Auerbach, Eric, *Mimesis* (New York: Doubleday Anchor, 1957).

Bacon, J. R., *The Voyage of the Argonauts* (Methuen, 1925).

Benjamin, Walter, *Illuminations* (Fontana, 1973).

Berlin, Isaiah, *The Proper Study of Mankind* (Chatto & Windus, 1997).

Bilmanis, Alfreds, *A History of Latvia* (New Jersey: Princeton University Press, 1951).

Bremmer, Ian and Ray Taras (eds), *Nations and Politics in the Soviet Successor States* (Cambridge: Cambridge University Press, 1993).

Breuilly, John, *Nationalism and the State* (Manchester: Manchester University Press, 1982).

Brundage, James (ed.), *The Chronicle of Henry of Livonia* (Madison, WI: University of Wisconsin Press, 1961).

Cunliffe, Barry, *The Oxford Illustrated History of Prehistoric Europe* (Oxford: Oxford University Press, 1994)

———— *The Extraordinary Voyage of Pytheas the Greek* (Penguin, 2001).

Davidson, H. R. Ellis, *The Viking Road to Byzantium* (George Allen & Unwin, 1976).

Dreifelds, Juris, *Latvia in Transition* (Cambridge: Cambridge University Press, 1996).

Eglaja-Kristone, Eva and Benedikts Kalnacs (eds), *Back to Baltic Memory: Lost and Found in Literature 1940–1968* (Riga: Institute of Literature, Folklore & Art, University of Latvia, 2008).

SELECTED BIBLIOGRAPHY

Eksteins, Modris, *Walking Since Daybreak* (Macmillan, 2000).

Gimbutas, Marija, *The Balts* (New York: Praeger, 1964).

Herodotus, *The Histories*, trans. Aubrey de Selincourt (Penguin, 1982).

Hiden, John and Thomas Lane (eds), *The Baltic and the Outbreak of the Second World War* (Cambridge: Cambridge University Press, 1992).

Hobsbawm, Eric, *Nations and Nationalism since 1780* (Cambridge: Cambridge University Press, 1990).

Hroch, Miroslav, *Social Preconditions of National Revival in Europe*, trans. Ben Fowkes (Cambridge: Cambridge University Press, 1985).

Kalnins, Mara, *The Ancient Amber Routes: Travels from Rīga to Byzantium* (Rīga: Pētergailis Press, 2012).

Kirkby, David, *The Baltic World 1772–1993* (Longman, 1995).

Lapidus, Gail W., Victor Zaslavsky and Phillip Goldman (eds), *From Union to Commonwealth: Nationalism and Separation in the Soviet Republics* (Cambridge: Cambridge University Press, 1992).

Lieven, Anatol, *The Baltic Revolution* (New Haven, CT: Yale University Press, 1993).

Mallory, J. P., *In Search of the Indo-Europeans: Language, Archaeology and Myth* (New York: Thames & Hudson, 1989).

Mallory, J. P. and D.Q. Adams (eds), *The Oxford Introduction to Proto-Indo-European and the Indo-European World* (Oxford: Oxford University Press, 2006).

Misiunas, Romuald J. and Rein Taagepera, *The Baltic States: Years of Dependence, 1949–1990* (Berkeley: University of California Press, 1993).

Mole, R. C. M., *The Baltic States: from the Soviet Union to the European Union* (Routledge, 2012).

Motyl, Alex J. (ed.), *The Post-Soviet Nation: Perspectives on the Demise of the USSR* (New York: Columbia University Press, 1992).

O'Connor, Kevin, *The History of the Baltic States* (Westport, CT: Greenwood Press, 2003).

Pabriks, A. and A. Purs, *Latvia: The Challenges of Change* (Routledge, 2001).

Page, Ray, *Chronicles of the Vikings* (British Museum Press, 1995).

Petersen, Nickolay (ed.), *The Baltic States in International Politics* (Copenhagen: DJOF Publishing, 1993).

Plakans, Andrejs, *A Concise History of the Baltic States* (Cambridge: Cambridge University Press, 2011).

Pliny the Elder, *Natural History: A Selection*, trans. John F. Healy (Penguin, 1991).

Renfrew, Colin, *Time Depth in Historical Linguistic* (Cambridge: McDonald Institute for Archaeological Research, 2000).

Rogers, Hugh I., *Search for Security: A Study in Baltic Diplomacy, 1920–1934* (Hamden, CT: Archon Books, 1975).

Rose, Richard and William Maley, *Nationalities in the Baltic States: A Survey Study* (Glasgow: University of Strathclyde, 1994).

SELECTED BIBLIOGRAPHY

Rowell, S. C., 'Baltic Europe' in *New Cambridge Modern History*, Vol. VI, ed. Michael Jones (Cambridge: Cambridge University Press, 2000)

———— 'Eastern Europe: the Central European Kingdoms' in *New Cambridge Modern History*, Vol. V, ed. David Abulafia (Cambridge: Cambridge University Press, 1999).

Schama, Simon, *Landscape and Memory* (HarperCollins, 1995).

Seton-Watson, Hugh, *Nations and States* (Boulder, CO: Westview Press, 1977).

Smith, Anthony, *The Ethnic Origins of Nations* (Oxford: Basil Blackwell, 1986).

Spekke, Arnolds, *History of Latvia: An Outline* (Stockholm: M.Goppers, 1957).

———— *The Ancient Amber Routes and the Geographical Discovery of The Eastern Baltic* (Stockholm: M. Goppers, 1957).

Sprudzs, Adolfs (ed.), *The Baltic Path to Independence: An International Reader* (Buffalo, NY: William S. Hein & Co., 1994).

Stamers, Guntis, *Latvia Today* (Rīga: Latvian Institute of International Affairs, 1993).

Starrels, John M., *The Baltic States in Transition* (Washington, DC: IMF, 1993).

Švābe, A. and E. Straubergs, E., *Latviešu Tautas Dziesmas*, 12 volumes (Copenhagen: Imanta, Hauzenberga-Šturma 1952).

Swain, Geoffrey [with Nigel Swain], *Eastern Europe Since 1945* [with Nigel Swain] (Macmillan, 1993; rev. & expanded 2003).

———— *Between Stalin and Hitler: Class War and Race War on the Dvina, 1940–46* (Routledge-Curzon, 2004).

Tacitus, *De Germania*, trans. J. B. Rives (Oxford: Clarendon Press, 1999).

Trapans, Jan Arveds (ed.), *Toward Independence: The Baltic Popular Movements* (Boulder, CO: Westview Press, 1991).

Turner, Victor, *Dramas, Fields and Metaphors: Symbolic Action in Human Society* (Ithaca: Cornell University Press, 1974).

von Rauch, Georg, *The Baltic States: The Years of Independence 1917–1940* (Berkeley: University of California Press, 1974).

The World Bank, *Latvia: The Transition to a Market Economy* (Washington, DC: The World Bank, 1993)

INDEX

[Page numbers in ***bold italic*** refer to maps]

INDEX

INDEX

INDEX